DEAD MAN'S CHEST

UNIVERSITY PRESS OF FLORIDA

Florida A&M University, Tallahassee
Florida Atlantic University, Boca Raton
Florida Gulf Coast University, Ft. Myers
Florida International University, Miami
Florida State University, Tallahassee
New College of Florida, Sarasota
University of Central Florida, Orlando
University of Florida, Gainesville
University of North Florida, Jacksonville
University of South Florida, Tampa
University of West Florida, Pensacola

DEAD MAN'S CHEST

Exploring the Archaeology of Piracy

Edited by Russell K. Skowronek
and Charles R. Ewen

UNIVERSITY PRESS OF FLORIDA

Gainesville/Tallahassee/Tampa/Boca Raton
Pensacola/Orlando/Miami/Jacksonville/Ft. Myers/Sarasota

Published in the United States of America.

28 27 26 25 24 23 6 5 4 3 2 1

Library of Congress Cataloging-in-Publication Data
Names: Skowronek, Russell K., editor. | Ewen, Charles R., 1956– editor.
Title: Dead man's chest : exploring the archaeology of piracy / edited by Russell K. Skowronek and Charles R. Ewen.
Other titles: Exploring the archaeology of piracy
Description: 1. | Gainesville : University Press of Florida, [2023] | Includes bibliographical references and index. | Summary: "This book presents a variety of approaches to better understanding piracy through archaeological investigations, landscape studies, material culture analyses, and documentary and cartographic evidence"— Provided by publisher.
Identifiers: LCCN 2023012267 (print) | LCCN 2023012268 (ebook) | ISBN 9780813069746 (hardback) | ISBN 9780813070513 (pdf) | ISBN 9780813072852 (ebook)
Subjects: LCSH: Underwater archaeology. | Coastal archaeology. | Pirates—History. | BISAC: HISTORY / Maritime History & Piracy | SOCIAL SCIENCE / Archaeology
Classification: LCC CC77.U5 D44 2023 (print) | LCC CC77.U5 (ebook) | DDC 930.1028/04—dc23/eng/20230330
LC record available at https://lccn.loc.gov/2023012267
LC ebook record available at https://lccn.loc.gov/2023012268

The University Press of Florida is the scholarly publishing agency for the State University System of Florida, comprising Florida A&M University, Florida Atlantic University, Florida Gulf Coast University, Florida International University, Florida State University, New College of Florida, University of Central Florida, University of Florida, University of North Florida, University of South Florida, and University of West Florida.

University Press of Florida
2046 NE Waldo Road
Suite 2100
Gainesville, FL 32609
http://upress.ufl.edu

This volume is dedicated to Meredith Morris-Babb,
former director of the University Press of Florida,
who launched the series and titled the books.

Contents

Figures

Tables

Preface

In our first book, *X Marks the Spot,* we told the story of how—at midcareer with tenure in hand—we were emboldened to explore the topic of the archaeology of piracy. Now, more than fifty years since we met in Naperville, Illinois, and half a century after our first archaeological project in 1973 at the Middle Mississippian Orendorf site in central Illinois, we are in the sunset of our careers.

We were in the middle of the post–World War II baby-boom generation. Some of our teachers in high school in Naperville, had served on Dwight Eisenhower's staff and one as a marine on Guadalcanal. The marine, Mr. Genovese, told us of atrocities committed on both sides of the battle. When he was not in class, we had a substitute teacher we called "Amazon Joe" be-

Figure P.1. Ewen and Skowronek at Fort de Chartres, Prairie du Rocher, Illinois, 1974. (Authors' collection)

cause he searched for gold when not teaching. During high school, we took classes at the nearby College of DuPage. Our professor there introduced us to Margaret Mead. It was a heady time to say the least.

In the early 1970s archaeologists were mostly men. The prevailing idea was that the only real archaeology was prehistoric archaeology. When we voiced interest in historical archaeology prior to excavating at the French colonial Fort de Chartres in Illinois in 1974, we were said to be doing not "real" archaeology but "hysterical" archaeology (Figure P.1). These biases persisted. Years later, following a decade of work (including MA theses on historic and shipwreck sites), those of us involved in underwater research were often teased by being called "Bubbleheads."

College at the University of Illinois and University of Minnesota gave us the basic academic grounding in our field. Our professors had seen service in World War II, but many had also been involved in the Works Progress Administration archaeological projects of the 1930s. They introduced us to Walter Taylor and the "Conjunctive Approach" and Thomas Kuhn and the paradigm shift to the "New (Processual Approach) Archaeology." We learned about Lewis Binford's "Middle Range Theory" for explanation, Michael Schiffer's "site formation processes," and the "new" fields of anthropologically focused historical archaeology and its cousin maritime archaeology, detailed by Keith Muckelroy. When we were freshmen in college, the movie *The Man Who Would Be King* was released. Though separated by hundreds of miles, we recognized ourselves in the characters of Danny Dravot and Peachy Carne-

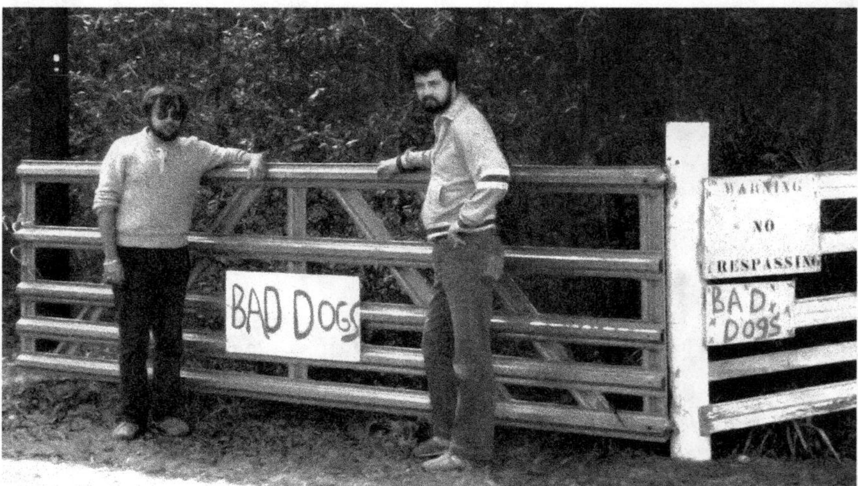

Figure P.2. Skowronek and Ewen, the "Bad Dogs," at an undisclosed location in Florida, 1986. (Authors' collection)

Figure P.3. Skowronek and Ewen in Williamsburg, Virginia, 2007. When they could not separate us, they found other means of keeping us out of trouble. (Authors' collection)

han. While we would never be "Kings of Kafiristan," we could be masters of our careers through our friendship.

We got our "band" back together at Florida State University in 1979. There we worked with Kathleen Deagan and George Fischer, earning master's degrees in anthropology and history before we headed off for our doctorates at the University of Florida and Michigan State and won tenured positions in historical archaeology on the East and West Coasts.

We often mused about how our deep friendship and less than reverent approach to the field earned us the title of "Bad Dogs" (Figure P.2). Both of us drew on our shared experiences in maritime archaeology through studies of the Manila galleon trade, smuggling in the colonial Caribbean and North American colonies, supplying Spanish California, and of course piracy.

The rest is history. Weddings, funerals, visits, and the annual Society of Historical Archaeology meeting have kept this friendship rock solid and locked in place (Figure P.3).

Soon we will relinquish our academic positions to a new generation of archaeologists trained in the postprocessual world. We will be watching, prepared to help or admonish.

RKS, Edinburg, Texas
CRE, Greenville, North Carolina

Acknowledgments

We wish to thank the University Press of Florida and our editor Mary Puckett for shepherding this project to completion. Special thanks are extended to Kathy Lewis for her excellent editing of the manuscript. We have been fortunate to work with her on all of these volumes. We are also grateful to the once anonymous reviewers of the manuscript for this book. The insights provided by Dr. Frederick "Fritz" H. Hanselmann of the University of Miami; Charles T. "Chuck" Meide, director of the Lighthouse Archaeological Maritime Program in St. Augustine, Florida; and Dr. Charles D. Bendig made this a much better book. We note a sort of symmetry in the University Press of Florida's selection of this team. Fritz contributed to our second pirate book, *Pieces of Eight*. Chuck came out of the Florida State University program that helped spawn our interest in maritime archaeology. And Dr. Bendig not only lent the eye of a Texas A&M nautical program graduate but has a connection to Naperville and the College of DuPage. What a small world and intertwined group!

OPENING SALVO

1

On Celebrating Piracy

But Should We?

Charles R. Ewen

On April 6, 2018, the *Charlotte Observer* published a story questioning why North Carolina would celebrate a murdering scoundrel like Blackbeard. The celebration revolved around the 300th anniversary of the death of North Carolina's most infamous pirate and, ironically, favorite son. The North Carolina Department of Natural and Cultural Resources went all out with a lecture series, a traveling museum exhibit, and pirate festivals in communities across the state. I even arranged for a cannon being conserved at the Queen Anne's Revenge Conservation Lab to be placed on a float in the East Carolina University (ECU) homecoming parade and brought to the stadium during the football game (our mascot is PeeDee the Pirate). I went out on the field with the chief conservator, Kim Kenyon, at half time, while the stadium announcer read a script about the cannon and the shipwreck. We received a hearty round of applause, and a good time was seemingly had by all. Blackbeard was once again as popular in North Carolina as when he was welcomed by Governor Charles Eden with a royal pardon in 1718.

A specific event prompted the newspaper article: the state-operated ferry system opted to fly Blackbeard's flag on three routes serving Ocracoke Island (ironically, where Blackbeard met his demise) as well as the route between the towns of Bayview and Aurora. Why would they do this? Pirates were the scourge of the southeastern American coast in the early eighteenth century. Scores of ships were captured and looted and an even larger number of individuals were either killed or captured. Blackbeard's banner supposedly depicted a skeleton holding an hourglass and spear and a heart dripping blood. When this black flag was raised, it struck terror in the hearts of honest merchants who knew their time was up. And now this evil ensign was to be flown by a passenger ferry?

The point is well taken. The article goes on to say, "Pirate lore charms tourists, but the former English privateer Edward Teach was known to torture the crews and passengers of merchant ships he plundered in the Caribbean and on the Atlantic coast" (Henderson 2018). We actually don't know that Blackbeard tortured anyone (see Kenyon, Chapter 2), but that is beside the point. Most members of the ferry-riding public *believe* that he did and are captivated by North Carolina's most notorious pirate. Have we no shame?

Apparently not, as the 2021 Pirate Invasion in Beaufort, North Carolina, showed us. In this continuation of the Blackbeard celebration, the schedule of events included a pirate "attack" on the Beaufort Hotel (beverages available in the lounge while you watch), "Breakfast with Blackbeard" for the kids, a parade through the town, a "battle" flotilla, and a pirate encampment. A memorial service was even dedicated to Blackbeard and his crew and all who fell during the Battle of Ocracoke (Beaufort Pirate Invasion 2021). It was a lot of fun and almost made you believe in Bartholomew "Black Bart" Roberts's view of piracy: "a short life and a merry one be my motto" (Johnson 1724a:214). But was it really?

Pirates as Terrorists

As we point out in the first two volumes of this series (*X Marks the Spot* and *Pieces of Eight*), the image of piracy in popular culture such as literature and movies has softened with the passage of time, but real pirates were far from jolly rogues. They were literal terrorists, intent on robbery and mayhem through intimidation and violence. As Rediker (2004:5–6) notes,

> Pirates consciously used terror to accomplish their aims—to obtain money, to punish those who resisted them, to take vengeance on those they considered their enemies, and to instill fear in sailors, captains, merchants, and officials who might wish to attack or resist pirates. . . . In truth, pirates were terrorists of a sort. And yet we do not think of pirates in this way. They have become, over the years, cultural heroes, perhaps antiheroes, and at the very least romantic and powerful figures in an American and increasingly global popular culture.

While you can confront an audience with the realities of piracy, it's difficult to convey the true horror they inspired.

Piracy in the eighteenth century was certainly terrifying, but was it what we would consider terrorism today? Modern terrorism is usually associated with political aims. Can we actually count pirates as terrorists or were they simply seaborne robbers? Burnett (2002:284) opines:

> There has been traditionally an ill-defined distinction between piracy and terrorism. Following the attacks on the World Trade Center and the Pentagon, governments world-wide finally began to take notice that there had been a war at sea long before September 11. . . . The attack [on the USS *Cole* in Aden] hammered home that we can no longer afford to ignore piracy, or deny its close relationship with terrorism.

Others make a similar point that piracy off the coast of Somalia is state-sponsored terrorism (Mueller and Adler 1985). The 2007 United States Policy for the Repression of Piracy and Other Criminal Acts of Violence at Sea was part of its global "War on Terrorism" (Marley 2011:180–181).

I was lecturing to my Caribbean Archaeology class at ECU a few years ago and tried to make this point about the reality of piracy. It was very hard to get past the Disney view of pirates that my students had grown up with. In a moment of inspiration, I decided to use the example of our football team's mascot, PeeDee the Pirate. I asked, "What if instead of being the ECU Pirates, we were the ECU Terrorists?" That got their attention. I let the students ponder this a bit and finished the lecture. At the end of class, a football player who sat in the back row came up to see me. He said that he'd been thinking of what I had said and wasn't sure he could play for the ECU Terrorists. Several of the students said it made them reconsider their image of piracy in light of how we revile terrorism, in all its forms, today. When I use this ECU Terrorist example in some of my local public lectures, it never fails to get a reaction—which is the point after all. The audience is startled, followed by nervous laughter. Good, it takes a jarring example to overcome a lifetime of gentle stereotyping.

An Archaeology of Piracy

So celebrating murder and mayhem can't be a good thing. Fortunately, archaeology gives us a legitimate opportunity to satisfy our guilty pleasure. Criminals, especially high-profile thieves, hold a fascination for many. Perhaps it is because they lead a life that most of us would not contemplate. We can vicariously follow their lives without actually hurting anyone. Or perhaps we admire how such people "got away with it" for so long (although most pirates' careers were brief). Whatever the motivation, archaeology is one of the socially acceptable ways that respectable people can enjoy piracy.

Legitimate Ways of Enjoying Piracy

We can get to know what the lives of pirates were like in the same way archaeologists get to know how any people lived in the past—through their stuff. Material culture studies allow us to throw off the tyranny of the historical record and see pirate lives as reflected in their belongings rather than merely through the writings of others. Kimberly Kenyon (Chapter 2) discusses some surprising finds from the *Queen Anne's Revenge* that illuminate everyday life aboard a pirate ship. Even a scrap of paper stuffed in a cannon breech block can tell a fascinating tale. The discussion of how the material recovered from the wreck was identified is as fascinating as the artifacts themselves. Though the purposes of their voyages differed, in many ways the activities of pirates at sea were similar to the shipboard life of legitimate sailors of the period. This has made connecting the shipwreck site to Blackbeard challenging (see Wilde-Ramsing and Ewen 2012).

Still, written history is integral to the study of pirates. As noted in our previous volumes, it is extremely difficult, if not impossible, to identify a pirate site without some help from the historical record. Jessie Cragg and Michael Thomin (Chapter 3) tackle this problem in looking at the material remains associated with nineteenth-century piracy. Unlike the Golden Age of Piracy (late seventeenth/early eighteenth century), these were smaller-scale operations involving out-of-work privateers and coastal bandits. Cragg and Thomin focus on terrestrial bases and compare "pirate villages" to coastal habitation sites. Again, working with both the archaeological record and the historical record is the key to identifying these lairs and comparing them to the homes of more honest seafarers.

Material culture studies can be used to inform popular culture as well. Film production companies routinely hire historical advisors to help portray the period of a television series or movie more accurately. Coy Idol and Katherine Thomas (Chapter 4) follow this progression to the next logical step and examine how video games have used and misused archaeology in their pirate-themed adventures. Serious scholars may find the idea of a video game's historical accuracy silly, but tens of millions of these games have been sold and influence our students earlier and more profoundly than we academics ever do. Perhaps playing *Assassin's Creed IV: Black Flag* might actually inspire a gamer to investigate the "rest of the story."

Jean Soulat (Chapter 5) reexamines pirate material culture from a European perspective. He perceives the context of piracy to be multicultural, in both the composition of the crews and the material culture they acquired. His summary complements the other offerings in this section.

Then there is the question of recognizing a pirate in the archaeological record. In fact, this was the central question for our first volume, *X Marks the Spot, in* 2006 and continued to be the main thread in *Pieces of Eight* in 2016. It remains an important issue in this volume. If anything, this shows the important role that historical archaeology plays in identifying illicit behavior in the past. As I often tell my students, archaeological sites are like crime scenes set in the past. The historians are the detectives, taking depositions from the witnesses. Sometimes those witnesses miss important clues or misinterpret what they saw or even outright lie for any number of reasons. The archaeologists are the crime-scene technicians gathering the physical evidence, which relies on one layer less of human bias (archaeologist versus historian plus author of the historical record) and tends to hold up better in court. Still, without the historical record, the archaeological record would be harder to interpret. You must know a crime has occurred before you can look for clues to solve it.

Even when you know that pirates were in the vicinity, it is still difficult to distinguish a pirate ship from a merchant vessel—especially since pirate ships were often repurposed merchant vessels. And how can you tell if their cargo was stolen? Courtney Page and I (Page and Ewen 2016) made these comparisons in a previous volume and found that—despite some anecdotal differences (loaded cannon, variety of cargo)—there were not enough data to confidently define a "pirate pattern." This is where connecting a site to known pirate activity is essential. With each new ship or lair discovered and excavated, more comparative data can be applied to the identification of undocumented sites. In this book we continue to make progress toward that end.

Megan Victor (Chapter 6) examines the blurred line between pirates and fishermen in two seaside communities in New England, following two different tracks as far as making an honest living. One is a solid Maine fishing plantation producing a steady supply of salt cod. The other is a loose confederation of fishermen sailing close to the line separating the legal from the illegal. Curiously, the sketchy community produced better salt cod, when not engaged in piracy.

Lundy Island would appear to fit the stereotype of a pirate lair. Located at the mouth of the Bristol Channel, it was an ideal place to intercept ships and raid the mainland or engage in smuggling. All of these activities are documented to have taken place. While certain features of the landscape could be connected with piracy, Patrick Boyle (Chapter 7) has found that identifying particular artifacts with them is not possible with any degree of certainty.

Bradley Rodgers and Jason Raupp (Chapter 8) appear to have solved a crime that would have gone unrecognized by archaeologists without both documentary and archaeological lines of evidence. In this case, a privateer was undone by Bermuda islanders, who saved the crew members from a storm then took their ship, stripped it, and made it look like a wreck (a salvaged ship looks much like a wreck unless you know what you are looking for, as Rodgers and Raupp do).

Another mystery solved involves a shipwreck off the coast of Brazil. The wreck was long believed to be a pirate ship, but its identification was in doubt. In an extensive investigation of the historical and archaeological record, Geraldo Hostin (Chapter 12) makes a compelling case for this ship being *La Louise*, captained by Olivier Levasseur, the notorious La Buse. He notes that this discovery opens new opportunities for further studies of a true pirate shipwreck, the only one of its kind in Brazil.

Several of the contributors to this volume begin with the historical record and suggest where and how archaeology might be used to verify the connections with pirates and illuminate their poorly documented lives.

It is almost comical how many place-names in the US Virgin Islands are related to pirates, both historical and fictional. Kenneth Wild (Chapter 9) investigates the veracity of these pirate geography connections, coining the term "pirateers" to characterize the blurred lines between privateers and pirates in the islands. Research involving the original Danish deed records attempts to connect these pirateers with their land holdings—with archaeological investigations to follow.

Daniel Finamore's (2006) chapter in *X Marks the Spot* characterizes the logwood cutters along the coast of Honduras as opportunistic pirates. He describes their temporary camps as makeshift in nature but often supplied with high-end items (such as porcelain) stolen from passing ships. Alexandre Coulaud, Nathalie Sellier-Ségard, and Martijn van den Bel (Chapter 10) find a similar situation on war-torn St. Martin island in the French West Indies. A protected anchorage out of sight of passing ships with lightly built structures and a rich array of artifacts add up to a pirate lair. A pattern is emerging.

Along these lines are the turtling encampments off the Miskito Coast, where pirates exploited a turbulent environment of international hostilities and ethnic tensions to partner with the native inhabitants and further their illicit enterprises. Lynn Harris (Chapter 13) describes how the intertwining of turtle harvesting, slave trading, and opportunistic pirating creates a complex ethnographic picture of the eighteenth-century Central American coast.

Few places have a stronger association with pirates and are less studied than Isle de la Tortue (Turtle Island: Tortuga) off the northwest coast of Haiti. The island was a notorious early buccaneer hangout prior to the rise of Port Royal in Jamaica and Nassau in the Bahamas. What made it a great hideout was its access to the sea-lanes and its remoteness from population centers. Its remoteness today has preserved its isolation. Laurent Pavlidis (Chapter 11) discusses the possibilities for productive research if investigators could gain access to the island.

The book winds up in another remote hotbed of piracy: Madagascar. Jean Soulat, Yann von Arnim, and Patrick Lizé (Chapter 15) revisit the *Speaker*, one of the first pirate ships ever archaeologically investigated. After forty years, new excavations are planned on the wreck to answer questions raised in *X Marks the Spot* (Lizé 2006). John de Bry and Jean Soulat (Chapter 14) also report on recent and additional planned archaeological investigations in and around Ambodifototra Bay on Sainte-Marie Island.

When we started examining the archaeology of piracy, Russ and I were forced to beat the bushes to find examples of such research. Even the authors who contributed to *X Marks the Spot* were sheepishly reluctant to admit to studying a topic as popular as pirates. It seemed the more popular the topic, the more suspect the science. Three volumes later, the archaeology of piracy has attained a legitimacy that has encouraged others to pursue the subject and add to the database that will allow future researchers to identify undocumented pirate sites in the archaeological record. We think that the latest additions are something to celebrate. Enjoy these guilt-free investigations of piracy!

Acknowledgments

We wish to thank the University Press of Florida and our editor Mary Puckett for shepherding this project to completion. Special thanks are extended to Kathy Lewis for her excellent editing of the manuscript. We have been fortunate to work with her on all of these volumes. We are also grateful to the once anonymous reviewers of the manuscript for this book. The insights provided by Dr. Frederick "Fritz" H. Hanselmann of the University of Miami; Charles T. "Chuck" Meide, director of the Lighthouse Archaeological Maritime Program in St. Augustine, Florida; and Dr. Charles D. Bendig made this a much better book. We note a sort of symmetry in the University Press of Florida's selection of this team. Fritz contributed to our second pirate book, *Pieces of Eight*. Chuck came out of the Florida State University program that helped spawn our interest in maritime archaeology. And Dr. Bendig not only lent the eye of a Texas A&M nautical program graduate but has a connection to Naperville and the College of DuPage. What a small world and intertwined group!

2

The Stories They Tell

Recent Finds from *Queen Anne's Revenge*/*La Concorde* (1718)

Kimberly P. Kenyon

Piracy greatly complicates the interpretation of the archaeological record. Material culture associated with pirates speaks of theft, an opportunistic exchange of goods, and an abrupt shift in how an object is used and its perceived value. These factors all contribute to obscuring an artifact's provenance. Few sites embody that complexity like North Carolina archaeological site 31CR314, the wreck of Blackbeard's *Queen Anne's Revenge*, which has been under investigation since its discovery in 1996. Initial research was focused on the identification of the wreck as undoubtedly that of the pirate's infamous flagship (Wilde-Ramsing and Ewen 2012), abandoned near Beaufort, North Carolina, in early June 1718 (South Carolina Court of Vice-Admiralty 1719:45–46).

Prior to its brief and ill-fated stint as a pirate's vessel to display force, the ship was employed for most of its service at sea in the French slave trade under the ownership of wealthy merchant René Montaudoin of Nantes (Moore and Daniel 2001). Over the course of four years and three slaving voyages, the vessel then known as *La Concorde* was used to transport 1,265 captive Africans from West Africa to the Caribbean to be sold into slavery (Emory University 2019: Voyage IDs 30028, 30059, and 30090). During the Middle Passage of the third voyage, the ship was seized by Blackbeard, renamed, and reoutfitted to serve as an unmistakable symbol of the pirate's power over the Atlantic.

Artifacts from *Queen Anne's Revenge* have the potential to tell a much greater tale than just the story of a feared pirate. Full excavation has produced over 400,000 artifacts, with half the wreck's footprint still unexplored. Many objects are obscured by concretion, a dense substance made of iron corrosion

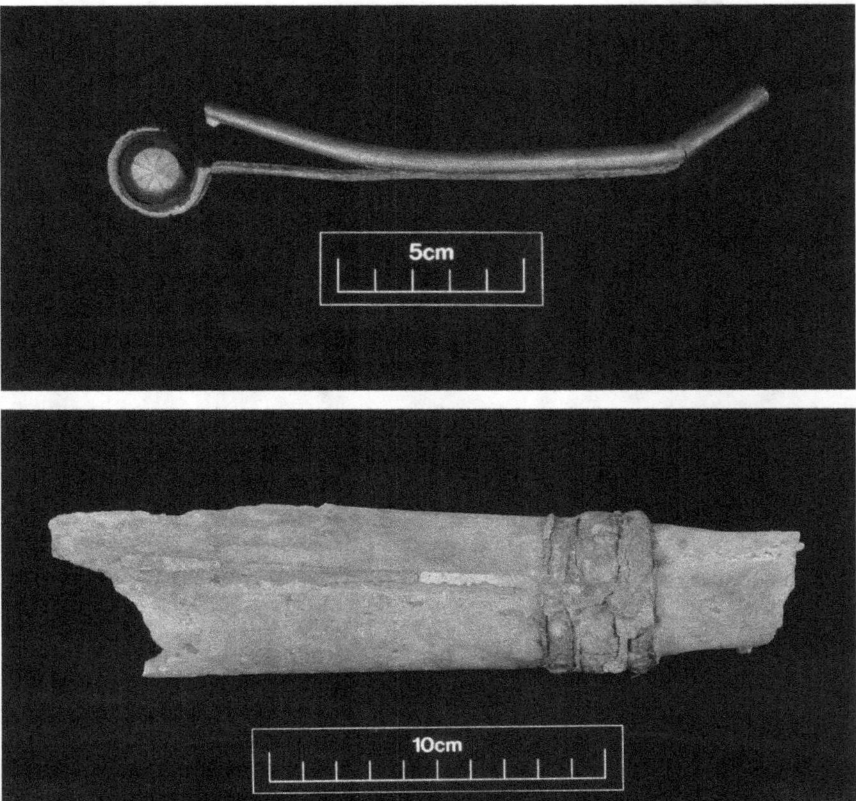

Figure 2.1. Boatswain's whistle (*top*) and speaking trumpet (*bottom*). (Image by North Carolina Department of Natural and Cultural Resources)

and marine growth. Concretions are X-rayed to identify the contents, but this sometimes creates more questions that can only be answered once an artifact is freed.

The abundance of archaeological evidence offers a chance to better understand a vessel whose conversion from slave ship to pirate ship shortly before its loss broadens the story revealed by those artifacts. New discoveries from the site represent a multidimensional social network, the transatlantic slave trade, English piracy in the Caribbean, and the chronicles of the many unsuspecting victims in Blackbeard's path.

Means of Communication

Communication at sea in the Age of Sail was limited to visual signals using flags and audible signals using speaking trumpets, whistles, and even signaling cannon. One bronze swivel gun, showing characteristics of English signal guns of the early 1700s, has been previously detailed (Brown 2007; Smith and Brown 2007), but two new artifacts (Figure 2.1) also relate to shipboard communications and may even connect to individuals on board.

Boatswain's Call

A small globe (QAR1108.010) was noted in X-ray in 2016. Its likeness was compared to a prosthetic eye and even a tiny version of Darth Vader's Death Star from *Star Wars*. Careful extraction from concretion has now allowed its construction to be studied. The orb is made of two sheet-copper hemispheres soldered together, with the join capped by an incomplete circumferential band decorated with diagonal and vertical lines. The sphere is not perfectly round but elongated toward the copper-alloy caps, which bear a pattern of eight spokes. A hole in the body corresponds with the gap in the band (Martindale 2018b).

Tentative identifications of the orb have included a bead or a sword pommel, but another possibility has come to light. Twenty-three whistles in the Portable Antiquities Scheme database (British Museum 2020) resemble QAR1108.010. Twelve are described as hemispheres of sheet metal soldered together with a raised equatorial rib. Another object discovered many years earlier (QAR345.001) in the same area as QAR1108.010 was described as a copper-alloy tube. When examined together, the two artifacts join cleanly, forming the buoy and the gun to a whistle. While whistles were considered tools, toys, and even mementos, a specific whistle named the boatswain's call was used for communicating orders at sea.

Historical documents disclose the identities of two boatswains whose lives became entangled with Blackbeard. Jean Goué was listed on *La Concorde*'s 1717 muster roll as the *contremaître* (Ernaud 1718; Ducoin 2001: Annexe XII) or ship's boatswain (Fusaro et al. 2020: Table of Roles on Board), which even records that he earned twenty-four livres per month. His ultimate fate—whether he joined the pirates or returned to France—is unknown (Moore and Daniel 2001: Table 1). Ignatius Pell served as the boatswain aboard Stede Bonnet's *Revenge* and was present when Blackbeard encountered Bonnet in September 1717 (South Carolina Court of Vice-Admiralty 1719:11–12, 38, 48); however, it is unclear whether Pell ever actually boarded *Queen Anne's Revenge*.

These calls were not exclusive to boatswains but were also carried by other officers and were often a symbol of the bearer's rank (Höglund 2019:43–44). It is possible that this whistle belonged to or was used by other crew members of both *La Concorde* and *Queen Anne's Revenge* or was a personal possession stolen along the way.

Speaking Trumpet

The X-ray of concretion QAR687.000 gave conservators much fuel for debate. The cylindrical artifact it contained was thought to be a spyglass, a powder horn, or even a type of carrying case. It is made of extremely thin, heavily corroded sheet metal and surrounded by glass beads within its dense concretion, making conservation time-consuming. The concretion was dismantled in 2018, producing seventy-nine beads and one fragile pewter speaker's trumpet, QAR687.030 (Figure 2.1).

Much like the boatswain's call, the speaker's trumpet was a symbol of rank and served an important function in relaying orders to the crew. This trumpet served as a megaphone rather than as a musical instrument, so the bearer assumed a certain amount of responsibility in its use. The ship's speaker was recognized by the crew as being respected and trusted by the captain (Höglund 2019:43).

Philippe Charles from Pont d'Arche (likely modern-day Pont-de-l'Arche) is listed on the muster roll for *La Concorde*'s final voyage (Ducoin 2001: Annexe XII), earning eighteen livres as the *trompette* (trumpeter). Ernaud (1718) mentions the *passager trompette* in his deposition, although he could not recall his name. Ernaud does provide one other interesting detail about the trumpeter: he was Black, making him (along with Joseph Alabard of Whydah in Africa), one of two Black members of *La Concorde*'s crew.

Paper

Some of the most puzzling objects from the site are remnants of printed paper removed from a breech block in 2017. Due to the fragility of waterlogged paper and its near nonexistence in the archaeological record, the paper has created unique and rewarding challenges in both its conservation and its interpretation (Farrell et al. 2018).

The paper was found layered within a textile gasket sealing the breech block (QAR1445.010), a reusable gunpowder chamber that enabled rapid reloading of breech-loading cannon. The legible text was transcribed, noting successive lines of words and letters. Keywords such as "fathom" and "*South*" suggested an English-language navigational treatise published before 1718, the

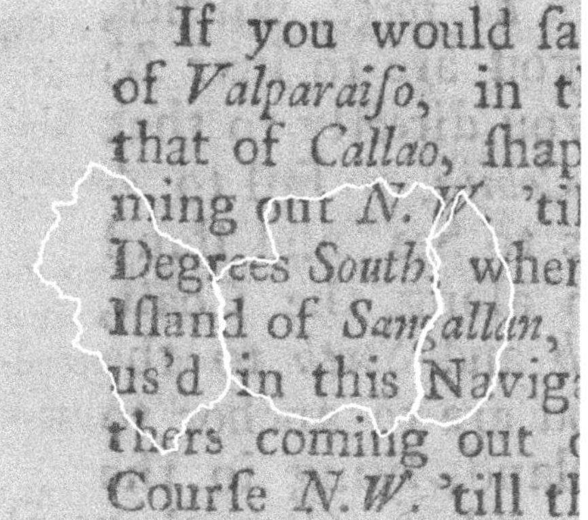

If you would ſa
of *Valparaiſo*, in t
that of *Callao*, ſhap
ming out *N. W.* 'ti
Degrees *South*, wher
Iſland of *Sangallan*,
us'd in this Navig
thers coming out
Courſe *N.W.* 'till t

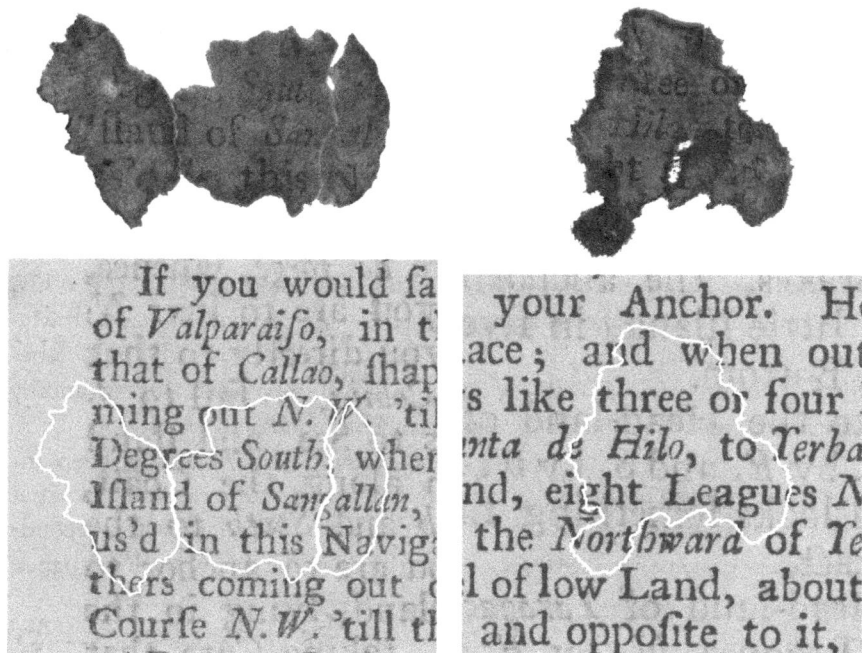

Figure 2.2. Fragments of printed text recovered from a breech block (*top*) compared with pages of Cooke's 1712 *A Voyage to the South Sea and Round the World* (*bottom*). (Image by North Carolina Department of Natural and Cultural Resources)

year the ship ran aground. Voyage narratives of the time were numerous, so to limit search terms the distinct word *Hilo* (the Spanish word for thread) was explored. Since it was capitalized and italicized, *Hilo* was thought to be the name of a location in the Spanish holdings. One candidate was the modern-day city of Ilo, Peru, which is mentioned as a stop in several seventeenth- and eighteenth-century accounts. Various authors (Ayres 1684; Exquemelin 1684, 1685; Dampier 1697; Wafer 1699; Funnell 1707; Cooke 1712; Rogers 1712; Frézier 1717) differ in their spelling of the same location (Hilo, Ely, Ylo, Heloe, Ilo, and He lo hé), which was verified by the proximity of each occurrence in a passage to other place-names such as Arica, Chile, and Arequipa, Peru. These variations assisted in further eliminating candidates.

The fragments were found to match pages 178 and 183–188 of Captain Edward Cooke's *A Voyage to the South Sea and Round the World*, published in 1712 upon his return from a three-year privateering voyage led by Woodes Rogers (Figure 2.2). No other historical information could be found on the fate of Edward Cooke, largely because Rogers later became a significant historical figure and thus overshadowed his fellow captain and author. Rogers was dispatched to the Bahamas in 1718 as the colony's first royal governor, with specific orders to put an end to the rampant piracy on the islands. In his own published book about that same 1712 voyage, Rogers (1712:xvi–xvii) makes clear his feelings on pirates: they are criminals who are not to be glorified or romanticized.

Historians have noted a likely connection between Rogers and Blackbeard, who were of similar background, education, and origins, even saying that Rogers might have been the only person in the Caribbean aware of Blackbeard's true identity and familial connections (Konstam 2006:13–15). While it is compelling that pages of a book written by the compatriot of a man who was vehemently antipiracy were discovered on a pirate ship, the motive behind use of the pages in artillery and a connection between Rogers (and by extension Cooke) and Blackbeard can only be speculative.

Additional paper in the form of coarse cartridge paper has since been unloaded from seven of the twelve cannon that are now fully cleaned. All paper from the site comes from artillery contexts, used as cartridges, with a secondary use as a gasket or wadding for a breech block in the case of the book paper.

Personal Arms

Popular culture is rife with imagery of swashbucklers armed to the teeth, and no review of artifacts from a pirate ship would be complete without mention of personal arms. Weapons were widely traded across the wilderness that was the Atlantic world in the early eighteenth century. Merchants needed to protect themselves and their cargos against raids. Pirates as the aggressors had an intrinsic need for arms to carry out their sole mission: to disrupt commerce and profit from the loot. Given the nature of the loss of *Queen Anne's Revenge*, portable items of value, including weapons, were likely offloaded before abandonment. This may explain the dearth of evidence for weapons to date.

Firearms

Personal firearms initially were only found in fragments: isolated gunlocks, brass furniture, a partial gunstock, the occasional broken barrel, and one stamped musketoon barrel (Lusardi 2002:37). This began to change as all concretions were X-rayed and the films were analyzed for content and inventoried (Kenyon 2016). Once the first semiarticulated musket was discovered, it was hoped that there would be others. A pistol and three additional muskets were subsequently identified. Unfortunately, the site is notoriously unkind to preservation of organic matter. None of the guns' wooden stocks are complete, and no butts have survived.

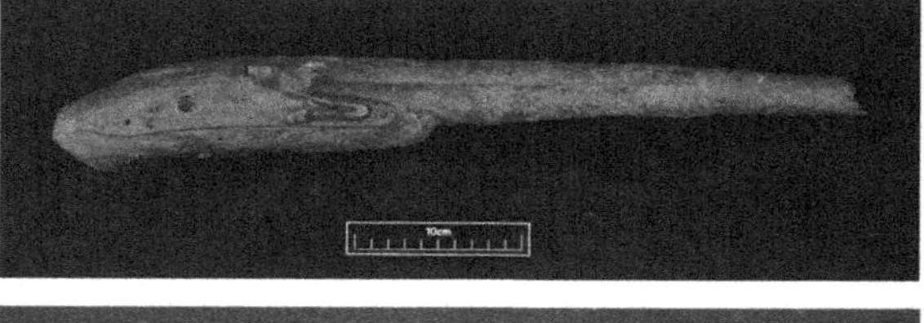

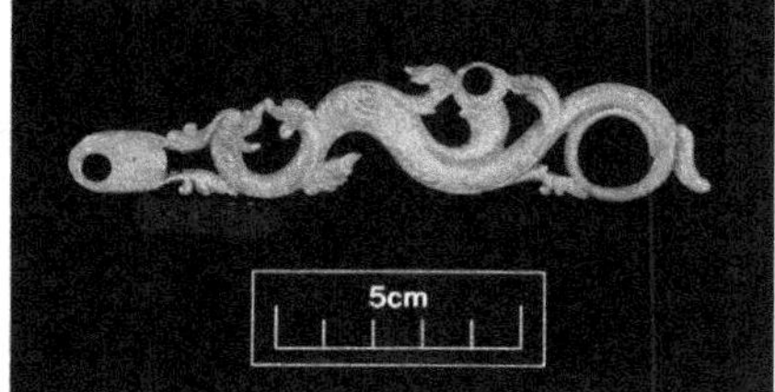

Figure 2.3. English doglock musket, QAR3111.008 (*upper left*); Dutch or English musket, QAR1402.005 (*lower left*) and its associated side plate, QAR2392.032 (*right*). (Image by North Carolina Department of Natural and Cultural Resources)

Two of the muskets have been deconcreted and have distinct features that aid in identification (Figure 2.3). QAR3111.008 was the first to be discovered and subjected to conservation, and its characteristics are typical of English muskets. A fastener hole behind the cock and near the bottom edge of the lock plate indicates that the lock was manufactured as a doglock, a type of gun made with a safety or "dog" that was favored by the English. These were only manufactured for a short period and were routinely modified to remove the safety (Bailey 2009:16–26). The face of the plate is flat, a feature that was discontinued by the middle of the eighteenth century (Blackmore 1961:42–43). The flat serpentine side plate with simple engraving, again of English origin, reveals that this gun was a lower-grade commercial trade gun (Gooding 2003:70–71).

The second musket to be cleaned, QAR1402.005, has a barrel that transitions from octagonal at the breech to round at the muzzle, with an engraved band commonly called a wedding band. It has one copper-alloy ramrod pipe still in place, with bulbous carving around it to serve as a grip for the steadying hand. Further decorative carving is found around the barrel tang. A gun of similar design dating to 1705 or 1706 is found in the Tower of London Armouries collection and bears the London hallmark and proof marks, along with the mark of English maker H. Pickfatt (Blair 1962: Plate 353).

While no side plate was attached, the finely carved mortise established that the missing plate was quite intricate. One such side plate (QAR2392.032) was found previously in concretion and fit perfectly into QAR1402.005 when the two were compared. This side plate and the remains of the carving signify that the gun was of higher quality. A fabric impression covers much of the barrel, perhaps evidence that the gun was carefully stowed at the time of the grounding.

The musket's features suggest either Dutch or more likely English origin, resembling late seventeenth-century English fowlers (Erik Goldstein, personal communication, 2021). Guns of the two nationalities share many characteristics, so it is usually the makers' marks that help determine origin. Unfortunately, the barrel has no surviving marks and no associated gunlock, where additional marks are typically found. The Dutch were prolific arms traders in the late seventeenth and early eighteenth centuries, so a Dutch gun could have come aboard the ship through several channels: procured in France prior to departure (Gooding 2003:49), purchased through trade in Africa, or acquired in the Caribbean and brought aboard by the pirates. There are also many explanations for the musket's presence on board if it is English.

The pistol (QAR1211.017) was only discovered when beginning to remove it from concretion. The copper-alloy "cup" was noted in X-ray, but its purpose as the pistol's butt cap was clear only after its removal. The barrel is octagonal at the breech and round toward the muzzle and was not outfitted with a side plate. The simple style of butt cap and plain iron trigger guard and the offset trigger are typical of military-issue English pistols of the late seventeenth or early eighteenth century. The rounded face of the lock plate was favored following the ascension of James II to the throne in 1685 (Blackmore 1961:36).

Edged Weapons

Evidence of bladed weapons remains sparse, but five relevant artifacts have been identified at present. A quillon block or cross guard bearing fine carvings, an antler grip with decorative copper-alloy caps belonging to a separate sword, and a copper-alloy scabbard clip were found independently. Another grip (QAR1853.000) made of boxwood with fine pewter inlay (Figure 2.4) has parallels in Amsterdam. Two similarly inlaid wooden handles of the same size, dating from the early to mid-eighteenth century and classified as table knives, were discovered in the Amstel riverbed during digging of a tunnel for the North/South metro line in the early 2000s (Gawronski and Kranendonk 2020: NZD1.00322MTL001 and NZD1.00422MTL004). As masters of makeshift weaponry, pirates likely would have used any available knife as a weapon. Given its diminutive size, however, it may have been intended for use as a table knife.

Another sword grip (QAR3170.013) is a recent find that, much like the pistol, was not obvious in X-ray. The only part visible was the wire wrap, now known to be decoration on the grip (Figure 2.4). The wrap is made of braided pewter wire with a twisted copper wire surround, which terminates at either

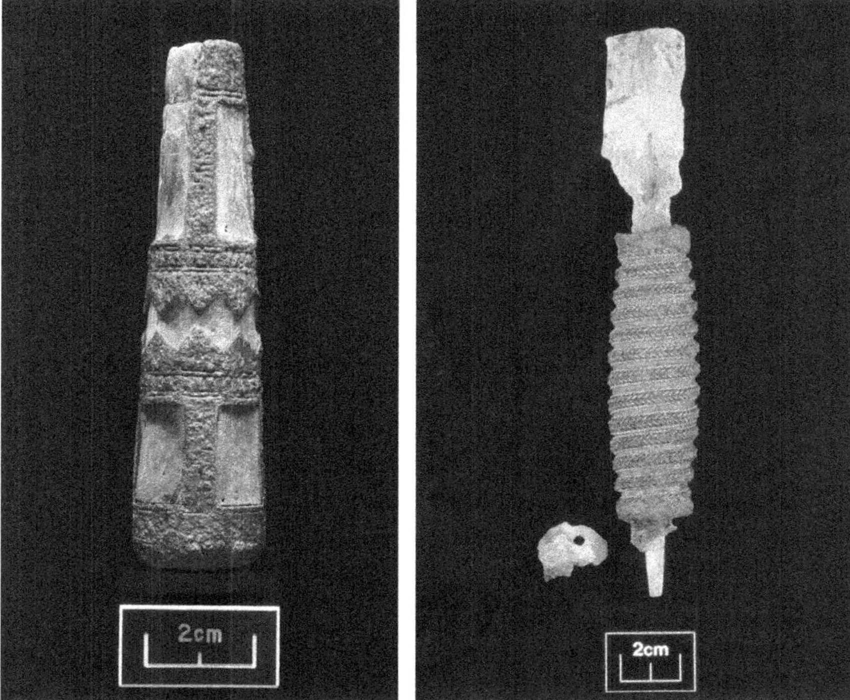

Figure 2.4. Table knife handle with pewter inlay (*left*) and sword grip with wire wrap (*right*). (Image by North Carolina Department of Natural and Cultural Resources)

end in a sailor's knot. Elemental analysis using portable X-ray fluorescence confirmed the metal identifications. Beneath the wrap is the well-preserved wooden grip. Part of the blade survived in the form of a concretion void, typical of wrought iron having completely corroded away. This void served as a mold that was used to faithfully re-create the lost blade in epoxy resin. Once the epoxy hardened, the concretion was carefully removed, preserving the shape and characteristics of the blade.

Braided grips appear commonly throughout the centuries and across the European continent. Archaeological parallels can be found on the French ship *La Belle* (1686) (Kampfl 2019:77–111) and *Dartmouth*. The latter grip was of much finer quality and no doubt a prized possession (Martin 2017:175–178). Grips of this type are found on English, Spanish, Danish, Italian, French, German, and Dutch swords, as early as the fifteenth century, with one example even known to have been manufactured in Japan and destined for the European market (Blair 1962: Plate 153).

Polearm

QAR2025.000 represents a simple shape: a two-tined wrought-iron fork hafted to a wooden rod. The tines are straight and form a V shape, with a distance of 5.08 cm between them. The fork is socketed to the rod, with remains of organic matting between the metal socket and the wooden rod. A small section of rope wrapped around the fork may or may not be incidental.

Four different forked implements common in the early eighteenth century were explored for identification. The fishing spear is an instrument of obvious utility aboard any sailing vessel. This tool was socketed to a wooden handle; however, fishing spears typically had multiple barbed tines. Meat forks were similar in form but were fully forged of iron because cooking occurred over an open flame. Another possibility was a musket rest, a socketed tool used to stabilize a musket when aiming and firing. The tines were set far apart to accommodate the width of the musket and were rolled outward rather than sharpened. The tines of QAR2025.000 are sharp and set closely together, so this possibility was eliminated.

Finally, QAR2025.000 was compared to a specific type of polearm called the fork. Polearms, also referred to as staves or hafted weapons, were staff weapons in use from the Middle Ages to the late seventeenth century and encompass a wide array of shapes, including the halberd, partisan, and pike. These weapons were likely derived from agricultural implements, which were easily repurposed with little to no modification. The fork resembles a farmer's pitchfork, with straight, sharpened tines. Military forks were specifically produced beginning in the fifteenth century but had fallen out of favor by the early eighteenth century (Blair 1962:21–24). So far, QAR2025.000 is the only example of a polearm in the collection. This comes as no surprise, as this style of weapon was already in decline.

It is difficult to attribute any weapon, as a whole, to one specific nationality or maker. Both firearms and bladed weapons were manufactured as separate parts, sometimes in different countries, to be assembled later and personalized by a prospective owner. There are also the issues of adaptation, replacement of parts, revivalism, and imitation (Blair 1962:75), which all muddle the interpretation of archaeological finds. Once weapons have then traded hands through piracy, their origins become even more obscured. The mix of weapons, from finer to more rudimentary, may indicate varying social status among members of the crew of a merchant vessel like *La Concorde* or even the happenstance gathering of looted weapons by Blackbeard and his band of pirates.

Personal Items

Some of the most stirring artifacts are those that people on board may have carried on their person. They serve as a poignant reminder of the human connection in archaeology. Despite the span of centuries, people have changed very little in our basic needs like clothing for protection or our personal attachments to objects we treasure.

Pocket Watch

Several delicate pieces found in concretion relate to timekeeping (Figure 2.5): a gilt brass filigree balance cock, a brass balance arbor setup wheel, and heavily corroded pewter rings, which are likely the remains of a watch case. The oblong shape of the balance cock and the design reveal that the pieces belong to a pocket watch manufactured between 1660 and 1675, making the watch somewhat of an heirloom at the time of its loss. Most pocket watches in museum collections are made of precious metals and were therefore more likely to be preserved and handed down through families. No other pewter examples have been found, although watch cases were routinely made of varying materials, such as crystal, amber, porcelain, iron, and leather, so other nonprecious metals are possible (Martindale 2018a).

Timekeeping at sea was typically the responsibility of the pilot (Gardiner 2005:264–267). There were five aboard *La Concorde*: Charles Duval, Pierre Sagory, Charles Ragideau, Pierre Emory, and Louis Dirpinosè (Moore and Daniel 2001: Table 1). Duval, the first pilot and probably the most experi-

Figure 2.5. Pocket-watch parts (*left*) and copper-alloy bird figurine, likely of Akan origin (*right*). (Image by North Carolina Department of Natural and Cultural Resources)

enced of the five, was forcibly retained by Blackbeard, implying a need for this role among the pirate crew. While a watch could have belonged to any of these men or to another crew member altogether, as with anything of value, it is also possible that a personal item like this was an obvious target for pirates seeking shiny goods to steal.

Bird Figurine

One small object has sparked much conversation since its discovery in 2006. A small copper-alloy figurine of a bird (QAR111.004), resembling a hen or rooster (Figure 2.5), was thought to be a decorative finial. Further research has offered another possibility. Gold dust was used extensively as currency in West Africa, and a necessary tool of this trade was the use of brass weights to determine the value of the dust. Though it is incomplete, the figurine's current weight of 7.0 grams falls well within the spectrum of known weight standards—typically ranging from 0.04 to 352 grams (Garrard 1973)—of the Akan peoples of West Africa. Its size at 2.55 cm compares favorably to two examples of bird-themed weights (measuring 3.5 cm and 4.45 cm, respectively) in the collection of the Metropolitan Museum of Art (2020: Accessions 1994.312.17 and 1994.312.16).

As early as 1400, geometric shapes were manufactured in copper alloy to weight standards used by the Akan. Copper-alloy figurine weights began to appear around 1700. However, lack of standardization among the figurines suggests that some may have been used secondarily as weights if they corresponded with known standards, but they were likely not made for this purpose. These figurines occur in many shapes (Metropolitan Museum of Art 2020; Smithsonian National Museum of African Art 2020) and were likely produced as "proverb stones": representative of proverbs or sayings in a culture with a rich oral tradition (Mollat 2003). A collection of proverb stones served as a sacred text to be passed down, conveying the collective wisdom of previous bearers (Kouadio 2018:30–33). Small figurines such as this and other tokens from their former lives may have been hidden by African captives as they boarded *La Concorde* (Handler 2009; Webster 2005:253) or even acquired by merchants and sailors in Africa as mementos of the voyage (Webster 2005:255–256).

Galley Wares

Evidence from the ship's galley includes glass bottles, pewter plates and spoons, ceramic vessels, and even animal bones, remnants of the shipboard diet. Three different types of cast-iron cooking pots have been identified: a pot-bellied cauldron of common form, a straight-sided pot with long legs similar to one found in Amsterdam dating from 1600 to 1750 (Gawronski and Kranendonk 2020:NZR2.00516MTL195), and a fragment of a third in the form of a thick, ribbed leg with a small portion of the body attached. Two new additions to this category continue to shape our understanding of the need for sustenance on long voyages.

Copper Pot

Small fragments of a riveted copper pot (QAR1895.001 and QAR2418.001) were recently unearthed (Figure 2.6). An estimation of size is not possible because the remains are fragmentary and were scattered across the site. A kettle ear (QAR1310.000) may belong to the same pot, along with several rivets and additional fragments of sheet copper. Copper cauldrons have been found on other sites in better states of preservation, such as the wrecks of *Mynden* (1718) (Auer 2004:273–275) and *Swan* (1653) (Martin 2017:121–124) in galley contexts, as well as an isolated find in the Amstel River (Gawronski and Kranendonk 2020: NZR2.00210MTL001). Two large copper cauldrons discovered on *Henrietta Marie*, an English slave ship that wrecked off the coast of Florida in 1700, were likely used to feed the hundreds of captive Africans on board during the Middle Passage (Webster 2005:252). Another from the Emanuel Point shipwreck (1559) contained remnants of pitch, indicative of its use in keeping the ship in good repair (Bratten 2018:141–144). Without similar trace evidence from *Queen Anne's Revenge*, it is not yet possible to narrow the pot's function, but either purpose would have been critical to a ship making the long Middle Passage voyage. *La Concorde*'s cooks, Pierre Peron and Georges Bardeau, or even the caulker, Jean Puloin, could have put such

Figure 2.6. Fragment of a riveted copper cauldron (*left*) and a personalized pewter spoon handle (*right*). (Image by North Carolina Department of Natural and Cultural Resources)

a cauldron to use. While both cooks perished during the voyage, Puloin was one of the crew kidnapped by the pirates (Moore and Daniel 2001: Table 1), which reflects the essential need for maintaining a watertight hull.

Personalized Spoon Handle

Several fragments of spoons and complete spoons have emerged through the years, but one small fragment stands out among the others (Figure 2.6). Parallels are found as intact pewter spoons from the wreck of *Dartmouth* in 1690 (Holman 1975:260) as well as fragments of spoon handles catalogued in the Portable Antiquities Scheme database (British Museum 2020: Objects DENO-7DC9DD and SUR-0A8CDA). These are variants of the trifid handle, with the same subtle lobes found on QAR3697.001. However, the example from *Queen Anne's Revenge* was customized by the owner with shallowly carved engraving. A lowercase "t" on one side resembles the symbol of Christianity, and on the reverse is a crossed pattern, reminiscent of corseted lacing, gradually widening toward the end. Engraved spoons, many with the owner's initials, have been found throughout the United Kingdom (British Museum 2020: Objects DEV-CC48BC, SWYOR-499614, SUR-F8CD29, SF-5305F9, and YORYM-E82056), suggesting that personalization was common. In the case of QAR3697.001, the meaning behind the marks will likely remain known only to the person who carved them.

Piracy and the Archaeological Record

Interpreting the remains of a ship known to have engaged in piracy is no simple task. Reports of what was taken from Blackbeard's victims range from tools, instruments, gold, cargos, and personal effects to the people themselves and the ships on which they sailed. *La Concorde*'s last journey is well detailed. Once the ship's story was unalterably stained by piracy, however, the interpretation of artifacts, how they came to be on board, and who used them becomes muddied. *La Concorde* was neither the first nor the last ship Blackbeard attacked during his reign of terror: as *Queen Anne's Revenge*, it was used to mercilessly plunder other vessels in the Caribbean and mid-Atlantic. Artifacts may have entered the narrative at any point—from the moment *La Concorde* departed Nantes, through trade along the way, or from victims of theft on the high seas. All are possibilities when interpreting such a collection. Each new discovery holds the potential to reveal more about the people connected to this complex vessel than ever before, giving a voice to the experiences of the many men and women impacted by the ship's fateful final voyage.

3

Sail Bags and Black Flags

Identifying Material Culture of Nineteenth-Century Pirates

Jessie Cragg and Michael Thomin

On May 14, 1794, Spanish captain Bartolome de Aranguren and his crew set sail on *San Juan Nepomuceno* from Florida to Matanzas. On June 3 the ship departed from Cuba to transport a cargo of corn back to Florida. Less than a week into the voyage, two boats crewed by thirty Anglo-American pirates (de Aranguren 1794) captured their ship near Key Biscayne. Several days later, a French privateer overtook the pirates and Aranguren's captive crew and transported them all to Charleston as suspected pirates. The Admiralty Courts cleared up the misunderstanding, freeing Aranguren while executing the pirates, but on the return journey south his men were once again captured by a French privateer (de Aranguren 1794).

San Juan Nepomuceno's voyage should have originally taken a few weeks, but it spanned nearly five months. In that single voyage the crew members were captured three separate times. While this might seem like an extraordinary series of events, it was all too common during the Age of Revolution. From the 1780s to the 1830s, a brutal wave of maritime crime erupted in the Caribbean and along the Gulf Coast. Both privateers and coastal bandits took advantage of a fluctuating political climate, spawning an intense period of piratical acts that are relatively understudied. These men were vastly different from the Golden Age buccaneers who conducted large-scale fleet operations. These pirates were adept sailors who preferred guerrilla warfare, often from a terrestrial base of operations. Difficult for contemporaries to locate even at the time of their raiding, these groups are enigmas archaeologically. One of the best hopes of identifying associated sites is through the corroborating documentary evidence.

Context

Following the War of 1812, a resurgence of maritime crime occurred (Gibbs 2012:83). Several factors, including the Napoleonic Wars and Latin American wars of independence, created a lawless frontier area in the Caribbean and Gulf of Mexico. Resulting economic conditions in the United States pushed former privateers south to accept commissions from Latin American revolutionaries fighting against Spanish rule (Davis 2006:70). When Spain lost its ability to control overseas territories, a period of weakened authority along the southern coast of the United States created an environment amenable to piracy.

As Spain's power waned in the Western Hemisphere, the United States began accelerating its naval program. A quasi-war with France initiated a wave of increased naval construction as a means of extending diplomacy and projecting confidence as a new country (Crawford and Hughes 1995). During the War of 1812, the United States began relying heavily on supplementing its forces with privateers. At least 100,000 Americans found employment through privateering during the war (Kert 2015:38). At war's end, these 100,000 people lost their revenue stream. With armed ships but no war to fight, the privateers needed a new plan. Coupled with out-of-work merchants in prominent cities such as Baltimore, a class of "patriot privateers" emerged: vessels sailed south to accept commissions from Latin American revolutionaries while fencing their stolen cargo through American merchants (Hopkins 2008). Patriot privateers generally followed the laws of the sea, only seizing prizes that were at war with their commissioning nation-state. Taking liberties with their authority became increasingly common, however, as the rebellions dragged on.

Eventually, maritime predations began impacting United States commerce, provoking backlash from the US Navy. While piracy was always outlawed by the United States, the justified use of privateers as an auxiliary to the regular navy increased the number of sailors versed in the practice of capturing ships and their cargos at sea. The initial authorization of privateering created a popular path for out-of-work sailors whose normal operations were interrupted by conflict. With so many vessels armed and operating under letters of marque or commissions, a natural progression in seeking prizes outside of their authority occurred with more frequency. By then the United States was struggling to author a policy that would combat piracy but not condemn its own citizens in acts of maritime crime (Cragg 2019:34–35).

Concurrently, the lack of strict regulation and enforcement by any nation on prize-taking reinforced the environment of piracy. The nations that had vested interests in the Caribbean and Gulf of Mexico focused their naval efforts on fighting each other, rather than suppressing maritime crime. As patriot privateers started going rogue, they encouraged coastal bandits to do the same. Local authority in the island territories of the West Indies, particularly Puerto Rico and Cuba, fluctuated between upholding Spanish rule and enabling illicit dealings (Goodrich 1916:1176).

Coastal bandits came from a maritime background but differed from the formally trained sailors who made up the patriot privateer class. They were coastal dwellers from the West Indies who saw an opportunity to prey upon commercial vessels. Ships laden with valuable trade goods often traveled to the United States from Latin America via the Mona Passage, between Puerto Rico and Santo Domingo. A predictable trade route resulted in numerous incidents of piracy by coastal bandits (Shoemaker 1976:158).

The bands could be large: upward of forty men would set upon a passing ship. After capturing the cargo, the men returned to shore and traveled inland to cities, where they fenced the goods through markets. Captain Barnabas Lincoln, who encountered pirates in 1821, made note of the way in which these raiders conducted business. After being held captive, Lincoln recalled:

> This lets us a little into the plans by which this atrocious system of piracy has been carried on. Merchants having partners on board of these pirates! Thus pirates at sea and robbers on land are associated to destroy the peaceable traders. The willingness exhibited by the seven above mentioned, to join our gang of pirates, seems to look like a general understanding among them; and from there being merchants on shore so base as to encourage the plunder and vend the goods, I am persuaded there has been a systematic confederacy on the part of these unprincipled desperadoes, under cover of the patriot flag. (Lincoln 1822:12)

Material Culture

While patriot privateers and coastal bandits differed to a certain extent, the two groups shared a number of similarities (Head 2015; Morales 2018; Thomin 2018). A vast amount of textual evidence about these maritime marauders is recorded in letters, newspaper accounts, logbooks, captivity narratives, court cases, pamphlets, and various other published sources and unpublished manuscripts from the early nineteenth century. Yet, so far, no evidence of material culture specific to privateers or pirates has been positively identified archaeologically from this period, although a number of terrestrial and underwater sites have potential to shed more light on the subject (Exnicios 2006; Borgens 2016; Horrell and Borgens 2014, 2017; Malcolm 2017).

The sheer number of documented cases of piracy in United States courts alone suggests that some physical evidence of their activities just be preserved within the archaeological context (Chet 2014:16–17). The cultural material that piratical groups left behind at shipwreck sites or terrestrial establishments might offer insights into these individuals' lives that the documentary record simply cannot capture.

While several efforts to locate and identify archaeological remains linked to pirates have been successful, relatively few studies attempt to interpret material culture specific to piracy (Skowronek and Ewen, ed. 2006; Ewen and Skowronek, ed. 2016). Soulat and de Bry (2019:89) conclude that no artifacts could be attributed specifically to pirates during the seventeenth and eighteenth centuries; they could be identified only as "objects of everyday life used by pirates in particular contexts." Nevertheless, an innovative study by Page and Ewen (2016) attempts to identify behavioral differences between pirate crews and nonpirate ships based on artifact frequencies recovered from different shipwrecks representing merchant, naval, and pirate vessels from the late seventeenth and early eighteenth century. Although Page and Ewen (2016:273) were unable to "discern a definitive artifact pattern for pirate shipwrecks" based on the sample size, they did find that pirate ship "assemblages may differ from those of other types of shipwrecks."

One question worth examining is whether the situation was the same for pirates operating during the nineteenth century. Wagner and McCorvie (2006:237–247) demonstrate the value of archival documents in attempting to identify artifact types of river pirates in the late eighteenth and early nineteenth century. More recent studies have examined material culture within the documentary record as a way to establish markers of gender identity within ships (Seaborn 2017). Similarly, identifying material culture of pirates during this same period through textual evidence could potentially help to interpret sites associated with piracy.

If one single object of material culture is most identified with pirates, then arguably it must be the "Jolly Roger" or "Skull and Crossbones" flag (Hatch 2016). Just as in the Golden Age of Piracy during the late seventeenth and early eighteenth century, red or black flags were commonly flown on pirate vessels that operated in the waters of the Gulf and Caribbean during the first decades of the nineteenth century (Warrington 1822). After naval sailors from USS *Peacock* boarded a suspected Spanish pirate schooner off the coast of Cuba in 1822, one of the pieces of evidence gathered that revealed a "piratical character plainly" was a "bloody red ensign and pendant" found hidden on board (S. Cassin 1822a). The captain of USS *Peacock* made sure to mention this evidence in a letter he wrote to the US district attorney in New Orleans, should there be any doubt of their guilt (S. Cassin 1822b).

Likewise, James Jeffreys reported of his time sailing aboard the Colombian privateer *Maria* in 1816 that they flew the Colombian flag for privateering purposes but raised the black flag when attacking ships not at war with Colombia (Gibbs 1831:4–5). Even though pirate flags are the most recognizable type of material culture mentioned in documents, they are unlikely to survive in archaeological contexts. Nevertheless, if specific objects like flags are mentioned in the documentary record as clearly being associated with piracy, then perhaps other forms of material culture were as well.

Personal Effects

Peg legs, eye patches, striped shirts, and cocked hats remain popular images still commonly, though inaccurately, identified with pirates (Babits et al. 2006:271–272). Personal effects such as clothing were certainly part of material culture as "expressions of social identities" across the Atlantic world (Duplessis 2015:3). However, the documentary record suggests that pirates in the early nineteenth century dressed no differently than ordinary sailors. During an 1822 federal court case held in New York, a witness was asked if he could recall what an accused pirate who attacked his ship off the coast of Cuba was wearing. The witness stated that the pirate "was dressed in rough sailor clothes." The prosecution and defense lawyers cross-examined witnesses in this case but turned their focus to whether the witnesses remembered scars on the hands of the accused (Perez 1823:15–16).

During a piracy trial in 1834, one witness described an accused pirate as wearing a tarpaulin hat, duck pantaloons, and a checked shirt during the commission of the crime (United States Circuit Court 1834:13). While some of the questions did concern the clothing the pirates wore (such as the color of their jackets), prosecutors and defense lawyers were more concerned about their physical appearance. Several accounts mention pirates stealing and wearing their victims' clothing (*Charleston Mercury* 1826; Hampton 1823; Lincoln 1822; Smith 1824:33, 159). This suggests that contemporaries did not appear to recognize any clothing or personal effects unique to pirates during the time.

Arms and Armament

Privateers and coastal bandits were frequently mentioned as being heavily equipped with small arms and edged weapons ranging from muskets to blunderbusses, pistols, cutlasses, hatchets, and long knives in various accounts. Pirates acquired these by buying them from local merchants, by taking them from the ships they seized, or even by raiding vulnerable fortifications (J. Cassin 1822; Gallegher 1823; Gregory 1823; Launders 1823). Regardless of how they procured arms and armament, surplus weapons from European and American manufacturers were widely available to revolutionaries, privateers, and pirates following the end of the Napoleonic Wars and War of 1812 (Blaufarb 2016; Regele 2019). Pirate ships were also armed with mounted guns, although evidently not as heavily as the naval warships that pursued them (Niles 1823).

Nonetheless, documents also demonstrate that even merchant ships could be armed at this time, especially to defend against pirates (*Charleston Daily Courier* 1825; Launders 1823). While having arms certainly increased their chances, merchant vessels fared better if they could find an escort with warships or traveled together in convoy.

Textual evidence often mentions the numbers and types of weaponry used by pirates but does not describe the particular manufacturer or model of any of the small arms or artillery. Privateers and pirates likely had a more heterogeneous assortment of firearms and edged weapons compared to naval crews due to their acquisition strategies. Although their ships were mounted with guns, they typically did not carry as many as government warships (Porter 1823). While merchant ships were armed during this period, they were much less equipped with small arms and guns compared to commerce raiders because their crews were generally smaller (Lords of Commons 1830: sections 719–720).

Cargo

The heavy armament protected all the valuable cargo. Merchant sailing increased exponentially in the first decades of the nineteenth century, particularly in the United States. Annual gross tonnage of commercial cargo reached 525,000 tons by 1800, and 96 percent of incoming cargo arrived on American ships by 1811 (Hutchins 1941:250). The sheer volume of merchant vessels traveling through the Caribbean waters provided ample opportunity for pirates to capture prizes.

Caribbean islands and Latin American territories supplied the bulk of trade goods in the form of sugar, rum, and molasses. Ships carrying spirits, tobacco, and even food fell victim to pirates. It is important to note that cargo also included enslaved Africans at this time, despite the outlawing of the slave trade in 1808. Smuggled enslaved or captive cargo could earn a large profit for privateers and pirates (Goodall 2016; Head 2015).

The booming economy of the United States relied on ships traveling regularly from the Caribbean to the eastern coast of North America. This boosted incidents of maritime crime, as pirates sought some of the cargo for themselves (Gibbs 1831; Gough and Borras 2018:23). Successful pirates could capture millions of dollars in trade goods by overtaking only a few ships. *Triton*, a Spanish merchant vessel, contained over $1.5 million in prize money by itself. A fleet of three ships caught by the privateer *Republicana* resulted in a $4 million payday for the crew (Head 2015:78).

Pirates captured the schooner *Exertion* in December 1821. The previously mentioned Barnabas Lincoln, bound from Boston to Cuba, detailed his encounter with pirates in the Florida Keys. The pirates, claiming to be privateers operating under the Mexican flag, used *Exertion* as a floating galley—eating and drinking the cargo before trading the rest of the goods to merchants. After a month of captivity, the pirates marooned the captive crew (Lincoln 1822). In instances such as this, the archaeological record would be nonexistent. The schooner, even though ransacked by the pirate crew, survived the encounter and continued its life as a merchant vessel.

Pirates traded or consumed perishable cargo, which would leave little evidence behind. Inventory lists identified within court records created from captured pirate ships do provide some insights into what items might be associated within shipwreck contexts. The lists located for this study are limited and vary widely but demonstrate that pirate ships carried items similar to those that might be found on any vessel from the period (*Argote* 1824; *Bru* 1819; Sands 1822; *United States v.* Pegasus 1820). Thus, most examples for this era of piracy prove Soulat and de Bry correct. However, many pirates at this time did not operate from a ship-based location. It is the raiders who practiced piracy from terrestrial bases that would leave behind the largest archaeological imprint.

Pirate Villages

In 1825, after the American brig *Betsey* was "cast away" on one of the Florida Keys, second mate Daniel Collins and his six shipwrecked crewmates eventually landed their long boat on an island close to Cuba (Porter 1825). According to a later newspaper account, "On said island were two houses, inhabited by a few male Spaniards, who pretended to be fishermen" (*Charleston Mercury* 1825). The five "fishermen" were revealed to be part of a pirate crew when they sprang into action to eliminate any witnesses who might identify the location of their hidden establishment. After being joined by a few other pirates, they tied up the survivors and took them by boat to a nearby lagoon. The pirates attempted to murder the shipwrecked crew. Collins was struck on the head and fell overboard but somehow managed to untie his restraints. After six days of evading capture through the woods, he successfully made his escape (Porter 1825).

The pirates' plot ultimately failed, because Collins boarded USS *Beagle* and showed the American naval crew the pirates' whereabouts. A few months later, US and British naval forces teamed up for an assault on the pirates. They took nineteen prisoners and recorded eighteen killed during the skirmish, but several "escaped into the mangrove bushes." Nearby they observed several "articles concealed in a thicket about 20 yards from the vessel, which was approached by a meandering path." The naval personnel "discovered a large schooner rigged Regla Boat" the next morning and eventually reached the pirates' "place of resort and establishment" (Porter 1825:n.p.). Reports described the pirate haunt as "consisting of two very large huts and some outhouses" (McKeever 1825:n.p.). While relatively rare, a few descriptions of nineteenth-century coastal bandit villages like this might suggest a pattern to look for archaeologically.

Joseph Cassin, lieutenant on USS *Peacock*, discovered a pirate landing site and base in Cuba in 1822. He provided one of the best descriptions of these sites from an American perspective. According to Cassin, at the pirates' landing place they discovered three empty rowboats as well as English and French manufactured goods. The landing site was near a cart road that led to the mountains, so the pirates could transport "their ill gotten goods." Cassin wrote that a few miles from the landing site they uncovered a "few firearms and cutlasses with a small quantity of French goods in trunks—not of much value." After seeing some smoke, Cassin and his crew "rowed through several intricate channels," where they discovered a badly damaged "large black schooner laden with coffee." On the land nearby they found one "old man" at the pirate camp, who provided them with a forged document The camp had several small thatched huts, with about fifty bags of coffee thrown about. Cassin claimed that it also had "a pair of stocks to contain 15 heads at one time" and estimated that between twenty and thirty people occupied the site, based on the evidence of food preparations (J. Cassin 1822:n.p.).

Locating pirate villages or establishments in remote areas that were difficult to access certainly had strategic benefits (Kelleher 2016:185). Even so, evidence suggests that at least some of these locations in Cuba and Puerto Rico were known by authorities but allowed to operate (Beechler 1890; de Comte 1825; McKeever 1825; Thomin 2018:17). While coastal bandits needed to keep their villages out of view from naval ships seeking their destruction, they still had to remain close enough to local markets to quickly dispose of the evidence and get paid (Parker 1825).

Future Avenues of Study

Pirate villages lend themselves to terrestrial rather than maritime archaeology, despite their context as a site of maritime conflict. However, determining the differences between a pirate village and other coastal sites such as typical fishing ranchos (coastal villages occupied by Cuban fishing communities) in the archaeological record needs further examination.

The Fishing Rancho period dates from 1760 to 1840, overlapping the time when the pirates occupied villages in the Caribbean. A fishing rancho would likely exhibit much of the same material culture as a pirate village. Not only were pirates from this period posing as fishermen, but eyewitnesses noted the presence of fishing items and similar fishing vessels at "piratical establishments" (Kearney 1823:n.p.). Archaeologists have only identified a handful of Gulf Coast rancho sites, due in part to the extensive development that has occurred on the Florida coasts where these sites exist (Stack 2011:71).

In a comparison of three rancho sites in southwest Florida, archaeologist Margaret Stack located similar assemblages. Rancho sites present a large number of ceramics, lead shot, glass fragments, and rusted metal pieces—all of which are typical of Spanish colonial settlements. Minute differences, most notably in the use of glassware and fishing material, distinguish fishing ranchos from other Spanish settlement sites (Stack 2011:122). Pirate village sites would provide the same scatter of artifacts as fishing ranchos but with a larger variety in trade goods and weaponry, reflecting the pirates' penchant for stealing cargo.

A second avenue for further study is looking for maritime archaeological contexts in the cave systems that dot the interior of Caribbean and Bahamian islands. One of the most descriptive accounts of a pirate village comes from a young David Farragut, at the time a lieutenant in the West Indies Squadron, before his rise to naval fame during the American Civil War. Aboard USS *Greyhound*, Farragut came across a pirate camp in Cuba that contained "all the necessary apparatus for turtling and fishing as well as for pirating." He also discovered several caves, well concealed, one of which was "filled with plunder of various kinds, including many articles marked with English labels, with saddles, and costumes worn by the higher classes of Spanish peasantry" (Farragut 1879:97).

Based on descriptions such as these, pirate village sites would be located in areas with intricate channels that only shallow-draft ships could access. There should be a related landing site, possibly indicated by remains of artifacts of English, American, and French manufacture, located near some type of trail or path. The base site would contain artifacts of English, American, and French wares as well as large numbers of artifacts related to arms. If any evidence of structures survives, it would include remains of thatched huts and outhouses that could accommodate a few dozen people and possibly stockades.

Perhaps the best possibility for locating an archaeological signature lies in the cave system. While it can be presumed that villages would eventually use or sell the goods gathered during pirate activities, trace identifying artifacts may remain concealed among the numerous caves scattered throughout the Caribbean islands. Ironically, pirates of the nineteenth century were more likely to bury their "treasure" than their earlier counterparts were, as a means of keeping stolen goods hidden until they could be fenced through friendly markets.

Coastal bandits, privateers, and pirates of the early nineteenth century not only evaded the mythos of history but also seem for the most part to have avoided leaving behind a trail of archaeological evidence. Fortunately, the ever-shrinking frontier where they operated resulted in frequent confrontation with judicial forces. Where the archaeological record might be slim or simply too difficult to identify, archival documents may pick up the trail and point archaeologists in the right direction. Court documents, military correspondence, and cargo manifests can help narrow down the type of material culture that would positively identify a site of a late eighteenth-century or early nineteenth-century pirate village or shipwreck. Inventories of items captured from pirates found in federal court cases might provide some of the best archival evidence of the material culture of these mariners. While common maritime items like "sail bags" appear in these lists, the large number of munitions and armaments demonstrates the predatory nature of their voyages. Analysis of more of these lists could reveal important patterns. Speculative archaeology, combined with carefully curated documentary research, can identify the potential sites of these rogue mariners who operated in a time that has long been understudied but is still so immensely intriguing.

4

“Running a Rig”

Pirates and Archaeology in Video Games

Coy J. Idol and Katherine D. Thomas

Archaeology as a discipline has become an important aspect of popular culture. Whether it is an important find or site entering into the mainstream discourse or being spun off into the realm of pseudoscience and conspiracy theory, archaeology has found itself enmeshed in at least part of the popular culture of any given period over the past century. More recently, this trend has not been limited to real-life archaeology: fictional archaeology has been of growing importance in popular culture.

When the use of archaeology in fiction is combined with the presence of pirates in fiction, historical accuracy becomes muddled. Acts of piracy have been around since seafaring first became possible (Skowronek and Ewen 2016). Pirates became a permanent fixture with the advent of written records, and their actual activities were manipulated for political purposes. The true rise of pirates in fiction occurred in the nineteenth century, with classics like *Treasure Island* (Stevenson 1883) and the musicals of Gilbert and Sullivan (1879). As movie theaters and television became more important aspects of popular culture, pirates made the transition: the Caribbean setting came to life more vividly (Ewen and Skowronek 2007; Skowronek and Ewen 2016).

Building on the popularity of piracy in other media, video games have tapped into the cultural fascination with pirates to craft very successful games. Through Steam (2022), close to a hundred different titles have been tagged by players with the term “pirates.” This number grows when considering publishers like Nintendo, who do not make their titles available on Steam.

Like books and film, video games have primarily drawn from the legendary aspects of pirating that have developed ever since *Treasure Island* was first published. The public imagination has largely been centered around a few decades at the beginning of the eighteenth century in the Caribbean, known as the Golden Age of Piracy (Ewen and Skowronek 2007). The focus on this time and place has carried over to video games, with the vast majority of pirate-related games being set in the Golden Age or featuring characters culturally influenced by it.

This chapter explores how pirates have been depicted in video games, with a focus on the way archaeology has influenced this representation. We discuss two primary games: *Assassin's Creed IV: Black Flag* (Ubisoft 2013) and *Uncharted 4: A Thief's End* (Naughty Dog 2016).

Video Game Studies, History, and Archaeology

There are two different types of historically based video games. The first type starts from a historical basis but allows the player freedom to diverge from the historically accurate timeline. Within this genre are two distinct approaches to history. Games built on conceptual simulation, like the *Age of Empires* series (Ensemble Studios 1997–2020) and *Sid Meier's Civilization* (MicroProse and Firaxis Games 1991–2021), use factions based on historical civilizations, with skirmish-based game-play (Chapman 2016; Peterson et al. 2013). Strategy games with grand campaigns, like *Total War* (Creative Assembly 2000–2020) and *Crusader Kings* (Paradox Development Studio 2004–2020), start from a historical year, with each civilization roughly beginning at a historically accurate location. Once these grand campaigns get started, the player is allowed to diverge from the historical narrative and create new "histories." These games are termed "counterfactuals." Peterson et al. (2013) argue that they are successful in developing the conceptual frameworks of historical knowledge, despite not being an accurate historical representation.

The other types of historically based games are role-playing games and action adventures, which aim for realistic simulation (Chapman 2016). These games use history as a plot device: the player interacts with historical people, events, and landscapes to drive the plot forward (Dow 2013; Schwarz 2014). Unlike conceptual simulation, history is followed all the way through in these games, which tend to have "truer" historical narratives.

Archaeology's early forays into studying games were focused on conceptual simulations. The *Age of Empires* and *Civilization* series have been of particular interest and generally remain so (Gardner 2007; Mol et al. 2017). Part of this early fascination is related to the true lack of games marketed as historical prior to *Assassin's Creed* (Ubisoft 2007). In the last decade or so, historical games have grown beyond this. Simultaneously, archaeologists have become engaged as video games have staked a stronger claim to being arbiters of history.

The early archaeologists, like Gardner (2007), looked to the educational opportunities of video games in teaching players about archaeology, as it relates to themes and civilizational developments. This educational focus is still a common theme in archaeological discussion of video games. Some historians, especially Chapman (2016), have tried to develop an understanding of the historical theory provided by video games by balancing the dichotomy of academic and popular history, exploring video games as a new form of popular history, and developing a forms-based approach to understanding different types of historically based games.

This understanding has largely been lacking in archaeological discussion. The one exception may be Reinhard (2018). He takes a much broader perspective on the interaction of archaeology and video games, viewing the multiple ways in which archaeology and video games intersect: in the real world as video games with an archaeological protagonist; in game worlds as archaeological sites; and in the immateriality of material culture produced both within and outside of video games. While this approach lacks the theoretical thrust of Chapman (2016), it also lacks the much deeper foundational work that historians have done in support.

Even so, Reinhard (2018) still has an implicit focus on the educational opportunities provided by video games, highlighting the status of archaeogaming as inherently a new venture in public archaeology. In this same vein, Mol et al. (2017) immediately identify the target audience beyond the traditional academic one, including video game players and designers. Rollinger (2020) takes a similar approach but melds video game studies with an already strong classicist field of reception studies. Once again, we are seeing a very public-based perspective developed by archaeologists who study video games. These studies, however, highlight a general void in looking at how the public is responding to and learning from video games. The desire to engage with this media form is growing, with an ever-increasing online presence, through blogs and other digital media. This has allowed for a free exchange of ideas not typically seen in academic communities, as the general public is being given more access to the researchers and the data to interpret and discuss.

The games examined in depth here fall into the latter category of realistic simulation. The presentation of pirates in popular culture makes them better suited to be explored through role-playing games. The more action-adventure nature of these types of games better taps into the Zeitgeist of pirates, presenting more compelling game-play, though future projects may consider how pirates are depicted in conceptual simulations.

The History of Pirate Video Games

The first pirate-based 2D video game was *Sid Meier's Pirates!* (MicroProse 1987). This game was in line with most other romanticized stories about pirates: a young man becomes an outlaw, for whatever reason, but still lives by a strict moral code and thereby performs some heroic deed, which allows him to reintegrate with proper society (Pfister 2018). Where *Pirates!* plays the pirate theme straight, the next pirate-based game published, *The Secret of Monkey Island* (LucasArts Entertainment 1990), is a parody not just of pirate mythos but of the entire romanticization of the early modern Caribbean.

Despite the success of these two games, the pirate genre did not take off. It was not until the release of Disney's *Pirates of the Caribbean* that pirate-based video games saw more prolonged success. The quest of returning to society gradually fell out of favor in this new generation of pirate games. They began to tap into another pirate narrative: treasure hunting.

With this new goal the player was set against the colonial powers of Europe and began questing for wealth accumulation. This involved actual treasure hunting or the establishment of economically strong centers of power (Pfister 2018). This trend was present in *Pirates!* (MicroProse 1987) but was balanced by the overarching narrative of the game. Later strategy games that copied *Pirates!*—like the *Port Royale* franchise (Ascaron Entertainment and Gaming Minds Studios 2003–2012)—lessened the overall narrative and put more emphasis on capital accumulation.

In all these games except the *Monkey Island* series (LucasArts Entertainment and Telltale Games 1990–2010), the player does not have to be a pirate. A player can choose to take on the marginally more legal profession of privateer, governor, or merchant. With the exception of *Pirates!* none of these games allow the player to commit acts of piracy. In *Assassin's Creed IV: Black Flag* (Ubisoft 2013), the game brings back the actual piracy of *Pirates!* but with more historical accuracy than was available in a 2D game setting.

Not all pirate games have had a historical focus. Japanese-produced games have used pirate imagery for comedic effect, with *The Legend of Zelda: Wind Waker* (Nintendo 2003) being the prime example. Another Nintendo production, *Donkey Kong Country 2: Diddy's Kong Quest* (Rare 1995), also uses a Caribbean pirate theme in a comedic style. The main enemy, K. Rool, stylizes himself as a captain, and his minions assume nautical pirate themes. This all combines with level design that reflects the pirate theme. Both these games reflect a trend toward pirates not actually pirating.

Other games tap into this. The *Total War: Warhammer II* DLC (downloadable content) pack *Curse of the Vampire Coast* (Creative Assembly 2018) is almost a direct rip-off of the style of *Pirates of the Caribbean* movie. The lack of naval combat in the game raises the question as to whether the primary faction could actually be identified as pirates were it not for their overt stylized connection to the Disney movie franchise. Creative Assembly's other *Total War* franchise DLC pack to focus on pirates came as part of *Total War: Rome II, Pirates and Raiders* (Creative Assembly, 2014). The game is set in antiquity, so piratical activities are performed differently. The political and imperial nature of primary sources from this time has also played a role in how we remember the "Illyrian" polities represented in this DLC and piracy in general (Dell 1967; de Souza 2008). In *Empire: Total War* (Creative Assembly 2009), pirates show up in the more traditional role and region, dominating the Caribbean at the beginning of the game, though they will cause problems in other regions.

Games like *Uncharted 4: A Thief's End* (Naughty Dog 2016) take a different approach to pirates. Instead of taking place in the historical period when they were active, these games more directly take on the historical memory and mytho-historical ideas about pirates that have developed in the modern period, basing their game-play on modern misconceptions of pirates.

Assassin's Creed IV: Black Flag

This game was released in 2013 to overwhelmingly positive reviews. Developed by Ubisoft, the game was nominated for and won multiple awards and has since gone on to sell over 20 million copies. Set in the northwest corner of the Caribbean, it covers a ten-year period between 1712 and 1722, with a few events taking place outside the Caribbean.

The main story follows Edward Kenway, a former privateer who stayed in the Caribbean to pursue his fortune as a pirate, despite having a wife in Britain. As in most pirate stories, Edward has suffered social death and lives outside proper society. A twist to this is his desire to re-create society. One of the early plot points is the creation of a pirate utopia free from the colonial powers of Europe, built on democratic principles but still driven by a quest for wealth. As the British begin to press their claims in the region, Edward's revolutionary vision disintegrates. He is brought more into an alliance with the Assassin Brotherhood. At the game's conclusion, Edward has finally joined the Assassins and rejoins proper English society.

A typical highlight of the *Assassin's Creed* franchise has been re-creation of historically important features on the landscape of the urban centers used as settings. This helps make the setting seem familiar to those who have visited or lived in the town or city represented in the game and makes these areas feel real. Some locations have caused problems because they are so different from their modern-day landscapes, like New York in *Assassin's Creed III* (Ubisoft 2012) and *Assassin's Creed: Rogue* (Ubisoft 2014). On the other hand, some buildings are put in games set in a time before they were historically built because they are so strongly associated with a city's landscape, usually in Italian Renaissance cities (Dow 2013).

The development of *Black Flag* had close connections to archaeological research. During the initial phases, Ubisoft sponsored the exhumation of Spanish privateer/pirate Amaro Pargo. While the exhumation did provide some interesting information about the local community's reverence toward Pargo, it had very little impact on the game. The possibility of using the results of the excavation to digitally re-create Pargo was discussed, but no Spanish pirates appear in the game: the excavation just became good publicity (Vallejo Jorge 2017).

The influence of archaeological information can be seen in a few areas of the games. Port Royal in Kingston, Jamaica, plays an important part in the final stages of *Port Royale* the game. Port Royal has developed a reputation in popular history as a haven for piracy in the early periods of English colonial efforts in the Caribbean (D. Hamilton 2006). *Black Flag* is set later: the role of pirate haven is filled by Nassau and Kenway's fictional base at Great Inagua, which seems based on the real-life Matthew Town. By the time of the game, Port Royal (Figure 4.1) had been devastated by the earthquake of 1692. Evidence of this destruction in the form of ruined buildings is scattered around the landscape. Appropriately, this area is part of a greater Kingston area, reflecting the historical movement of the economic and political center of the harbor across the water to the town of Kingston.

For the most part, Port Royal in the game lacks any reference to a piratical past, other than being burned by pirates in 1703. This is in line with the archaeological evidence, which does not support a large pirate presence before 1695 (D. Hamilton 2006). The settlement is greatly overshadowed by the much larger Kingston and the much more ominous presence of Fort Charlotte on the town's side of the harbor.

Fort Charlotte brings up a much larger feature of the Caribbean landscape, both in the game and in the archaeological records: the presence of forts. Skowronek and Ewen (2006:265) identify the proliferation of forts in the Caribbean during this period as reflective of a "culture of fear," directly linked to the rise and influence of piracy. While they mostly discuss the rise of forts in the sixteenth century, the continual use of forts by colonial powers proved decisive not just against pirates but against other European powers active in the Caribbean. Two of the forts mentioned, Castillo San Salvador de la Puerta

Figure 4.1. View of Kingston Harbor from Port Royal. The ruins and rebuilt Port Royal are in the foreground, with Kingston in the background, across the harbor. *Assassin's Creed IV: Black Flag* (Ubisoft). (Screenshot by Coy J. Idol)

and Castillo de los Tres Reyes del Morro, both in Havana, serve as locations for major story events at the beginning and toward the end of the game.

The other forts in *Black Flag* take on a key aspect of naval game-play. Most of the forts are subject to siege, first at sea through naval combat then transitioning into a land assault. A successful siege leads to the forts being taken over by the pirates. Prior to this they serve as major obstacles covering choke points of nautical travel, forcing the player to either take longer routes or make daring runs past them. There is no evidence of any forts being taken over by pirates during this period, much less held for multiple years. Historical evidence, however, indicates that pirates did besiege cities and forts for short-term gains.

Even though the forts are not historically accurate in form, they function to provide landscape features that represent archaeological realities. This is furthered in the game-play mechanics surrounding forts. The way they implement the historic realities of pirate sieges is not accurate but functions to convey a historic reality of the time.

In addition to re-creation of the past, other aspects of archaeological research are present in the game. It offers collectibles that reflect real archaeological finds. Most are related to the native inhabitants of the Caribbean Islands and Yucatán Peninsula. One object in particular is very relevant here: the *Whydah* Bell. This bell is an important archaeological artifact, as it was the smoking gun in identifying the associated shipwreck as the *Whydah Gally*.

If the bell and its engraving had not identified the ship, it is doubtful that its identity would have ever been conclusively proved (C. Hamilton 2006). Including the *Whydah* Bell as a collectible in the game demonstrates the developers' understanding of what was archaeologically important and helps to draw the player's attention to these areas.

All these elements represent cases where the game does a good job of exploring pirates. Buried treasure is one game element that plays more into lore than history. Maps can be found at various locations maps, including coordinates for a different location and drawings of different aspects of the landscape, with an "X" marking where the treasure chest is buried. These chests contain either money or special upgrades for Kenway's ship, the *Jackdaw*.

Uncharted 4: A Thief's End

While *Assassin's Creed: Black Flag* focuses on the lived experiences of pirates, *Uncharted* focuses on their material culture. *Uncharted 4: A Thief's End* was released in 2016 as the final installment of the series. Individually it had sold over 16 million copies as of 2020, the third most of any Sony PlayStation 4 game. The game also received fifty-five award nominations. The entire four-game series has sold over 41 million copies and is widely regarded as one of the best series released for PlayStation.

The *Uncharted* series (Naughty Dog 2007–2016) follows treasure hunter Nathan Drake as he and his ragtag group of friends attempt to solve some of history's greatest mysteries. Previous installments found him searching for El Dorado, Shambala, and the lost city of Ubar. In each game, Drake and his team follow an intricate series of clues that take them all over the world to find a great lost treasure. In the end, though, Drake and the gang decide that the treasure is not worth it for one reason or another and walk away with few or no riches, only stories. In the fourth and final installment, Drake and his long-lost brother, Sam, are trying to solve a mystery that has haunted them from childhood: Henry Avery's lost treasure. The game begins in a Panamanian jail. The brothers follow a series of puzzles to Scotland, Madagascar, and finally a small island off Madagascar's coast.

They find the remains of Libertalia hidden deep within the jungle (Figure 4.2). The clues that Drake and company follow are not just placed there for them: Henry Avery created a series of puzzles for only the best pirate captains to solve, with their reward being Libertalia. Ten other captains did solve the puzzles and landed at Libertalia: Adam Baldridge, Richard Want, Anne Bonny, Christopher Condent, Edward England, Joseph Farrell, Tariq bin Malik, William Mayes, Yazid al-Basra, and one simply identified as "G. W."

Figure 4.2. Nathan Drake's first look at Libertalia. *Uncharted 4: A Thief's End* (Sony Computer Entertainment).

It is revealed that Thomas Tew, who helped Avery raid the *Ganj-i-Sawai* and its escort, survived and became his right-hand man, confidant, and friend. Together, they created Libertalia and welcomed the other ten captains and a whole slew of colonists. Avery and Tew also created another city, New Devon, within the settlement of Libertalia, just for the pirate captains. Although Libertalia was supposed to be an egalitarian utopia for all those who lived there, there is a clear class difference between the colonists who lived in the settlement and the pirate captains who resided in the lap of luxury in New Devon. The theory is that the colonists realized that the captains had stolen their money and rebelled. However, upon further examination of New Devon, it appears that Henry Avery was overcome by greed, poisoned the other captains, and attempted to leave with all of their combined treasures. Avery was not successful and died before he could escape. His ship filled with gold, jewels, and other treasures sat in the water underneath the island for centuries. The player finds the ship on fire in a cave about to collapse. The game's villain succumbs to his greed like Avery, while Nate, Sam, and the others escape to safety with only a handful of *reales* to show for it.

The *Uncharted* series (Naughty Dog 2007–2016) twists historical facts and rumors to make a compelling story. *A Thief's End* is no different from the rest of the installments. It uses the biography of Henry Avery and a loose interpretation of the historical record to create a compelling narrative to end Nathan Drake's journey. In actuality, Henry Avery did raid the *Ganj-i-Sawai* and its escort with Thomas Tew. However, Tew died during the fight and Avery became a wanted man. After this raid, he seems to have disappeared. No later records of him exist, with rumors swirling that he went back to his homeland England, lived the rest of his life on a tropical island, or died penniless after squandering his riches. His disappearance is not entirely unusual for a pirate, as the previous two volumes in this series have covered the difficulty of finding archaeological evidence of piracy and squaring it with a questionable historical record riddled with grandiose myths and tales.

Each *Uncharted* game is associated with an iconic location. The first one mainly takes place in the jungle, the second on a snowy mountain, and the third in the desert. Using Scotland (snow), Madagascar (desert), and the island (jungle) as the main game locations functions both as a reference to previous games and as an attempt to utilize historical facts, with the locations serving the story rather than historical knowledge. This contrasts with the *Assassin's Creed* (Ubisoft 2007–2020) series, which focuses on creating an accurate representation of the past and then creating a story within that location. *Uncharted*'s historical facts are simply convenient for Drake's narrative.

The major location of the game is Libertalia, a so-called pirate utopia that has plenty of myths surrounding it. It is first mentioned in *A General History of the Pyrates* (Johnson 1724a), considered a more than questionable source of historical information. Johnson describes Libertalia as having two elevated forts on opposite sides of a harbor, with the living quarters located under their guard. Supposedly, Libertalia was only about 13 miles from the nearest town. He also identifies the founders of the colony as Captain James Mission and Thomas Tew. An earlier pamphlet by Van Broeck (1709), who claimed to be a victim of Avery and his crew, identified Henry Avery as the founder of Libertalia. A *Thief's End* marries the two myths to create the narrative.

Thief's End's interpretation of Libertalia is much different. It is a colonial town hidden in the jungle on a secret island. The colonists had to use an intricate system of pulleys in order to move material to Libertalia's location, as the colony is essentially on the side of a cliff. Within Libertalia, New Devon is a neighborhood of mansions surrounded by walls. It is neither an immediately defensible position, as described by Johnson, nor a place for a group of people to create a self-sustaining colony. Here the concept of Libertalia is a vehicle to illustrate the overall series theme of the corruption of human power and greed.

In a 2016 interview with writers Neil Druckmann and Bruce Straley, interviewer Dean Takahashi asks the duo if the parallels between Henry Avery and Thomas Tew—a relationship ending in betrayal and murder—and Nathan Drake and his brother were purposeful. According to Druckmann, "they were very deliberate" (Takahashi 2016). In a separate interview with writer Tom

Bissell, he says that the productions' philosophy is that "design follows narrative" (Brown 2016). Their focus is clearly on the narrative, with historical fact either fitting or being modified to fit their story. As previously discussed in Skowronek and Ewen (ed. 2006) and Ewen and Skowronek (2016), sites of piracy are difficult to discern in the archaeological record, and the historical record is filled with stories that are not easy to confirm as factual. *A Thief's End* takes the spaces in the archaeological and historical record to try to create a narrative in which the audience members can begin to familiarize themselves with the lives of a few of the real-life pirates rather than the fictional ones.

Conclusion

Pirates have captured our imaginations for centuries: we have followed their fictional adventures through books, movies, television, and now video games. The two games discussed in this chapter attempt to use facts in creating their pirate stories, to different ends. Like Kapell and Elliott (2013), we have tried to focus not just on what video games get wrong. That would have been easy but uninteresting. While pointing out inaccuracies, we have connected them, when possible, with the developers' adjustment of archaeological data to create more engaging game-play that relates archaeological realities. With the success of both *Black Flag* and *A Thief's End*, pirates will clearly be a popular video game subject. We hope that developers will continue to rely on facts rather than on Hollywood's perception of pirates.

5

The Material Culture of Pirate Wrecks and Lairs

A Reflection of Colonial Archaeology through Multicultural Assemblages from the Seventeenth and Eighteenth Centuries

Jean Soulat

The examination of archaeological objects from sites identified as being associated with pirates can provide insight into their daily life and adaptations in the seventeenth and eighteenth centuries. Life aboard pirate ships is probably best known from the numerous wrecks identified on the east coast of the United States, in the Caribbean Sea, on the coast of southern Brazil, and in the Indian Ocean. Nevertheless, new terrestrial archaeological sites provide additional data, notably in areas of the Caribbean and the Indian Ocean.

Did the life of these outlaws on ships or on land differ from the life of other sailors? Whether they were pirates or sailors, these seafarers crossed the oceans and were therefore in perpetual motion. Depending on whether the archaeological sites are shipwrecks or land-based settlements, the artifacts collected may vary significantly in terms of the functional categories represented. The analysis must also take into account that these postmedieval artifacts, like the seafarers themselves, were constantly moving fr]om a European sphere to new geographic and maritime areas such as the Americas, the Caribbean, and the Indian Ocean, creating new colonial archaeological contexts. While archaeological sites linked to pirate activity remain rare, colonial archaeological sites in North America and the Caribbean are richly documented and can provide very detailed evidence of the lives of those living on the "right side" of the law. The nature of the archaeological site (wreck, camp, or fortification) does not change with the occupation of pirates: it remains, above all, a colonial archaeological site of the seventeenth and eighteenth centuries. It must therefore be approached in this sense.

In addition to the study of the architectural configuration of structures encountered on archaeological sites, the examination of the associated material culture makes it possible to draw parallels between these shipboard and terrestrial contexts to delineate the evidence that would separate legal and illicit behavior in these varied types of sites. The aim of this chapter is to synthesize the main issues, based on examples of specific archaeological sites linked to piracy and case studies of objects and assemblages that shed light on the criminal phenomenon.

Underwater and terrestrial sites from various geographical areas are compared here. Thus, this study of objects related to piracy is part of an international phenomenon of contacts wherein objects originating in Europe, Africa, the Americas, or Asia are juxtaposed in a manner unlike objects associated with the mercantilism of the era. Multiculturalism within the same chronological framework, which extends from the second half of the seventeenth century to the first quarter of the eighteenth century, is clearly visible on these sites. Ceramics and coins are the main evidence for this. But other elements such as weapons or clothing accessories may contribute to this observation.

The Archaeology of Piracy: A Branch of Colonial Archaeology

The archaeology of piracy originated in the study of shipwrecks. These wrecks have allowed us to identify pirates in the archaeological record. Nevertheless, terrestrial sites in the Caribbean Sea and in the Indian Ocean are providing evidence for the terrestrial expression of these freebooters. These sites take different forms: fortifications, careening areas, and remains of camps. Just like the wrecks, land occupations where pirates settled are difficult to identify.

To date, less than a dozen pirate wrecks from the seventeenth and eighteenth centuries have been discovered and verified through underwater archaeology. Their identification is of course linked to an exhaustive examination of archival documentation and accounts of seafarers in the targeted geographical area. The wrecks are located along the east coast of the United States, in the Caribbean Sea, along the Brazilian coast, and in the Indian Ocean. Among the main wrecks found are the *Whydah Gally* (1717) and the *Queen Anne's Revenge* (1718) excavated on the east coast of North America and the *Quedagh Merchant* (1699) and *Great Ranger* (1722) in Caribbean waters. Two pirate wrecks have been discovered in southern Brazil. The first was found in the 1960s near the island of Cotinga. Archives mention a ship that sank in 1718. Some elements yet to be confirmed could identify it as *La Louise*, captained by the pirate Olivier Levasseur, known as La Buse. The second wreck was discovered near the island of Santa Catarina. Historical and archaeological research in 2004 identified a Spanish ship that sank in 1687, probably the *Aranzazu*, captured first by the English pirate Edward Davis and then by the buccaneer Thomas Prince or Frins. Finally, two wrecks were found in the Indian Ocean: a wreck in Ambodifototra Bay on Sainte-Marie Island in Madagascar, supposedly the *Fiery Dragon* (1721), and the *Speaker* (1702), found on the east coast of Mauritius.

All of these underwater contexts are very well dated time capsules, due to the precise date of the shipwreck reported in the maritime archives between 1687 and 1722. In addition to the surviving architecture of the vessel (in this case, the wooden structure of the ship, which comes mainly from Europe), each shipwreck contains a very large quantity of objects. These artifacts both reflect the life of the sailors and testify to the geographical origin of the crew, goods, objects on board, and personal artifacts in relation to the different prizes taken. Examination of these objects allows us to identify the area of their production but also, by extrapolation, to determine the nationality of the sailor who, for example, would wear a certain type of jacket button or shoe buckle. Research on the geographical origin of the objects necessarily widens the field of study and requires developing a comparative method extending from wrecks and contemporary regional land sites to sometimes very distant land production sites. This approach brings the theme of the archaeology of piracy closer to colonial archaeology across the Atlantic and in the Southern Hemisphere.

Placing the wreck in its historical and associated terrestrial archaeological context, especially when it is located close to the coast, can be particularly interesting in identifying other pirate sites, through comparison of similar objects and evidence of ephemeral or sedentary settlements in proximity to the wreck. In this respect, two examples from the Indian Ocean are notable.

The main pirate lair of the Indian Ocean is located on the northeast coast of the island of Madagascar, along the southwest coast of Sainte-Marie Island near the town of Ambodifototra at inside Îlot Madame. Between the end of the seventeenth century and the 1720s, the Bay of Pirates offered a perfect anchorage point, sheltered from attacks and capricious weather conditions. Sieur Robert, a former French officer who collected a number of testimonies, provides a seemingly very accurate vision of this area (Robert 1730). Readers can learn how pirates lived through his detailed descriptions of their fortified huts and careening areas. The landlocked location of the bay also attracted defensive installations, such as a pentagonal fort overlooking the bay, built by the French Royal Navy in the 1640s and then occupied by pirates led by Adam Baldridge in the 1690s.

Although these dwellings or camps and defensive installations have not yet been uncovered by archaeology, a shipwreck found in the bay has been identified as the *Fiery Dragon*, sunk in February 1721 by its captain, Christopher Condent (alias Edward Congdon). The sinking can be explained by a document found in the Morbihan departmental archives in Vannes (Brittany, France). An amnesty ordered by the governor of Bourbon, Joseph Beauvollier de Courchant, and signed on November 25, 1720, stipulates the conditions that must be respected by the pirate in order for him to be pardoned (Archives du Morbihan 1721). Thanks to this document, we know that more than 135 pirates and nearly 80 Black slaves from Guinea were still living on Sainte-Marie Island at that date. The discovery of the wreck and a small part of its cargo indicates probable intercontinental activity and multiculturalism in terms of the identified origins of the ceramics (South China, Asia, and Europe) and gold coins (Cairo, Venice, and the Netherlands).

On January 7, 1702, the *Speaker*, captained by John Bowen, was wrecked off the east coast of Mauritius. This wreck was partially excavated between 1980 and 1991. For several weeks, the pirates were hosted by the Dutch colony under the governance of Roelof Diodati in order to accommodate and care for the crew. The colony was situated around Fort Frederik Hendrik, founded in 1638 in Vieux Grand Port in the southeast part of the island. Excavated between 1997 and 2005, the fort has yielded numerous remains from successive Dutch, French, and British occupations between the seventeenth and nineteenth centuries. Examination of artifacts from the earlier archaeological levels reveals interesting comparisons with objects found during the *Speaker* excavation: ceramics, beads, and armaments. Exchanges between the Dutch colonists and the pirates are known to have taken place. Indeed, the pirates paid 2,500 piastres to the colonists to buy a new ship, the sloop *Vliegendehart*, and left Mauritius two months after the sinking of their original ship. Surprisingly, however, archaeologists from the University of Amsterdam have not yet established a link between the two archaeological sites. Future research will be undertaken to compare the archaeological collections and highlight potential evidence of the pirate presence in Fort Frederik Hendrik.

The Material Culture of Pirate Sites: A Witness to Multiculturalism and Piracy

The recognition of an archaeological site occupied by pirates, whether it be a wreck or a land occupation, is above all linked to research carried out in the

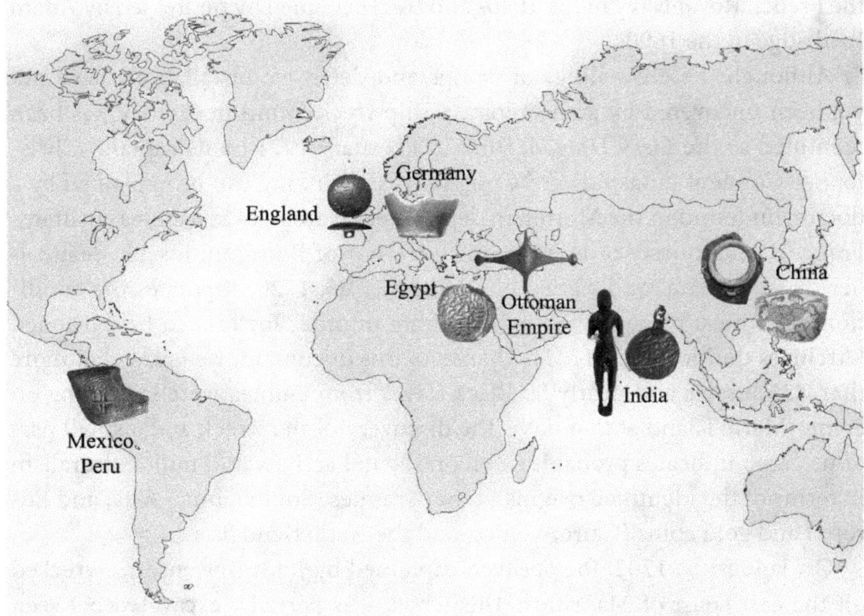

Figure 5.1. Some objects of various origins from the *Speaker*. (© Jean Soulat)

archives associated with geographic references. Archaeology then confirms the presence of a colonial site occupied at a given period with a marginal population defined as pirates. Apart from the type of site discovered, the artifacts encountered are important in supporting the hypothesis of a pirate presence, in particular based on the diverse origins of the artifacts.

Indeed, whether it is a pirate wreck or a pirate settlement site, the discovery of an assemblage of objects from a variety of localities dated to a narrow chronological interval may be the consequence of an accumulation of artifacts related to piracy. For pirate wrecks, these multicultural artifacts are generally associated with a large quantity of ammunition and weapons but also with some evidence of the sharing of booty among the crew (ingots or fragments of jewelry). For land sites, ephemeral or sedentary installations (defensive works, dwellings, camps, or even careening areas), it is mainly the combination of a brief occupation and the presence of multicultural artifact such as ceramics, coins, and other objects of daily life that allows us to hypothesize that a site was occupied by a marginal pirate population. Some case studies of object categories that are distinguished by their multiculturalism are discussed here. Objects of British and French material culture are mixed with objects from Spain, Germany, Holland, Scandinavia, Asia, India, the Arabian Peninsula, and Egypt (Figure 5.1).

England supplied a large number of items, such as guns, jacket buttons and various buckles, London pewter associated with various identified makers, wine bottles, wine glasses, kaolin clay tobacco pipes from Bristol workshops, monetary weights, and various coins (shillings and guineas, among others). The majority of the objects come from Port Royal and the wreck of the *Speaker* in 1702 and *Whydah Gally* in 1717.

For France, we note the presence of infantry swords made in Saint-Étienne, muskets from the workshops of Tulle, green glaze ceramics of Saintonge, a syringe and a pewter clyster produced in Paris and Rouen by known artisans, a nesting weight set from Montpellier, a lead shipping seal from Narbonne, and coins of the reigns of Louis XIII and Louis XIV. It should be noted that most French objects come from the *Queen Anne's Revenge*.

For the rest of Europe, the Venice workshops have produced many varieties of stemware and glass beads disseminated to the transatlantic colonies of the Americas. The artisans of Nuremberg marketed monetary weights, tokens, and nested scale weights throughout Europe, while bellarmine stoneware jugs from the Rhine Valley are as common in shipwrecks as Chinese porcelain. Pirate shipwrecks yield cannon cast in Sweden and Denmark as well as coins from various countries such as Holland and Spain or from the Spanish colonial mints of Peru, Mexico, and Bolivia.

Finally, the Asian sphere is also well represented. Chinese porcelain became a luxury item during the second half of the seventeenth century, thanks to the export of porcelain from Jingdezhen (Ching-te Chen, southeastern China). It is encountered in very large quantity in Port Royal and in the shipwrecks of the Indian Ocean like the *Fiery Dragon*, but also in the shipwrecks of the Caribbean area. Of course, artifacts from India and the Ottoman Empire (ceramics, coins, and statuettes) are also present in large numbers in the archaeological contexts of the Indian Ocean, on Sainte-Marie Island (Madagascar), and on the *Speaker*.

Ceramics

All types of archaeological sites yield ceramics. Colonial and/or pirate sites are no exception. However, in most cases, this material is neglected in the analysis in favor of metal artifacts. Indeed, no ceramics have been studied in the few works published on *Whydah Gally*. This was also the case for the *Speaker*, whose ceramics were examined much later. After reexamination of the ceramics, 97 sherds were inventoried and studied (Soulat et al. 2019:261–262). Among the items are fragments of Rhenish bellarmine-type production jugs, sherds of storage jars made in the Fujian region (southern China), and Chinese porcelain bowls produced in Jingdezhen (Figure 5.2). Apart from the

Figure 5.2. Coins and ceramics from the *Speaker*: (*from top left to bottom*) dirham from Cairo, ducat from Venice, *reales* from Peru, (*right, counterclockwise*) fragment of bellarmine jug, fragment of storage vase from Fijuan, and fragment of Chinese porcelain bowl from Jingdezhen. (© Jean Soulat, collection from the National History Museum in Mahébourg, Mauritius)

numerous Chinese porcelains found on the supposed *Fiery Dragon* wreck and a pilgrim's flask made of Islamic stoneware (de Bry 2006:124–127), the bags of common ceramics from Asia or Europe have not been carefully examined. Relatively few ceramics from *Queen Anne's Revenge* have been extensively studied, showing their varied origins. The ephemeral camp on Saint-Martin Island has yielded more than 200 sherds of ceramics with different origins: France, England, Germany, the Netherlands, Portugal, and China. The study of colonial ceramics of the seventeenth and eighteenth centuries in the Caribbean has been greatly enhanced by the excavations at Port Royal (Jamaica), the main British trading post known to have welcomed many sailors and freebooters in the seventeenth century (Donachie 2001). The different sites of Port Royal allow good comparisons with ceramics from pirate wrecks.

Coins

Like ceramics, but in a more precise and detailed way, the coins found on pirate archaeological sites testify to a wide variety of origins. The quantity of coins from sites varies, ranging from one to more than fifteen thousand. The wreck of the *Whydah Gally* is the one that has yielded the most. However, like the rest of the artifacts, none of the coins have been the subject of a detailed analytical study accessible to the scientific community (Jambu 2019:372–

373). The study of this exceptional lot would provide many answers about the different prizes of Samuel Bellamy's team. However, of the 5,658 coins analyzed by Christopher Hamilton (2006:155), the question of multiculturalism is clearly visible in *reales* struck in Spanish colonial mints in Potosí, Nuevo Rieno, Lima, and Mexico City; shillings, crowns, or half-crowns from England; and even French coinage, including centimes, silver Louis, pennies, and *écus* (from Saint-Menehould, Bordeaux, Paris, Limoges, and La Rochelle).

The wrecks of the *Speaker* (thirty-four coins: eight gold, twenty-two silver, and four copper alloy) and the possible *Fiery Dragon* (thirteen gold coins) are also very interesting, because the monetary issues are similar (Figure 5.2). We find examples from Europe (Venice, colonial Spain, France, Holland, Germany, England), Egypt, Yemen, and India, all dated 1602 to 1699 (except for a dirham, a silver unit of currency in the Islamic world, dated between 1687 and 1718) for the *Speaker* and from 1649 to 1718 (except for a Venetian ducat dated between 1709 and 1722) for the possible *Fiery Dragon*.

Sharing the Booty

In addition to the multinational origin of the artifacts, the phenomenon of booty sharing can attest to the presence of pirates. Several wrecks that belonged to a pirate crew have revealed evidence of this division of stolen goods, including gold and silver bars and gold nuggets, also called gold dust or gold grains. The *Whydah* shipwreck yielded at least seven pieces of gold bullion and three silver ingots (Clifford and Kinkor 2007:16, 124) and the *Speaker* wreck two gold ingots, one of which is cut (Figure 5.3). Melted and molded into transportable pieces, the gold ingots revealed knife marks, likely evidence of a pirate testing the gold for its purity and true nature, making sure it was not gold-coated lead.

Gold powder is found on the *Whydah* and also on the *Queen Anne's Revenge*. The presence of this gold dust aboard these ships is surely linked to their slaving activity before they were captured by pirates like Samuel Bellamy and Edward Teach. When Teach and his crew took *La Concorde*, they stole more than 20 pounds (9 kilograms) of gold dust (Wilde-Ramsing and Carnes-McNaughton 2018:150). The French slaver went to the West African coast several times between 1713 and 1717. It is quite possible that the grains of gold come from these localities, as fragmentary pieces of Akan jewelry were also found on both the *Whydah* and the *Queen Anne's Revenge*. The *Whydah Gally* also moored in the same waters between the end of 1715 and the beginning of 1716. Excavations on the *Queen Anne's Revenge* were able to bring to light only 0.7 ounce (20 grams) while nearly 7,000 grains were discovered on

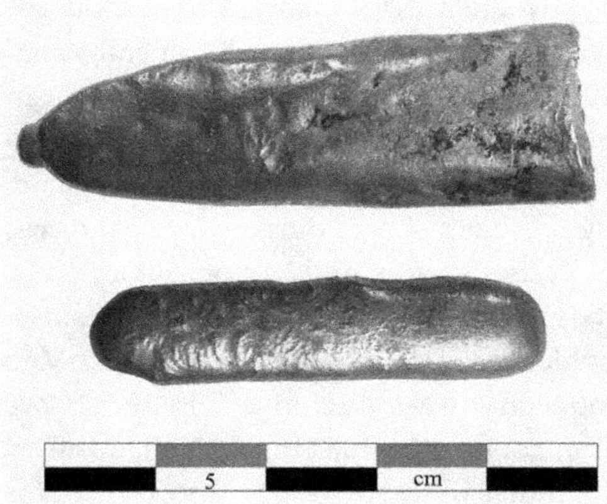

Figure 5.3. Gold ingot from the *Speaker*. (© Jean Soulat, collection from the National History Museum in Mahébourg, Mauritius)

the *Whydah* (C. Hamilton 2006:144). The discovery of these grains of gold can also be related to the presence of remnants of African gold jewelry on these two wrecks, belonging to the Akan tribes who lived on the West African coast, between the current Ghana and Ivory Coast. African gold was prized by international pirates because of its purity and consistent quality.

Conclusion

My objective here was to try to understand and recognize archaeologically recoverable evidence of pirate-related sites, whether a wreck or terrestrial. Study of these sites must be based on analysis of the material culture, compared with the documentary record. Study of the objects found allows us to appreciate a way of life, generally over a short period: a synchronic snapshot, in relation to the traditions and customs of the seventeenth and eighteenth centuries. This archaeology of the material culture of pirate sites must be integrated into colonial archaeology because it is part of a historical phenomenon, known as piracy, which is at the heart of the political conflicts of this period. Globalization and commercial exchanges between the European powers of the time, whose goal during the seventeenth century was to develop and even accelerate their domination in the new colonies across the Atlantic and in the Southern Hemisphere, led to a large-scale transit of goods and consumer goods. Thus, the archaeological sites occupied by the pirates are replete with these multicultural objects, whose presence is linked to the capture of merchant ships during the period of their illicit activities. The discovery of ceramics, coins, weapons, and objects of daily life of varied origins within such short-lived occupational contexts appears to be significant in recognizing pirate archaeological sites dating to the seventeenth and eighteenth centuries.

TRANSATLANTIC PIRACY

6

Casting Piracy a Line

An Examination of the Influence of Piracy in the Archaeological Record of Two New England Fishing Settlements

Megan Rhodes Victor

The mere mention of colonial New England fishermen and sailors conjures up raunchy, salt-soaked scenes of taverns, with ale and coins scattered across creaking, sticky wooden tables. Such taverns are frequently inseparable from the stereotypes of seventeenth- and eighteenth-century fishing towns. Historically, there is solid evidence for this association. The centrality of these institutions on the social landscape of the English colonial world makes them ideal locations in which do what archaeology does best: search for the material remains of human behavior. Within the evocative, alcohol-laced environment of the tavern, an early modern period patron could find the ideal atmosphere for sociability and commensal politics (defined as the sharing of food and drink in a structured way so as to facilitate social negotiation). A keen-eyed archaeologist can find the remains of these negotiations, including agreements both legal and illicit.

Through a comparative study, this chapter examines the material remnants of such negotiations of social and economic capital at two sites to highlight the presence—or absence—of illicit trade and piracy in the archaeological record. The fishing station of Pemaquid, Maine, resembled many contemporary English colonial fishing plantations of the seventeenth and eighteenth centuries, while the fishermen of Smuttynose Island, in the Isles of Shoals on the Maine/New Hampshire border, ran a fishing station consisting of a loosely organized confederation of fishing masters. These expert fishermen combined their knowledge with a new innovative fish-drying technique, dunning, to create a lucrative business enterprise. Further, unlike Pemaquid, the

Shoals were a well-known haven to smugglers and pirates, including Thomas Larrimore and John Quelch. The archaeological assemblages from the taverns and domestic areas at the two sites reveal the presence (and absence) of piratical patrons.

Historical Background

Now the site of present-day Bristol, Pemaquid was one of the earliest fishing villages in Maine, established in the 1620s (Figure 6.1). While it is difficult to ascertain an exact date of founding, a permanent settlement likely was present by 1629, with enterprising fishermen exploring the area for as much as a decade earlier (Camp 1975; Hackelton 1869; Maine Department of Agriculture, Conservation, and Forestry 2013). As a fishing plantation, Pemaquid endured a series of land conflicts and uprisings, each of which damaged its economic prosperity and its population density. The fishing station weathered at least four major uprisings: King William's War (1688–1697), Queen Anne's War (1702–1713), Lovewell's War (1722–1725), and the French and Indian War (1754–1763) (Camp 1975; Coolidge and Mansfield 1859; Hackelton 1869; Maine Department of Agriculture, Conservation, and Forestry 2013).

Organizationally, Pemaquid was very similar to other seventeenth-century fishing plantations, such as Maine's Richmond Island, near Cape Elizabeth, and Newfoundland's St. John's on the English Shore (Camp 1975; Harrington 1992; Pope 2004). The fishermen at Pemaquid labored as residents of a fishing plantation, defined as a "waterfront premises from which the fishery was conducted" (Pope 2004:1). They worked under a local agent who regulated nearly all aspects of their daily lives, standing in for the (usually absentee) "planter," who owned the land on which the community stood and the fishing boats. The planter for Pemaquid and other such English fishing plantations generally held high social and economic status, while the fishermen themselves operated under the perpetual threat of job loss due to the planter's financial hardships or whims (Hamilton et al. 2009; Harrington 1992; Pope 2004). Finally, Pemaquid—like many mainland fishing plantations—was organized and funded as an entrepreneurial enterprise. Within the broader framework of Atlantic world trade systems, it was one of many fishing plantations that were part of a trade network consisting of "two steady streams" of economic flow "and one trickle" (Pope 2004:91). Pemaquid and other stations supplied Europe, especially southern Europe and the Mediterranean, with dried codfish; European centers, in turn, exported both fruit and wine to English and Dutch ports on the North Atlantic. These are the "steady streams" about which Pope writes. Finally, Dutch and English ports then sent goods back to

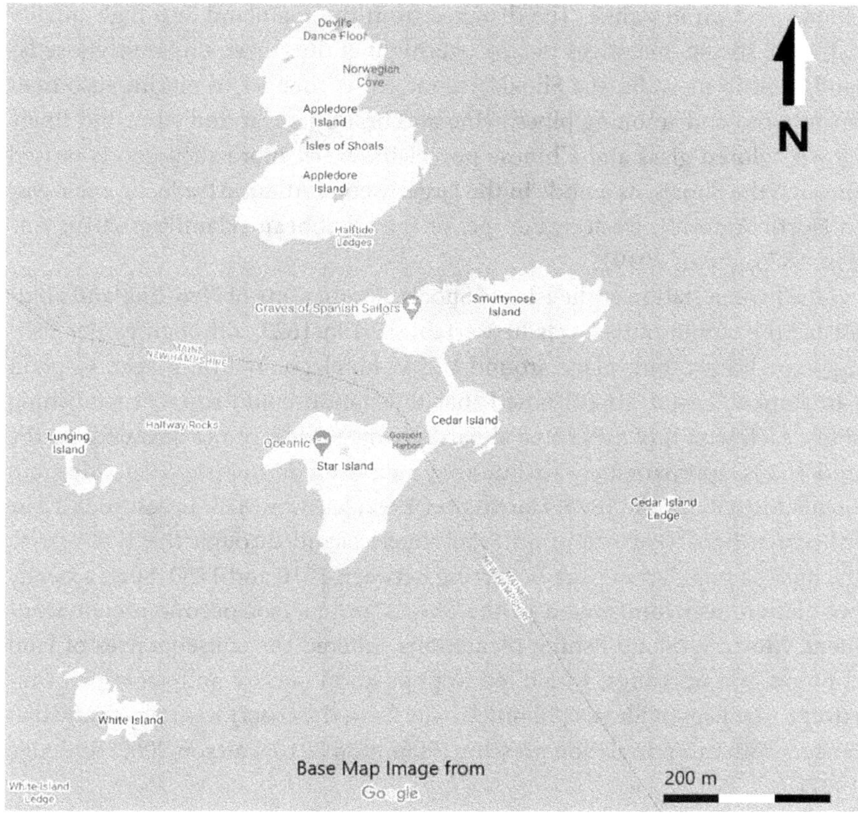

Figure 6.1. Map of the Isles of Shoals, Maine/New Hampshire, United States.

fishing plantations like Pemaquid, in a "trickle" of much smaller proportions than the fish exported.

This unequal flow of goods made it difficult for the fishermen at Pemaquid to acquire large amounts of wealth, despite fishing the rich waters off Pemaquid Beach (Pope 2004). The activities and strict social organization of fishing plantations like Pemaquid generated a unique settlement pattern: the fishermen lived in a large communal building known as the Great House. This structure was the center for domestic activities in the community and also sheltered the fishermen from the elements while they carried out other tasks, such as net mending.

The Isles of Shoals consist of nine craggy islands, located approximately 10 miles off the coast of the present-day Maine and New Hampshire border. Located in a deepwater harbor, the Isles were well situated for the enterprising Shoalers to establish a tavern, which catered to travelers, fishermen, merchants, and pirates alike. The distance from the mainland and high-quality fish were strong incentives to stop overnight at the tavern on Smuttynose Island. Within its walls, the Shoalers arranged exchanges of marine resources for tobacco and smoking pipes, wine and brandy, sugar and rum, and finely blown colored glass and Chinese porcelain. Many more such goods passed through the Shoals, as a node in the larger web of Atlantic trade, on their way to North America, western Europe, or the Caribbean (Hamilton 2010; Jenness 1875; Victor 2019).

The fishing station at the Isles of Shoals, another one of New England's oldest fishing communities, was first established in 1623, although earlier fishing expeditions took place around the archipelago. Within a year, Captain Christopher Levett (1628) noted that the station could support six fishing ships, each with fifty fishermen aboard. By the middle of the next decade, the mid-1630s, approximately six hundred men lived on the Isles (Coolidge and Manfield 1859; Drake 1875; Harrington 1992; Jenness 1875; Levett 1628). The fishermen lived year-round on Smuttynose Island through the 1780s, with the highest population peak occurring between 1710 and 1750. Such a steady population also contributed to the Shoals' unique socioeconomic environment. Most mainland fishing plantations suffered the consequences of land conflicts and uprisings, which led to population decline and subsequent recovery. The Isles of Shoals (10 miles away from the coast) were physically distanced from this population pressure (Hamilton 2010; Lawson 2007; Rutledge 1997).

The Shoalers' most potent resource came from the plentiful schools of fish that lived around the archipelago. Regularly weighing approximately two hundred pounds (which far exceeds today's six- to ten-pound specimens), codfish (*Gadus morhua*) dominated the Shoals' economy. The master fishermen at the Shoals used a new technique, known as dunning, to dry the fish they caught in such abundance; dunning dried each fish with less salt and rendered each one thinner than other processes, which allowed more fish into each wooden barrel shipped out from the Shoals. The reduction in salt not only reduced costs for the fishermen but also made the final product far more palatable. Once soaked and boiled, as was the practice with saltfish, Shoals fish retained much more of its inherent plumpness, giving it a fresher taste. This taste was so appreciated that Isles of Shoals cod was soon seen as the best available, resulting in Caribbean and European merchants using the product as something of a standard against which they could measure other salted cod and set prices (Hamilton 2010; Jenness 1875; Lawson 2007; Rutledge 1997).

The Shoalers also owed their success to their social organization. Rather than operating as a fishing plantation, the fishermen at the Isles of Shoals worked together as teams of fishing masters to build capital and were consequently distanced economically from the pattern of streams and trickles mentioned by Pope. The Shoalers were not "planted" colonists but, instead, could compete with the wealthy planters due to the volume and quality of the saltfish that they produced. At the height of the fishing station's productivity, they were exporting 3,000 to 4,000 quintals of fish per year (Coolidge and Mansfield 1859). A quintal, it should be noted, contains between 100 and 112 pounds of fish. The fishermen operated with "almost unrestrained civil and religious liberty" (Jenness 1875:107). Initially, they lived in privately held, lightly built wooden structures on the Isles as bachelors. Eventually, a few more substantial structures came to the Shoals, along with wives and children for some of the men (Hamilton et al. 2009; Harrington 1992; Jenness 1875). Many of the Shoalers eventually retired, wealthy, to the mainland.

Pirates and Fishermen: Two Different Stories

The fishing communities at Pemaquid and at the Isles of Shoals had widely varying views of piracy and colonial authority, no doubt influenced by their different socioeconomic structures. The Shoalers frequently were at the heart of colonial complaints for disrespecting officers of English colonial law, often even assaulting them, and generally showing "utter indifference" to their authority (Jenness 1875: 124; see also Drake 1875). In contrast, the fishermen at Pemaquid were known to comply readily with colonial authorities and cooperated to settle the constant land disputes over the bountiful fishing waters off of Pemaquid Beach. They also viewed English colonial authorities as a source of protection from the violent uprisings that they suffered. At least two forts were erected by such authorities to aid in these efforts, including Fort William Henry, which was likely the first stone fortification in New England (Coolidge and Mansfield 1859; Hackelton 1869; Maine Department of Agriculture, Conservation, and Forestry 2013).

Given this background, it is unsurprising that the inhabitants of the two settlements harbored very different views on piracy. Just as they were the victim of many land conflicts and uprising, the fishermen at Pemaquid were also attacked by the pirate Dixey (or Dixie) Bull (Dow 1969; Hackelton 1869). The first fort constructed at Pemaquid, known as Abraham Shurte's Fort, was erected in 1630 as a wooden palisade. Unfortunately, it "proved an insufficient defense against the marauding acts of the noted pirate, Dixie Bull," who attacked the settlement in 1632 and burned the fort to the ground (Hackelton 1869: 22; see also Cartland 1914). Bull fled with £500 in goods from Pemaquid, but the fishermen were far from piratical sympathizers. As his crew was weighing anchor, one of the men from Pemaquid successfully shot and killed Bull's second in command. Reportedly, an angry crowd gathered in Bull's wake as the ship left Pemaquid's shore (Cartland 1914; Dow 1969; Hackelton 1869).

In contrast, the Isles of Shoals had a reputation for being inhabited by a "motley, shifting community of fishermen . . . sailors, smugglers, and picaroons," all of whom chose to make the Shoals "their rendezvous and their home" (Jenness 1875:123). In fact, these fishermen were as "unconcerned with ideology or national borders as the fish they caught" (Smith 2006: 27). They would often "escape into the open sea" to "elude" officers of the law (Jenness 1875: 119-123). As such, pirates found a welcome home among the Shoalers. Jenness (1875:122) bemoans that "the islanders were generally indulgent, and sometimes friendly and serviceable in their intercourse with the numerous pirate ships which visited their harbor."

Dow (1969: 31) recounts multiple instances of piracy at the Shoals. In 1691 Governor Simon Bradstreet of the Massachusetts Bay Colony commissioned Captain Christopher Goffe to sail the *Swan* between Cape Cod and Cape Ann as well as "off the Isles of Shoals for the safeguard of the coast." Later that same year, Captain Thomas Griffin and Captain George Dew (also known as George Hout or George d'Hout), initially commissioned as privateers, captured Captain Thomas Wilkinson's ship and claimed that they believed it was a French vessel. Rather than relinquish their wrongfully stolen goods, the two men slipped from privateering to piracy and avoided Boston altogether. Instead, they "carried their prize into the Isles of Shoals" first, before heading into Portsmouth and upriver, "where part of the cargo was disposed of without trial or adjudication" (Dow 1969: 31). These were not the only pirates to seek shelter at the Shoals. Thomas Larrimore, pirate captain of the *Larrimore Galley* and part of pirate John Quelch's crew, traveled to the Isles of Shoals to gain men and provisions (Beal 2007; Dow 1969). Beal (2007: 134) notes that "this was not a surprising destination" because "since the early seventeenth century the Isles had been a favorite waypoint for people looking to disappear." Larrimore was confirmed to have returned to the Shoals, laden with Portuguese gold, after Quelch and his crew were pursued by Major Stephen Sewall (Beal 2007; Dow 1969).

Archaeology at the Two Sites

Unlike other early New England fishing stations, the site of Pemaquid underwent thorough excavations. Camp (1975) excavated there for ten years, with the goal of refining the station's chronology and identifying the places of manufacture of the artifacts found. The project yielded extensive information on the metals recovered, particularly those pertaining to fishing equipment and ships. The crew also recovered a large amount of pipe fragments, glass, and ceramics, which Camp (1975:78) focuses on in detail as "datable artifacts." Drawing on these data recovered, Camp (1975:79) concludes that the site's strata dated to a "range from the early 1600s through the period of the American Revolution." This period of occupation is almost the same as for the Isles of Shoals, which makes the archaeological comparison a sound one. Analysis of the artifacts allowed Camp (1975:79) to deduce that the inhabitants of Pemaquid were indeed "for the most part fishermen," as is fitting for a fishing plantation. In total, during the ten years of excavation, she uncovered the foundations of fourteen buildings, which included a tavern and a domestic activity area. The ceramics from these two areas are the main focus on this analysis.

The data from the Isles of Shoals come from three years of excavations on Smuttynose Island (2009 through 2011), under the direction of Nathan Hamilton. Excavating in three phases, the project first confirmed the presence of an intact site on the island dating to the seventeenth and eighteenth centuries, then identified activity areas, including a fish-processing area, a domestic area, and a tavern (Figure 6.2), and finally conducted small-scale data recovery (Victor 2019). The tavern-related activity area lay on Smuttynose Island's western shore, likely once constructed of brick with lead window casements and a nonlocal stone floor. The domestic architecture, as alluded to earlier, was archaeologically ephemeral. The fishermen's small wooden homes left little architecturally in the archaeological record. This was a problem exacerbated by the island's rocky soil, which made identifying postholes difficult. The fish-processing area was identified by the hundreds of fish remains (especially articulated cod vertebrae) recovered there, as the wooden racks and other equipment would also have left little trace archaeologically. The soil in this area was thick with fish oil, even centuries later.

Comparing the Data

The analysis done for this chapter drew on the ceramic assemblages from Pemaquid and Smuttynose Island in the Isles of Shoals. The ceramics were organized by ware type and comparative contemporary value (DAACS 2004; FLMNH 1995–2010; Stelle 2001; St. Mary's University Archaeology Lab 2010). Excavations by Camp (1975) yielded 15,215 sherds in total, of which nearly 5,000 (*n* = 4,967) sherds came from the fishing plantation's tavern, believed to be John Earthy's Tavern. The excavations at Smuttynose Island yield-

Figure 6.2. Ceramics from 2009 excavations at the Isles of Shoals, showcasing the variety of ware types present at the site. (Photo by author)

ed 11,004 sherds, of which almost 5,000 (n = 4,761) came from the tavern assemblage, which makes the size of the two tavern assemblages very similar. Coarse earthenwares composed the vast majority of the Pemaquid tavern's ceramic assemblage. Of these, 2,403 sherds were lead-glazed red earthenware vessel sherds, 241 sherds came from North Devon gravel-tempered vessels (of which 18 sherds were vessels decorated with an incised sgraffito pattern), and 3 sherds were identified as North Italian sgraffito-decorated slipware. Additionally, 22 sherds were classed as European slipwares and 55 sherds as Iberian storage jars. Staffordshire slipwares were also present, consisting of 212 sherds. Finally, 26 sherds of Buckley and a single sherd of Border Ware were identified in the assemblage. Camp (1975) also notes the presence of 11 sherds of unidentified coarse earthenware.

The tavern from Smuttynose Island yielded 2,413 sherds of coarse, lead-glazed red earthenware. North Devon wares were also prevalent in a rather high proportion, including the smooth (*n* = 954) and gravel-tempered (*n* = 125) varieties, as well as sherds with an incised sgraffito pattern (*n* = 33). A minimum of 54 North Devon vessels were recovered, of which 8 contained this decoration. Iberian storage and small olive jars (*n* = 4 sherds, representing at least 3 vessels), New England slip-trailed redwares (*n* = 31, representing at least 2 vessels), and 7 sherds of North Italian sgraffito-incised marbled slipware from a single vessel were also recovered. Additionally, European polychrome slipwares were represented by 2 sherds. Staffordshire slipwares were also present, consisting of 60 sherds (from at least 5 vessels). Finally, 24 sherds (representing at least 3 vessels) of Border Ware were recovered from the tavern assemblage.

Less represented at both taverns were refined, white-bodied earthenwares. No refined earthenwares were recovered from the Pemaquid tavern. The contemporary tavern assemblage on Smuttynose Island contained Jackfield (*n* = 2 sherds from the same vessel), Jackfield-type (*n* = 38 from at least 4 vessels), creamware (*n* = 304 from at least 18 vessels), plain pearlware (*n* = 509 from at least 23 vessels), painted pearlware (*n* = 160 from at least 22 vessels) and Whieldon Ware (*n* = 9 from at least 2 vessels).

Tin-glazed earthenwares were the second most common ceramics. The Pemaquid tavern yielded a total of 403 sherds, representing vessels from England, the Netherlands, and Spain. The tavern at Smuttynose Island had a total of 534 sherds of tin-glazed earthenwares, representing at least 34 vessels from Portugal, Spain, the Netherlands, and England.

Stonewares compose almost all of the remainder of the assemblages at both taverns. Just under a third (31 percent) of the assemblage from Pemaquid consists of stonewares. Many of these stonewares were Rhenish, including Westerwald and Bartmann-style Frechen. A notable 641 sherds from the assemblage were English Staffordshire white salt-glazed stonewares, of which 16 sherds were decorated with a scratch blue design. These ware types were also present at the Smuttynose Island tavern. Westerwald (*n* = 8) and Bartmann Frechen (*n* = 5) vessels were recovered. It is noteworthy that several sherds of the more expensive all-white Westerwald (a prestige good) were found at Smuttynose. Additionally, 46 vessels of English Staffordshire white salt-glazed stoneware were represented, of which 5 were decorated with a scratch blue pattern. Some stoneware types not present in the Pemaquid assemblage were found at Smuttynose Island, including Nottingham and Fulham.

Finally, a total of 35 sherds of porcelain came from Pemaquid's tavern, all of which were Chinese. Smuttynose Island's tavern assemblage contained 4 tea-ware vessels (*n* = 16 sherds), which were Chinese and English in origin.

The domestic assemblages for the two sites look quite different from one another, marking the main contrast in the two sites' assemblages. Most expensive ceramics are found in the tavern assemblage at Smuttynose Island. At Pemaquid, however, a fair number of finer wares were found in the domestic spaces as well, although they clustered in one or two domestic locations rather than being evenly spread, which speaks to a wealth inequality within the domestic spaces. A total of 4,693 ceramic sherds came from the dwelling spaces excavated at Pemaquid, compared with 6,243 sherds recovered from the domestic spaces at Smuttynose Island. Of these, coarse red earthenwares still represent the largest proportion of the domestic ceramics (n = 3,003): their volume is almost double the volume of the redwares from Smuttynose Island's domestic spaces (n = 1,601 from 41 vessels). The domestic assemblage from Pemaquid contains a total of 591 sherds of tin-glazed earthenware, as opposed to only 63 sherds at Smuttynose Island. In all, 253 Staffordshire slipwares were recovered from the domestic spaces at Pemaquid as well, while only 37 such sherds were found at Smuttynose Island. The only refined white-bodied earthenwares at the site come from the domestic assemblage, although they are present in much smaller numbers than at Smuttynose Island.

Finer stonewares, such as Westerwald and English Staffordshire scratch blue white salt-glazed stoneware, are present in larger abundance at Pemaquid, with 528 sherds. Smuttynose Island's domestic spaces have only 182 such sherds. Finally, the most expensive ceramic of the period, porcelain, was found in higher proportions in Pemaquid's domestic assemblage (n = 29) than at Smuttynose Island (n = 4).

Remnants of Piracy in Sherds? The Data Discussed

The datasets from the two sites reveal somewhat similar tavern assemblages but very different domestic ones, although Pemaquid, as a whole, was a far less wealthy settlement. The artifacts recovered speak to the definitive presence of taverns at both sites: assemblages filled with vessels related to alcohol consumption as well as the preparation, serving, and consumption of food. The tavern at Smuttynose Island yielded a far wider variety of ceramic types and places of manufacture. It contained wares not found at Pemaquid's tavern, such as Portuguese tin-glazed earthenwares, white Westerwald sherds, Jackfield and Jackfield-type ceramics, Nottingham stoneware, and refined white-bodied earthenwares. This wide variety of ceramics stands as a testament to the myriad trading routes and contacts associated with the independent fishing station at the Shoals; it also helps show their distance from the trade patterns discussed by Pope (2004) as typical for fishing plantations.

More of the comparatively expensive wares, such as tin-glazed earthenwares and porcelains, were found in the domestic spaces of Pemaquid than were recovered from Smuttynose Island's domestic area. These were not found at every domestic building, however, but were clustered at only a few such structures. While less valuable overall, the ceramics found at Smuttynose Island were rather evenly distributed. This showcases the hierarchical structure of the traditional fishing plantation organization at Pemaquid and the more balanced organization at the Isles of Shoals.

The ceramic assemblage of the domestic area speaks to household quotidian activities and features a correspondingly utilitarian array of ceramics. The vessels in the tavern indicate large-scale eating and drinking, which is expected at the alcohol-related establishment. Notably, though, the great wealth of the Shoals is also seen in the tavern. The Shoalers were fishing masters who, based on the archaeology, chose to invest their wealth in the tavern rather than in their homes. The more particular wares—like the white Westerwald and the Chinese porcelain—may very well have been a product of the traders, sailors, and pirates who came through the tavern in the course of their affairs, enticed by what was offered therein: good food, fine alcohol, and a sympathetic attitude, away from governmental regulations and—at times—pursuit.

7

The Archaeology of Lundy Pirates

A Case Study of Material Culture

Patrick J. Boyle

Lundy Island is located 12 miles off the coast of Devon, England, at the mouth of the Bristol Channel. Possession of this small island was sporadic: at various times, it was under the control of kings, knights, and pirates. A variety of historical sources suggest that English, French, and North African pirates occasionally used Lundy as a haven. Yet there is a significant lack of archaeological evidence to support these claims (Harfield 1996; Langham 1994). Multiple archaeological investigations have been undertaken on the island, documenting a variety of material culture dating from the twelfth to nineteenth centuries, when piracy was common on the island. None of the artifacts, however, were attributed to piracy.

To understand the lack of material culture relating to piracy on Lundy, it is necessary to characterize English pirates to determine what types of objects they may have left behind. Through historical research, areas on the island that were used by pirates were identified to determine the extent of the archaeological excavations. This chapter reassesses the previously excavated material to determine whether the objects are relatable to piracy.

Piracy in Southwest England

Piracy in southwestern England relied heavily on specific land bases that the pirates used to sell stolen cargo and to resupply their ships (Earle 2006:17). From these havens, English pirates were able to make voyages to the Mediterranean, Newfoundland, and the Caribbean (Appleby 1990:76). The organization of piracy within such havens ranged from disorganized groups that raided opportunistically to large outfits financed by wealthy supporters (Appleby 2009:17). English piracy began to decline, however, in the early seventeenth century, when harsher punishments were implemented (Senior 1976:134–143).

The decline of English piracy led to a rise in activity in other nations, such as the corsairs from the Barbary Coast (Appleby 1990:85). The Islamic Barbary States of North Africa, for instance, relied on slavery, although the enslavement of Muslims was forbidden (Konstam 2008:76–77). The Barbary pirates would therefore abduct and enslave European Christians. Barbary piracy in England is unique, because the pirates did not use English land havens to sell cargo. Instead, they raided the coastal villages and used secluded areas such as Lundy as temporary bases (Hamilton and Lomas 1897:546; Vitkus and Matar 2001:15).

Pirates used the same objects as ordinary people, sailors, and merchants, so distinguishing pirate material culture from that of society in general is difficult. Objectification material culture theory, however, is one approach to identifying such differences. This theory focuses not only on objects but also on the landscape, to determine what can be learned from the people who created, used, or even destroyed the cultural material (Tilley 2013:60–61). As such, the structures and locations that pirates used on Lundy can be interpreted as pirate material culture. If the objects used by pirates cannot be identified, the landscape itself can be examined and treated as material culture.

Historical Narrative

Lundy was a strategic location for capturing ships traveling in and out of the channel at the prominent port of Bristol (Jones 2012:63). The ships within the Bristol Channel were at the mercy of the tides, which made the timing and routes of ships very predictable (Jones 2012:65). Thus, when there were no ships to capture, the Lundy pirates were known to raid the nearby coasts of Devon and Wales (Owen 1920:209).

Pirates were not the only people who used the island of Lundy, which was sometimes inhabited by nonpirate groups in between the phases of pirate occupation (Bruce 1858:86). This mix of habitation resulted in a large assortment of artifacts dating from the thirteenth to nineteenth centuries. Not knowing how many inhabitants were on the island during these periods adds to the difficulty in determining which objects are relatable to piracy. This study therefore only examines the pirate groups that established Lundy as a base, because they have the highest probability of leaving behind material culture.

William de Marisco

In 1237 William de Marisco began using Lundy as a base to attack passing merchants, some of whose ships belonged to King Henry III (Black 1901:187). The king had no immediate intention of capturing Marisco's island stronghold, but on September 8, 1238, a man claiming to have been hired by Marisco was caught attempting to assassinate King Henry (Langham 1994:16). The king did not want the assassination attempt to go unpunished, so he retaliated.

Fifteen men under the command of William Bardolf sailed to Lundy in February 1242, invaded the island, and detained Marisco (Langham 1994:16–17). On July 25, 1242, Marisco was gibbeted: his body was publicly hanged from a hook. His entrails were cut out and his limbs were cut off and "sent to four principal cities in the Kingdom" (Langham 1994:17).

Captain Thomas Salkeld

Captain Thomas Salkeld attempted to make Lundy his permanent base in the early seventeenth century. While based on the island, the pirate abducted sailors, raided the coasts of England and Wales, and crashed stolen ships onto the steep cliffs of Lundy. Salkeld's small fleet of seven ships and a crew of nearly 130 sailors made Lundy "a place so dangerous for all passengers . . . it is almost impossible for them to escape him" (Owen 1920:209).

William Young, a local merchant, was taken from his ship and forced to work as a slave on Lundy. Salkeld's pirates raided Young's vessel near Milford Haven and took the ship and its passengers to Lundy. The pirates spent the next few days raiding the small villages around the nearby coast. They burned down houses, destroyed ships, and took as much loot as they could carry (Urban 1839:354). This desolation soon gained the attention of the authorities. Once the pirates were finished devastating Milford Haven, they made their way south to Lundy.

On March 23, 1609, the pirates and the captive passengers arrived on the island. Salkeld made sure that his ships were flying their flags when they landed on Lundy, "in defiance of the King of England" (Urban 1839:355). To further demonstrate his complete lack of respect for the English monarchy after taking Lundy, Salkeld "called himself King of it" (Green 1857:601). Only two days after landing on the island, the new "king" of Lundy commanded his captives to build a quay for his ships to dock. To prevent the captives from rising against the pirates, Salkeld divided them into three different groups, had the prisoners' heads shaved, and threatened to kill any of them who spoke to a member of a different group (Urban 1839:355).

Soon after the slaves were put to work, a 200-ton ship on its way to Bristol landed in the Lundy Roads, the area of water east of the island that is protected from the currents. Captain Salkeld sent some of his crew in a longboat to capture it, but the ship was able to escape the pirates with the help of a storm. A couple of pirates were even taken with the ship during the escape (Urban 1839:355). Because the pirate crew was slightly diminished, the captives began to plan an escape.

Salkeld constructed a platform to hang any person who did not accept him as king (Urban 1839:355). Instead of being deterred, a prisoner named George Escott rallied his fellow captives and coordinated an attack on the pirates (Green 1857:601). The rebellion of slaves, along with Escott, "who alone was armed having a poniard [a stiletto or dagger] in hand," attacked the fort (Langham 1994:35). The uprising resulted in the deaths of multiple pirates, but Captain Salkeld and the remaining crew members fled on Escott's captured ship.

The English authorities searched the Bristol Channel for months before they heard any news of Captain Salkeld. After making his escape from Lundy, he sought help from a former partner and fellow pirate, Captain Peter Easton. Instead of aiding Salkeld, Easton killed him for losing Lundy and threw his body into the sea (Russell and Prendergast 1974: Letter 871).

Captain Salkeld's occupation of Lundy is now a common folktale shared with tourists who visit the island. Although many of the exact details are not commonly known, the influence of pirates on the island is evident. The narrative of Salkeld's occupation of Lundy is important because the primary sources describe possible archaeological remains.

Jan Janszoon and the Barbary Pirates

Pirates from the Barbary Coast of North Africa used Lundy as a temporary base in 1625 while raiding the surrounding areas (Bruce 1858:86). Although the Mediterranean was the main region of Barbary pirate attacks, they ranged as far north as Iceland, attacking merchant ships to abduct Christians to sell into slavery (Vitkus and Matar 2001:8).

On August 18, 1625, three Turkish pirate ships took control of Lundy, abducted all of the inhabitants, and threatened to raze the nearby town of Ilfracombe. A few days later, the Barbary pirates captured a Danish ship and took eight captives somewhere off the southwest coast of England. The Barbary pirates had no intention of long-term occupation of the island and most likely used Lundy as a temporary base during their long raids (Bruce 1858:86).

A few years after the Barbary pirates first began raiding the English coasts, Jan Janszoon, a Dutch privateer turned Barbary pirate, arrived on Lundy: "for the next five years he used the island as a base to prey on coastal communities and shipping as far away as Iceland" (Konstam 2008:91). Janszoon and his crew undertook massive raids around the British Isles in order to abduct Christians. Some 230 Barbary pirates armed with muskets and firebrands stormed the town of Baltimore in 1631 and abducted over a hundred citizens (Mahaffy 1900:621–622).

The Barbary pirates intermittently pillaged the southwest coast of England and continued to use Lundy as a temporary base (Hamilton and Lomas 1897:546). Local merchants wrote a petition in 1636 to declare that they would no longer attempt to sail in the area because the waters were "much infested by Turkish pirates from Algiers, and especially from Sally in Barbary." By that time, the pirates had taken 87 ships and 96,700 pounds worth of cargo in the few preceding years. The number of sailors taken as slaves was estimated to be nearly two thousand (Hamilton and Lomas 1897:546).

There is no way to determine the exact length of time that the Barbary pirates made use of Lundy. Primary sources, however, explain that at one point the Barbary pirates were there for at least a fortnight (Hamilton and Lomas 1897:546). It is possible that archaeological remains of their activities might have been deposited during that brief time, although these have yet to be found.

Thomas Benson

One final pirate who committed crimes at sea while using Lundy as his own personal base was named Thomas Benson. Originally a merchant from Bideford, Benson leased the island in 1748 to aid in his clandestine endeavors. He continued his business as a merchant but accumulated multiple fines and penalties for illegally importing tobacco (Langham 1994:47). Once he obtained Lundy, the financially failing trader quickly discovered the lucrative potential of having a secluded offshore island.

Benson became a prominent figure in government and was elected as a member of Parliament for Barnstaple (Langham 1994:47). He used the position to obtain government contracts in order to earn extra income to repay his debts. One of these contracts required him to transport convicts to Virginia on his merchant ships. After retrieving the convicts in England, the devious smuggler would simply drop off his human cargo on Lundy. The ships would continue on to Virginia without them. The convicts would then be used as his own personal slaves on the island. Like the captured merchants used by Salkeld, Benson's slaves were forced into hard labor and kept in the ruins of the Marisco Castle (Baring-Gould 1926:234). It is unknown whether or not Benson chose to lease the island for the sole purpose of using slaves, "but the convicts were put to good use in farming and building, and for some years all went well" (Langham 1994:47).

Benson did not attempt to hide his slaves from the public. A small group of unidentified visitors to Lundy in 1752 documented their stay on the island. The author explains that "the old Fort was occupied by the convicts, whom he had sent there some time before, and employed in making a wall across the island; they were locked up every night when they returned from their labour." It is clear that in Benson's mind he was fulfilling his contract by taking the captives to Lundy because it was "the same as sending them to America" (*North Devon Magazine* 1824:55). The similarities between Captain Salkeld and Thomas Benson do not end with enslaved labor. Benson also "regarded himself as king of Lundy and ruled with a high hand" (Baring-Gould 1926:234). He was even known to fire at ships that did not hoist their colors while passing his fort (*North Devon Magazine* 1824:55).

The false king smuggled not only people to Lundy but also tobacco to the mainland. Once his ships returned from the American colonies, he would unload and store the tobacco in a small cave on Lundy located just south of the castle (Baring-Gould 1926:234). Customs authorities became suspicious of Benson in 1751 after his ship *Vine*, which was loaded with tobacco in Milford Haven, ended up in Cardiff without any cargo (Langham 1994:48). The customs authorities traveled to Lundy, where they found evidence of tobacco in a cave. They fined Benson over £5,000 and seized his property in Bideford (Baring-Gould 1926:234).

Benson attempted one last ruse to gain enough money to pay off his debts and thereby officially committed piracy. In 1752 he overly insured one of his merchant ships, the *Nightingale*, which was supposed to transport valuable cargo from England to America. Benson secretly stopped off at Lundy, however, and hid the cargo in the cave. He then ordered the crew to set sail and scuttle the ship so that he could claim the insurance money. An unknown crew member confessed to the crime, which was committed at sea and was therefore considered piracy. Many of the crew were hanged at Execution Dock, but Benson managed to flee to Portugal and avoid punishment (Baring-Gould 1926:235). After Benson lost the island, Lundy fell into disarray and changed ownership multiple times. Other smugglers used the island for a few decades more, but none of them made as much impact on Lundy as Thomas Benson.

Archaeology and Material Culture

The archaeology of Lundy began in 1856 when skeletal remains were found during the construction of buildings in the area known as Bull's Paradise

(Thackray 1989:113). It was not until the 1950s, however, that scientific archaeological investigations were carried out on the island (Ternstrom 2008:15). The current location of many artifacts excavated in this early period is unknown.

Bull's Paradise

The Marisco family created a stronghold in the area that is now known as Bull's Paradise (Figure 7.1). It is the only area on the island where twelfth- and thirteenth-century potsherds have been discovered (Thackray 1989:109–113). The stronghold area consisted of multiple buildings and a watering hole surrounded by a wall 2 m thick made from the island's granite (Gardner 1972:8). There is evidence of a large defensive structure believed to be a manor house (Thackray 1989:115–117). Research suggests that the Marisco stronghold

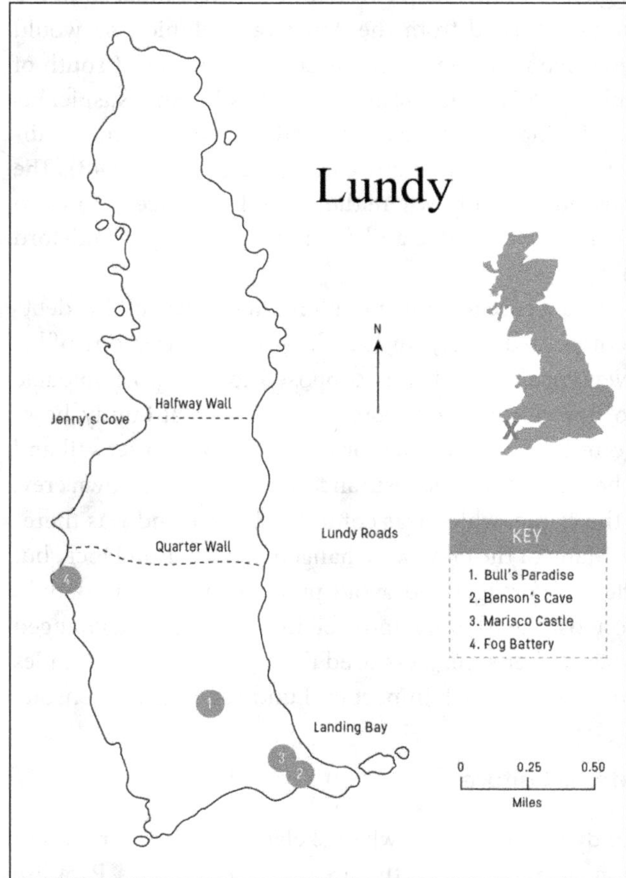

Figure 7.1. Map of Lundy archaeological sites relating to pirates (amended from Gardner 1972:12).

area was purposefully destroyed at some point, most likely when King Henry III retook Lundy in 1243 (Gardner 1972:9).

Multiple archaeological investigations have taken place at Bull's Paradise, the area that has seen the greatest amount of human activity on the island. Large quantities of thirteenth-century potsherds were recovered from an excavation in 2000, and many were identified as Devon and Somerset types (Allan 2001:136). The pottery was most likely obtained through legal trade even though the objects were found in a location used by pirates in the past. Pirates used the same everyday objects as everyone else, so it is impossible to distinguish potsherds from the vessels they used from those used by the other island inhabitants.

Three silver coins dating to the medieval period were also found in the same midden deposit as the pottery. All of these, however, were dated much later than William de Marisco. These artifacts indicate that the area of the Marisco stronghold was clearly used after the island was retaken from him. Whether or not the coins were obtained by pirates is uncertain. The excavated coins are dated to periods of no known pirate activity, so it is more likely that they reached Lundy through legal trade.

Benson's Cave

Thomas Benson's illicit history on Lundy can be seen in the cave at the base of Marisco Castle (Figure 7.2). Named after the pirate himself, Benson's Cave is located on a cliff on the southern end of the island. Although the entrance makes it appear small from the outside, the cave is 19.5 m long, 2.5 m wide, and about 4 m high (Langham 1994:116; Thackray 1989:141–142). Multiple groups of inscriptions carved into the walls of the cave consist of letters and

Figure 7.2. Benson's Cave. (Photo by author, 2016)

numbers that have been theorized to be the initials of some of Benson's slaves (Langham 1989:50).

Records indicate that Benson received £20 per convict that he transported as a fee from the government and that he brought at least two ships carrying convicts from England to Lundy: the first in 1749 and the second in 1752 (Langham 1994:49). A. F. Langham surveyed the entirety of the cave in 1960 and identified at least thirty-eight different carvings of initials. He found the records of prisoners deported from England during the years that Benson controlled Lundy: "seven or eight of the initials date from a 1749 passage to the island, and ten of the initials from a 1752 shipload" (Langham 1989:50).

Marisco Castle

Marisco Castle was originally built in 1243 at the request of King Henry III (Stevenson 1916:162). It was most likely in a ruinous state when Captain Salkeld occupied the island, since he used captives in an attempt to repair the castle by "building walls for a fort." Evidence for this also comes from Young's deposition, in which he explained that the captives were not even kept in the castle at night (Urban 1839:355).

The castle was not in a habitable state during Benson's occupation: he used it as a makeshift prison for his slaves (*North Devon Magazine* 1824:55). It is possible that the slaves used the stones from the castle walls to construct the Halfway Wall, as the stones show similarities (Langham 1994:116).

The parade grounds located on the east side of the castle were excavated in 1984 and 1985 (Historic Environment Record 2012:MDV41). The Lundy Museum contains multiple objects from different periods that were discovered during the parade-ground excavations, but no published reports pertaining to them are available. Further excavations of the areas surrounding the castle could produce material remains that may be linked to piracy (Figure 7.3).

Fog Battery

Two early eighteenth-century 18-pound cannon are located on a small platform on the west side of Lundy. Originally located on Beacon Hill, the cannon were moved, to be used as a fog signal for ships passing in bad weather (Thackray 1989:76–77). The cannon are muzzleloaders with a 5-inch (12.7-cm) bore and were created during the reign of George I from 1714 to 1727 (Historic Environment Record 2012:MDV69114; Thackray 1989:76–77). It is possible that the cannon were on the island at the time of Thomas Benson's occupation if they were brought there within a few decades of being made. As previously noted, Benson was known to fire cannon from the castle upon

Figure 7.3. Reconstructed Marisco Castle. (Photo by author, 2016)

vessels that did not raise a flag as a sign of respect when passing (*North Devon Magazine* 1824:55). Perhaps the fog battery cannon were on the island at the same time as Benson, but it is impossible to know.

Distinguishing Pirate Material Culture

The pirates of Lundy were not the stereotypical swashbucklers portrayed in modern culture. Instead, they were murderers, thieves, and slavers. Yet they are remembered as pirates only because of representations in the primary sources, which are the only extant fragments of their legacy. After all, pirates operated in the shadows and "have always been elusive figures. They came out of the blue. They attacked, they looted, and they vanished. They left no memorials or personal belongings behind" (Cordingly 2006:xiii). This case study, however, suggests that Lundy pirates did leave behind objects, which have yet to be studied in archaeological detail because it is almost impossible to identify them.

Objectification theory shows that material culture can be adaptable and inconsistent but socially significant. Thus, a certain object can have different meanings in multiple social contexts rather than belonging exclusively to one group. The theory also proposes that structures, landscapes, and places can be considered material culture if they were used by a group in a certain way (Tilley 2013:70). Therefore, a clear separation between particular groups must be made when attempting to identify pirate material culture. In this case study, the landscape, structures, and objects were all examined individually to determine whether they could be identified as material culture associated with piracy.

To identify areas of Lundy used by pirates, primary documents and previous excavation reports were examined. Studying the primary documents that mention precise locations from each phase of occupation helped to identify which sites possibly held material culture relevant to piracy. The sites that were identified only through primary documents but have yet to be excavated were also used to determine whether they could be considered pirate material culture. The spatial distribution analysis also explains why some of the sites were heavily used by one pirate group but neglected by others.

Lundy, as a whole, can be defined as pirate material culture because different pirate groups used it in different ways. Marisco and Benson both used the island as a permanent base, from which they conducted illicit activities. Salkeld tried to use Lundy as a permanent settlement but was forced to leave after only two weeks (Urban 1839:355). The Barbary pirates as well as other pirate groups briefly used the island as a temporary haven (Harfield 1996:65–69).

The landscape areas on Lundy are also difficult to define as pirate material culture, with little evidence of how pirates used them. For example, the gun platforms around the island date to the period when piracy was common, but no primary documents indicate that pirates used the platforms. As such, these geographical areas cannot be unquestionably related to piracy because there is no direct evidence that pirates used them in a unique way.

One such area often mentioned in primary sources is Marisco Castle. Salkeld used his captives to try to rebuild areas of the structure, presumably in an effort to use it as a permanent base (Urban 1839:355). Benson later used the castle as a makeshift prison for his enslaved laborers (*North Devon Magazine* 1824:55). According to the objectification theory, the castle can be related to piracy because two pirates used the castle in unique ways and the evidence to support this claim comes from separate eyewitness accounts (*North Devon Magazine* 1824:55; Urban 1839:355). Marisco Castle, therefore, can be identified as pirate material culture simply because primary sources confirm its use by pirates.

Similarly, Benson's Cave was used specifically to hide smuggled goods, and its walls are covered with carvings of initials that belong to convicts that Benson abducted (Langham 1989:50). Even though multiple groups of people likely used the cave throughout the centuries, Benson's particular use of it to aid in his clandestine activities suggests that it can be considered pirate material culture (Thackray 1989:141–142).

Figure 7.4. View of Lundy, looking south at Marisco Castle. (Photo by author, 2016)

Even though some specific sites on the island can be identified as pirate material culture, it is important to note that the objects found within these areas cannot automatically be attributed to piracy. Primary documents would need to indicate exactly which objects were used by pirates in order for the material culture to be identified.

Conclusion

Since the island of Lundy has a long history of pirate occupation, it is probable that it contains material culture relating to piracy. Identifying landscapes, structures, and objects that can be relatable to piracy, however, is difficult, regardless of the location. Identifying pirate material culture relies entirely on direct evidence from primary sources. Archaeological investigations at Lundy have yet to identify pirate material culture, even though primary historical sources indicate use of the island by pirates. Through both primary sources and excavation reports, it is possible to identify some structures as well as some objects that pirates perhaps utilized. Without primary sources indicating use of objects by pirates, however, it may be impossible to determine whether they are related to piracy. In this specific case, although the cultural landscape of Lundy can be recognized as pirate material culture, it is impossible to distinguish objects used by pirates from the other excavated material (Figure 7.4).

8

The Mystery of Morgan's Island

Archaeological Insights into a Possible Pirate Wreck at Somerset, Bermuda

Bradley Rodgers and Jason T. Raupp

Bermuda governor Nathaniel Butler commented in 1622 that one of his predecessors might have been involved in a nefarious plot with west-end islanders to capture a Dutch privateer and its crew for personal use. While official records convey witness accounts describing the loss of this vessel near Somerset, Butler's written accounts clearly indicate his doubts about the veracity of islanders' stories regarding the event. Although the crew was rescued after the grounding, testimonies falsely suggest that the vessel itself was wrecked and sunk in a storm on the western reef, with no effort made to save it. This is particularly curious because the population of west Bermuda commonly engaged in wrecking and salvage. The western reef is 20 miles from the capital of St. George's, so the story was apparently not easily verified by officials and eventually became one of the many colorful episodes in the early records of Bermudian colonization.

Data recovered from recent archaeological investigations of a shipwreck situated in shallow water just off Morgan's Island in Somerset may provide support for Governor Butler's suspicions. Examination of the Morgan's Island Wreck revealed numerous exposed timbers that appear to represent the remains of a single disarticulated wooden ship. Construction techniques and building material suggest that the vessel was likely constructed in the unique northern European bottom-based shipbuilding tradition sometime in the early seventeenth century. The vessel was armed, as indicated by the small number of artifacts identified at the site related to this period.

Furthermore, the highly disarticulated nature of these surface remains and the many unique marks visible on the timbers suggest that it was hand salvaged to recover hardware and lumber: it appears to have been literally torn to pieces through human intervention, not by a storm process. Thus, it seems quite possible that Bermudian locals at Morgan's Island managed to "out-pirate" a pirate ship, while fooling their own government into believing the vessel was wrecked in a storm.

Setting the Scene

It is not our intent here to rewrite the entire history of Bermuda from discovery to settlement but rather to highlight those historic activities and episodes that seem to correspond with data presented in the archaeological record near Morgan's Island. It should be noted, however, that the early history of the island chain is intrinsically linked to navigation of the Atlantic Ocean. Pilots in the Age of Sail knew well that sighting Bermuda, more than 1,000 kilometers east of Cape Hatteras, North Carolina, signaled the need to turn east out of the Gulf Stream and on to the Azores and then to Europe (Quinn 1989:4). Although the islands of Bermuda were discovered by Spanish navigator Juan de Bermúdez in 1505, they remained uninhabited until the seventeenth century (Barreiro-Meiro 2002). Prior to settlement, human encounters with Bermuda resulted from episodes of exploration or shipwreck, where crews were forced to survive on the island until they could repair damaged ships, build vessels from wreckage, or signal passing ships for help.

Though Spanish colonization of the islands was proposed in 1527, there is no evidence to support any serious attempt at doing so (Lefroy 1877:xlvi). But the islands are known to have hosted both pirates and privateers during the sixteenth century. Furthermore, numerous charts and maps indicate that Spanish, French, Dutch, and English navigators were familiar with Bermuda as a strategic waypoint in Atlantic shipping. The question of colonization was finally forced on the English early in the seventeenth century by the wreck of the Virginia Colony supply ship *Sea Venture* (Quinn 1989:1).

Perhaps the reason why Bermuda was not settled sooner was its dire reputation: from the early 1500s Spanish mariners referred to it as the "Island of Devils" (Hallett 2007:30). This is hardly surprising, as navigators had no reliable way to plot longitude until late in the eighteenth century. Thus, encountering the archipelago on a moonless night or in foul weather would have been risky. An unexpected rendezvous with reefs that extend out for several miles could spell disaster. Limited sources of food or water, as well as dense underbrush, were additional factors that made survival difficult (Quinn 1989:3). The huge outer reef system that surrounds Bermuda resulted in many calamitous and well-known shipwrecks in the sixteenth and seventeenth centuries. It is likely that other wrecking events went unrecorded due to a lack of witnesses or survivors. Oviedo (1851) recorded the first accounts of shipwreck survival in the sixteenth century when he interviewed sailors who had rescued themselves from the Bermuda reefs by building vessels out of pieces of wrecked ships and native cedar trees. All of these challenges have contributed to historians' long reliance on secondhand accounts of wrecking activity (Quinn 1989:4).

Archaeological data from the Morgan's Island site suggest an association with an early seventeenth-century Dutch vessel, making the reports of Bermuda's fifth governor, Nathaniel Butler, invaluable. Written in 1622, Butler's history of the islands covered the first decade of the colonization period. Among the most pertinent information contained within that volume, as it relates to this discussion, is the description of an event that perhaps most closely dovetails with the archaeological data revealed at Morgan's Island. Butler notes that in 1619 a "handsome pinnace" with a mostly Dutch crew was reportedly stranded on the rocks of the northwest shoals (Hallett 2007:118). Though the definition of the term "pinnace" changed over time, in the early to mid-seventeenth century it can generally be described as a heavily armed version of a Dutch fluyt. Fluyts were flat-bottomed, relatively narrow, and round-sterned vessel cargo carriers (Landstrom 1961:154). Pinnaces were used to escort convoys of merchant vessels and allowed the Dutch to expand their trading empire in a cost-effective manner. Though much like the flat-bottomed fluyt in form, the pinnace was more heavily constructed to accommodate additional ordnance and was a favorite class of ship for privateers and pirates. Most importantly, however, seventeenth-century pinnaces were made of hardwood, unlike the fluyt. Interestingly, it is thought that the term "pinnace" and the ship class it represented later evolved into the type of vessel known as the frigate.

Reportedly a privateer/pirate vessel operating in the Caribbean, the pinnace described by Butler approached Bermuda in search of food and supplies, because the few English sailors on board expected fair treatment in the British colony. The ship and crew arrived without a pilot familiar with the reef system, however, and soon the ship sailed "among the outlying rocks" on the reef. The crew of this pinnace was "rescued" by Bermudians who flocked to the stranded ship in small boats. Oddly enough, however, "no real attempt was made to salvage the ship": the vessel reportedly disappeared with the "next storm." Butler's text suggests that he did not believe the explanation given by previous governor, Miles Kendall. Instead, he speculated that the islanders might have worked in league with Kendall and deliberately allowed the ship to wreck so that it could be salvaged and any booty hidden within it could be recovered for personal gain. The Dutch crew members were sent to St. George's, where they reportedly lived in servitude for approximately one year before being shipped first to England and then home (Hallett 2007:118).

Evidence recorded during the recent archaeological investigation of the Morgan's Island Wreck site suggests that human intervention could have been the ultimate factor in its formation process. It would have been unlikely, if not impossible, for a ship without human assistance to slip its anchor lines, navigate or be blown by storm inside the reef, pass through the narrow channel that leads into Ely's Harbor, and then glide into the shallow, protected waters surrounding Morgan's Island. It should be noted that Bermuda was scarcely populated at the time. Morgan's Island was more than 30 kilometers from the main population center of St. George's. Passing ships would not have seen a vessel hidden behind Morgan's Island, and land travel through the brush and over the steep slopes around Ely's Harbor would have been nearly impossible. The presence of salvage marks on the extant timbers at the site supports the probability that clever islanders managed to deliver the vessel from the reef and move it to a protected spot for shipbreaking, while concurrently reporting it as lost after the next storm. This explanation would also have allowed Governor Kendall to avoid explaining the whereabouts of this valuable ship to his superiors.

As noted in the preliminary report of investigations for the Morgan's Island Wreck, historic sources indicate the loss of two Dutch-built vessels near one another on the western reef (Rodgers et al. 2017). The first, known as the Flemish Wreck, was lost in 1615 near a promontory referred to as Wreck Hill (Figure 8.1). The second is the pinnace referred to by Governor Butler as being lost in 1619. Construction features documented at a shipwreck located on the western reef and referred to as the New Old Spaniard (NOS) indicate a Dutch origin (Watts 2014:109). It is probable that the NOS site represents the remains of the lost Flemish Wreck, so the vessel remains documented at Morgan's Island are likely those of the 1619 Dutch privateer.

Perhaps It Is the Pirate Ship

Archaeology, like physics, operates on the principle of "Conservation of Information." Information from human interactions is recorded in artifacts, as are the alterations to the natural environment in areas where human activity takes place. If researchers are well versed in data collection and clever enough to interpret the evidence—and the environment has not erased it—then an

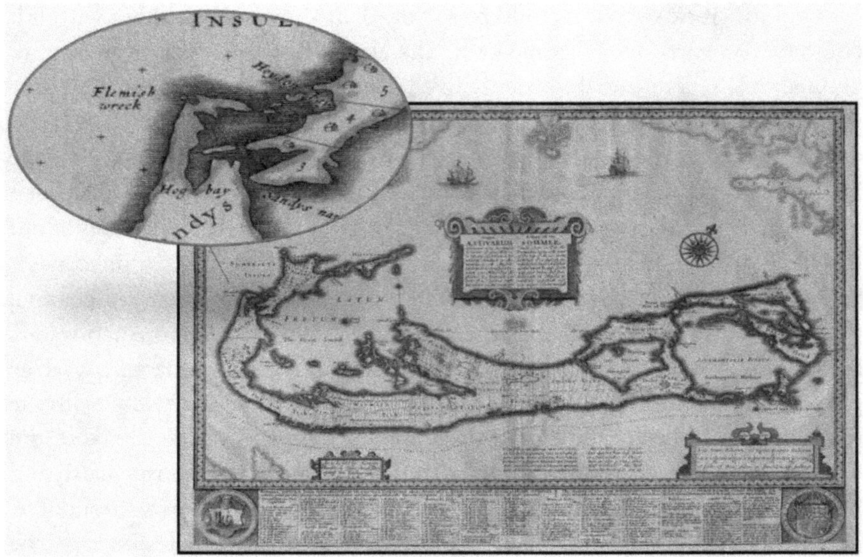

Figure 8.1. John Speed's *A Mapp of the Sommer Islands, Once Called the* Bermuda (1626/1627), with the location of the Flemish Wreck highlighted. (Courtesy of the Bermuda Maritime Museum)

analytical interpretation should be possible, much like a forensic cold case study at a crime scene. In the case of the Morgan's Island Wreck, the remains of a wooden ship are interpreted here on both a macro and micro level.

Located in Ely's Harbor, the wreck site extends over an area approximately 75 by 45 m, situated in very shallow water (Figure 8.2). The survey of the wreck included noninvasive techniques of illustration, photography, and standard archaeological site mapping. Situated west to east, the Morgan's Island Wreck site is composed of a surface scatter of several remarkably well-preserved timbers that retain the distinctive shapes of their original scantlings. Among the easily identifiable timbers are numerous floors, futtocks, and crotch timbers, as well as a single hanging knee, rudder, and portions of the bow assembly. Other timbers have yet to be identified but likely represent mast supports, a stem assembly timber, and part of a possible knighthead. Furthermore, numerous timbers undoubtedly lie buried beneath the sand and turtle grass, as indicated by a section of partially exposed and consecutive floor timbers.

The following discussion notes the diagnostic timbers and features singled out as the most important archaeological attributes at Morgan's Island. This analysis is based on a careful examination of collected data, including measured sketches of exposed timbers. This approach has revealed information

Figure 8.2. Aerial photo of the Morgan's Island Wreck site. (Courtesy of the Bermuda Maritime Museum)

related to ship construction techniques, the shape of the exposed scantlings, and associated artifacts. Most importantly perhaps, although much of the wreck is disarticulated, the shape of individual scantlings demonstrates, in puzzle-like fashion, the original form of the ship and how it was assembled using the unmistakable flat-bottomed northern European tradition.

Vessel Construction Features

Among the more intriguing timber remains surveyed are those of a partially intact piece of the vessel's bow (Figure 8.3). This feature includes bulwark timbers, a possible portion of the stem, and four iron-lined hawseholes situated with two on each side of the stem. Attached to these remains in several places are sections of lead sheathing that are fastened using copper tacks. Aside from those seen on the largely intact seventeenth-century vessels found in the cold and deep waters of the Baltic Sea, the preservation of this portion of a vessel is unique. For wrecks that occurred in shallow and/or tropical waters, ship features like bow timbers and hawseholes are generally lost when upper works are broken away, either in the wrecking event or in subsequent environmental decay.

The double hawsehole per side arrangement noted at the Morgan's Island Wreck was common in the seventeenth century, as indicated in many con-

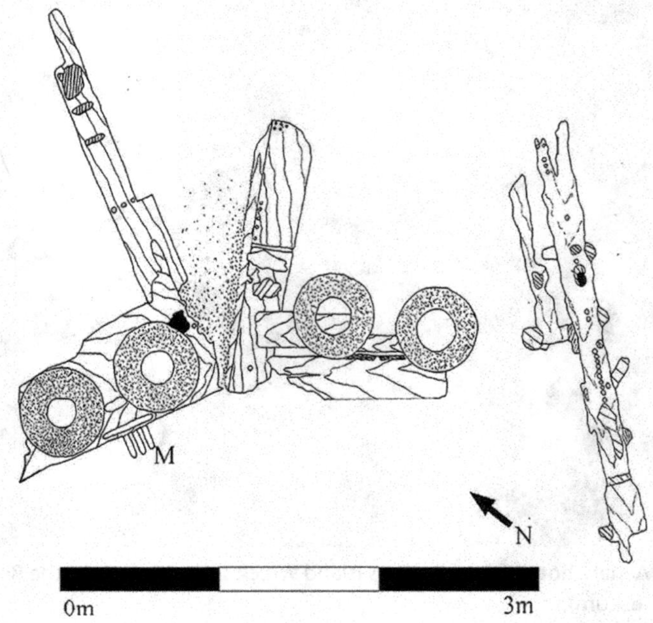

Figure 8.3. Bow feature of the Morgan's Island Wreck. (Image by the East Carolina University Program in Maritime Studies)

temporary illustrations depicting working ships, ship treatises, and ship plans (Bellamy 2006; Hoving 2012). Hawseholes are cylindrical holes cut into a vessel's bow through which anchor cables are passed (Steffy 1994:272). Although the use of iron for hawse hole liners during this period is not well documented, similar materials such as wood, lead, and copper were commonly used to reduce chafing of cables and wear on bow timbers (Goodwin 1987; Hoving 2012). Thus, iron would have provided a cheap alternative. Perhaps more important than the hawse configuration is the fact that the remaining timbers represent a type of construction in which the bow is supported by a single large wooden apron piece. This technique ended in the beginning of the seventeenth century and therefore suggests sixteenth-century or early seventeenth-century construction.

Possibly the most important evidence concerning the Morgan's Island Wreck site began to take shape when the detailed drawings of individual scantling timbers were completed. Of interest for this discussion are the remains of framing timbers, particularly the floors and futtocks that made up the midships portion of the vessel skeleton. These connected at the chine, where the side of the ship rose at a 130° angle from the nearly flat bottom: the

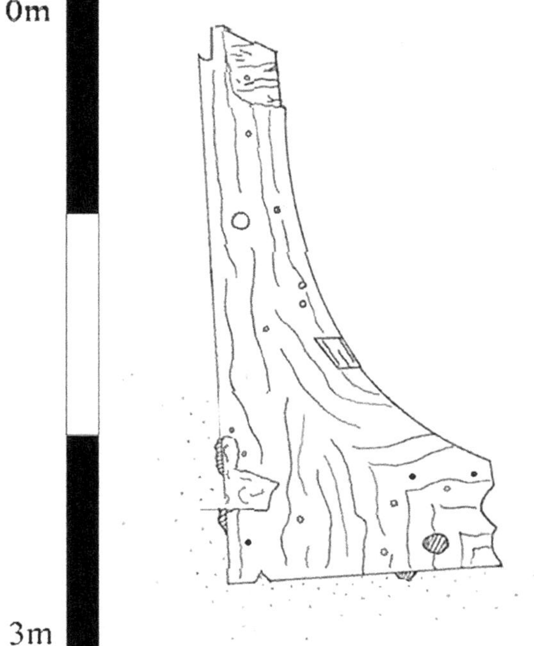

Figure 8.4. Rudder feature of the Morgan's Island Wreck. (Image by the East Carolina University Program in Maritime Studies)

unmistakable anatomy of a seventeenth-century northern European (Dutch or Danish)–built vessel, a very unusual find in English colonial waters.

The rudder, or a portion of it, is also a very important find (Figure 8.4). Features of the shape of the rudder and the remains of lead sheathing both indicate Dutch construction. The rudder blade nearest the ship is not mortised to accept the angular heel common on most European-built ships of this period, suggesting that it may not be complete (Witsen 1671:40). The rudder not only indicates that the ship was lead sheathed but, according to Witsen's 1671 shipbuilding treatise, can provide the size of the ship that carried it. According to Witsen's formula, the total length of this ship was 36.58 m, with a beam of 9.1 m (Hoving 2012). This is a sizable ship for the early seventeenth century and would have been a formidable warship for those times. Yet the fact that the rudder is still intact and remains part of the site gives our analysis an entirely new archaeological interpretation. When a ship wrecks, even if the wrecking event is intentional, as in Governor Butler's speculation (Hallett 2007:118), the rudder is generally the first scantling to detach. The fact that the rudder is present on the Morgan's Island Wreck site strongly suggests that the ship was floated unharmed to its resting place. As such, this site likely represents not the remains of a wrecking event but rather the remains of a salvage event.

Supplemental Evidence

Aside from the northern European influences noted in the construction of the vessel represented at Morgan's Island, several documented features support the association with the loss of the Dutch privateer/pirate ship in 1619. These include the species of wood used in its construction, the material used in its sheathing, a small number of artifacts identified at the site, and evidence of postwreck shipbreaking activities.

The unique character and unusual preservation of the various timbers inspected prompted the collection of wood samples from the site. These were analyzed by researchers at the Forestry Products Laboratory of the United States Forest Service. The results of this analysis indicate that all appear to be greenheart (*Ocotea rodiei*), a dense hard tropical wood native to Guiana, Surinam, and northern Brazil (Michael C. Wiemann, personal communication, 2016). Often confused with teak and lignum vitae, greenheart is an excellent shipbuilding material due to its hardness and the fact that its growth forms alkaloid compounds within its cellular structure (Humphrey 1915:205). These compounds are poisonous to living things, so the wood can survive virtually unchanged in the archaeological record for very long periods. Importantly, the Portuguese control of greenheart-producing areas in the sixteenth century was gradually supplanted by the Dutch when they began trading in the area in 1581 (Williamson 1923). The predominance of greenheart at the Morgan's Island site suggests that either the wood was harvested in South America and sent to Europe for fabrication or the vessel was constructed in the Americas, possibly as an *afreekboot*: a prefabricated ship for use as a portable "construction kit" (Parthesius 2010:81).

As mentioned, many of the timbers documented at the Morgan's Island Wreck site show evidence of shipbreaking. Clearly, any ship deposited in very shallow water would have presented an easily accessible and valuable resource. Islanders would have seen the wreck as a source of building materials, providing a windfall of artifacts or other materials brought in by a shipwreck. This vessel was undoubtedly no exception to that practice. The Morgan's Island Wreck timbers are so sturdy and resistant to rot that some are in use today around the harbor to shore up seawalls and delineate gardens (Anson Nash, personal communication, 2017). Extensive chop marks and conical threaded indentations on the ship's scantlings were likely made by axes plus a brace and bit screw pry. This indicates the value that these bits of hardware offered to people living on a frontier with limited means of accessing such material. It should also be noted that thus far there is no sign of planking anywhere on the wreck site, as seasoned planking would have been extremely valuable to islanders for construction.

Lead sheathing was found in situ on several of the bow timbers and, as mentioned, on the rudder of the Morgan's Island Wreck. A small section of disarticulated lead sheathing (with copper tacks attached) was also found in a modern anchor scar on the seabed near the main concentration of timbers. The use of lead for sheathing to protect hulls is well documented in various ship construction treatises. Though it was utilized extensively by ancient Mediterranean shipbuilders, its use waned by the Middle Ages and did not reappear in the archaeological record until its reemergence with sixteenth-century Spanish and Portuguese shipwrights (McCarthy 2005:102). Likely influenced by the southern European designs, the Dutch incorporated the use of lead sheathing for vessels at the end of the sixteenth century. Importantly, they discontinued using only lead sheathing around 1606 and thereafter combined it with sheet copper in alternating layers (Van Duivenvoorde 2015:350). Lead was also used as primary sheathing by English shipwrights for a short period beginning around 1670, but they found that it did not work well with iron fittings and soon discontinued the practice (Borrelli 2020:361; Harris 1966).

The last bit of supplemental evidence comes from two artifacts noted lying on the seabed at the Morgan's Island Wreck site. While the presence of these objects at a site so easily visited seems odd, they may be an indicator that much of the site lies protected under the bottom sediments. A singular piece of earthenware ceramic was located on the surface near the eastern end of the site. Through visual observations, artifact recordings, and typological research, the ceramic fragment was identified as a piece of Spanish lead-glazed coarse earthenware (Deagan 1987:47). Though this red-bodied dark-glazed ceramic is generally considered to date from the sixteenth century, its terminus post quem appears to be 1622. In addition to the ceramic, a single wooden wheel from a gun carriage was found on the surface at the site's eastern extent. Although this type of artifact was ubiquitous on armed vessels of the sixteenth and seventeenth century, it does suggest that this vessel was armed. Interestingly, this wheel also appears to be fabricated from greenheart wood. Further corroborating this point, a hanging knee timber (also apparently of greenheart) recorded at the site includes an eye bolt mounted through its throat, suggesting that it was used to attach gun tackle. If these objects prove to indeed be crafted from greenheart, it could indicate that the ship was completely built and fitted out in the Americas.

Discussion

Fortunately, while the historical record of the Morgan's Island mystery dimmed 400 years ago, modern archaeological evidence shines. The vessel remains at Morgan's Island are undoubtedly those of a single ship, constructed of an unusual tropical wood. The site does not technically represent a shipwreck, however; instead, it is the remains of a vessel impacted by salvage efforts. Furthermore, the remains indicate that the vessel was built using the northern European bottom-based tradition. This tradition certainly produced archaeological signatures that are different from those generally seen in shipwrecks located in the western Atlantic and are an unexpected find in a British colonial area such as Bermuda.

Initial visual observations added to the mystery at Morgan's Island. On the surface, what can be seen of the wreck simply looks too pristine to be 400 years old. Furthermore, other parts of the ship look—and actually feel—like iron due to the chemistry and tremendous hardness and density of the greenheart wood used in its construction. Additionally, the absence of wood-borer attack and total lack of degradation by ligniferous marine fungae caused a great deal of confusion about the vessel's possible age. Yet in all probability this site represents perhaps one of the oldest Dutch-built vessels found in the Americas and possibly the oldest colonial-built vessel discovered in the region.

Further investigation of the Morgan's Island Wreck could offer some insight. Dutch vessels were built using preconceived mathematical ratios of ship components. The formulas in Witsen's (1671) treatise, for instance, allow for the deduction of all the major dimensions needed for a theoretical reconstruction of the vessel remains at Morgan's Island. If Witsen's formulas hold true for rudder size, the original overall length of this ship was 36.58 m and the beam was up to 9.1 m—making it much larger than originally theorized. Because it was armed and constructed of hardwood, this ship was, by definition, a Dutch pinnace. This is how archaeological research can confirm historical narratives and help solve the 400-year-old mystery of the disappearance of a large and powerful warship under the nose—or at the behest—of a colonial government. Archaeological investigation could also help explain the wrecking or disarticulation process through detailed study of the salvage marks. While historic sources allude to the vagaries of human intervention in wrecking events on the island (Hallett 2007:1180), Butler's historic account of a wayward Dutch pinnace lost on the northwestern shoals in 1619 seems to dovetail nicely with evidence recovered from the wreckage left at Morgan's Island. In this instance, human agency is also undoubtedly involved with the ship's loss (or intentional hiding), again with both archaeological and historical research aligning to explain the evidence.

Final deductions from the archaeological evidence must take into account use of historical sources, which are fairly complete and steady after Bermuda became a colony in 1612. Indeed, historical sources indicate that there should be two Dutch-built wrecks on the western reef from the early seventeenth century: the Flemish Wreck lost in 1615 and the Dutch pinnace lost in 1619 (Rodgers et al. 2017:8). The discovery of two Dutch wrecks in Bermuda could only be explained by happenstance if not for the historical record.

The Morgan's Island Wreck site, however, is anything but a classic shipwreck site: salvage marks, the total disarticulation of scantlings, and its position all but rule out anything but human intent. Archaeological evidence from Morgan's Island confirms Butler's 1622 historical speculation that this ship was recovered intact from the reef, since the floors (representing the bottom of the ship), bow, and rudder are all present on the site. It seems doubtful that these scantlings would survive a wrecking event that took place over a shallow reef. These physical remains seem to corroborate Governor Butler's thinly veiled suspicions that the ship was intentionally wrecked or stolen and salvaged, perhaps a "cleverly planned trick of the Governor's cunning advisors to let the ship become a wreck" (Hallett 2007:118).

PIRATES OF THE CARIBBEAN AND TERRA FIRMA

9

What's to Become of Me?

Pirates and Refugees in the Archaeological Landscape of the Virgin Islands

Kenneth S. Wild

Many archaeological sites of the seventeenth and early eighteenth centuries have been discovered in Virgin Islands National Park on St. John, US Virgin Islands. These findings prompted a closer look at early European settlement of the Virgin Islands. Associating St. John's sites with individuals on the landscape is made possible by the meticulous records that the Danish kept throughout their 1672–1917 occupation of today's US Virgin Islands.

Many place-names across the Virgin Islands archipelago suggest the pirate/privateer activities that played a large role in early European presence in the West Indies for more than two centuries (Figure 9.1). In the British Virgin Islands are Dead Chest Island and Deadmans Bay, Freebooters Point, Bellamy Cay (named for Black Sam Bellamy's pirate lair), and Hamm's Creek, where a pirate friend of Captain William Kidd resided. Norman Island is named after a pirate, although the locals know it as Robert Louis Stevenson's *Treasure Island* (1883), the spot where buried Spanish treasure was found and the home of Spyglass Hill. On St. John are Rendezvous Bay, Privateer Point, and Privateer Bay, while St. Thomas has the fictitiously named Blackbeard Castle and Bluebeard Castle.

It is surprising, however, just how little information about this era regarding St. Thomas, St. John, and all the British Virgin Islands is found in popular history and books used in local classrooms. For the US Virgin Islands, this may be because much of this past has not been translated from Gothic Danish into modern Danish, and a lot of what has been translated is not available in English. Historical research, however, suggests that all the Virgin Islands

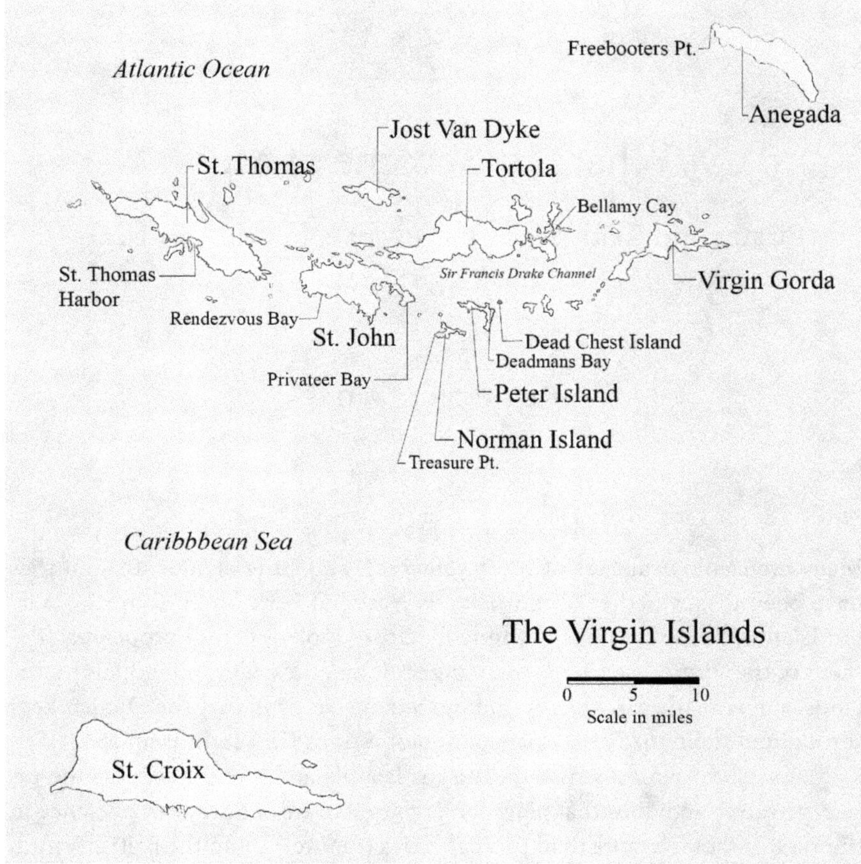

Figure 9.1. Map of the Virgin Islands with place-names associated with the era of pirates and privateers.

served as an epicenter of piracy, human trafficking, international conflict, and refuge for people who needed to live outside the law.

Historical Background

Understanding seventeenth-century and early eighteenth-century archaeological sites in the Virgin Islands starts with an appreciation of Caribbean cultural dynamics during this era of European expansion. Colonization required maritime combat, often motivated by desire for personal political power and wealth, involving naval forces, pirates, and privateers. The distinction between "pirates" and "privateers" was usually blurred; often a mariner was both. The term "pirateers" appears more suitable.

The Virgin Islands' geographical features and strategic location were key factors in the European powers' struggles for control of the Caribbean islands and maritime routes. This archipelago consists of approximately ninety islands, islets, and cays, all no more than a day's sail from each other and many within sight of Puerto Rico. The islands were left mostly uninhabited by the Spanish in the sixteenth century. Being uninhabited and near Spain's wealthy Puerto Rican port, these small islands with excellent anchorages surrounded by high hills were perfect rendezvous and hideaway places for interloping foreign powers (Wild 2019).

Throughout the sixteenth century and well into the seventeenth century, European powers used the Virgin Islands for staging assaults aimed at plundering Spanish shipping or capturing San Juan, Puerto Rico. Spain maintained control of Puerto Rico despite relentless attacks by pirateers that included French corsairs, Dutch freebooters, and Queen Elizabeth's English sea dogs. Sir Francis Drake's Channel, located along the south shore of Tortola, commemorates his presence during this period.

The Virgin Islands' proximity to Puerto Rico made them a dangerous place to settle. In 1621, for example, French corsairs on St. Croix were captured and executed in Puerto Rico. Around the same time, pirateer Jost van Dyke had established a Dutch settlement on Tortola and assembled other Dutch, English, and French filibusters engaged in illicit activities. The Spanish laid waste to the island because of the increasing threat posed by the pirateers and in retaliation for the Dutch siege of San Juan in 1625 (Pickering 1983). When the English tried to colonize St. Croix in 1631, they were soon attacked and imprisoned in Puerto Rico. The Spanish ships sent to destroy this settlement were themselves attacked at sea by French corsairs and took note of marauding Dutch pirates. The French tried to take St. Croix three years later, but the Spanish killed most of them. The Spanish troops left on St. Croix were attacked by English pirates in 1636, from the island of Tortuga off the north coast of Haiti (Figueredo 1978).

The English, Dutch, French, and Spanish destroyed each other's settlements several times over from 1641 to 1647 as they battled back and forth for ownership of the various Virgin Islands. By the 1650s, the French under Philippe de Longvilliers de Poincy gained control of St. Croix. De Poincy had already taken Tortuga by sending Huguenot corsairs whom he wished to banish from the French Catholic islands (Crouse 1940). Huguenot pirates, already refugees expelled from their homeland, are an example of those likely to have taken up residence on unsettled or ungoverned islands like the Virgins, if they survived piracy.

By this time the Dutch inhabited some of the northern Virgin Islands, including St. Thomas and Tortola. The Puerto Rican governor expressed concern over the large number of English ships in the Virgin Islands on their way to Tortuga, which was developing into a base for pirates. Its growing population was bolstered by the deportation of Europe's unwanted citizenry (Figueredo 1978).

Affluent statesmen obtained governorships in places where pirates congregated, such as Tortuga, Petit-Goâve, Jamaica, and Curaçao, in order to partake in the lucrative "pirateering" commissions that came with the title. Often, under a self-imposed sovereign flag, they granted letters of marque against an enemy nation to a captain who then obtained a crew from a mixed populace from across Europe and Africa. Sovereign loyalty was often determined by who could grant letters against a nation from which rich prizes could be captured. For example, the English governor of Jamaica recognized that retaining British sovereignty of Jamaica would have been impossible without the presence of the illicit fleet of pirates at Port Royal. To keep them there, he needed the ability to grant letters of marque (Barbour 1911; Haring 1910).

The Virgin Islands were completely enmeshed in this business. St. Croix was directly involved with conflicts for territorial control, both there and elsewhere, conducted by pirateers legitimized by governmental authorities such as de Poincy (Crouse 1940). Meanwhile, the northern Virgins were a dynamic smorgasbord of transient pirateers and short-lived settlements during much of the seventeenth century. In 1665 the Danes attempted to colonize St. Thomas. The Danish cleric of this failed settlement recorded that they were soon attacked by English pirates, who took all their food and ammunition. Few survivors made it back to Denmark (Jens Villumsen, personal communication, 2016). At this time the governor of Jamaica recruited true buccaneers of Haiti and Tortuga to attack islands inhabited by the Dutch, such as the Virgins, and many of these pirates stayed in the islands (Bro-Jørgensen 1966:9).

A turn of fate thrust the Virgin Islands to center stage, however. Over a thousand pirates from Tortuga and Jamaica under Henry Morgan were sacking Spain's richest ports in the West Indies between 1668 and 1671 (Esquemeling 1967 [1684]). Morgan had been imprisoned in London as a pirate but was freed, knighted, and appointed the lieutenant governor of Jamaica by 1674, with a mission to suppress pirating in the Caribbean (Black 1983:46–48). England's course reversal from being a supporter of pirateers to a nation bent on stopping them opened the door wide for a new Danish colony on St. Thomas to become a favored place for pirates and privateers.

St. Thomas

When Danes arrived again on St. Thomas in 1672, the English pirates had just left the island. The Danes found it inhabited by some Dutch. The English, who had just gone to war with the Netherlands, were in the process of capturing many of the Dutch islands, including Tortola, St. Eustatius, Saba, and St. Martin (Knox 1852). The Dutch had been one of the greatest sea powers. Their maritime smuggling network was worldwide, with contraband stored across the globe in warehouses such as those they later built on St. Thomas (Christensen and Jessen 2012; Klooster 1998:4). Their passion for Calvinist revenge motivated piracy aimed at their former Spanish oppressors, which helped to fuel their riches (Goslinga 1971). During the period when the Danes laid claim to St. Thomas, the Dutch contraband (smuggling) trade that revolved around small islands such as St. Thomas and St. Eustatius helped them survive the conflicts in the West Indies (Bro-Jørgensen 1966; Christensen and Jessen 2012; Klooster 1998). The Danes also were able to attract those escaping justice, immigrants, and refugees by remaining neutral, opening trade to everyone, endorsing freedom of religion, and offering the incentive of land without taxes for the first eight years.

The promoters of the Danish colony were provided as many men condemned in the Danish prisons, women from the spinning houses (government houses primarily for prostitutes), and indentured servants as needed to maintain the population of the colony. For decades, the Danes continued to bring in prisoners and servants, whose chances of survival were slim. The first governor of the island, Jorgen Iversen, was brutal to those brought there, and many died under his command (Westergaard 1917). Indeed, when the Danish West India Company tried to return Iversen to St. Thomas after an absence, the convicts and indentured servants on the ship pitched him overboard, knowing of his brutality (Heisen 2016).

Iversen, however, was successful in establishing the new Danish colony on St. Thomas by conducting illegal trade with the enemy, the French on St. Croix (Highfield 2013:289–318). The true pirate character of the inhabitants on French St. Croix became apparent in 1678. Feeling cheated in these illegal dealings (though they had actually had been cheated by their own governor), the St. Croix citizens attacked St. Thomas. Iversen had just completed a tower (Trygborg) in the colony's fort and was able to fend off this pirateering assault. Soon after the attack, he ordered another tower (Skytsborg) to be built on a hill that could spy down into the fort (Figure 9.2). He forced the landowner Carl Baggaert, whom he suspected would turn on the colony, to move down

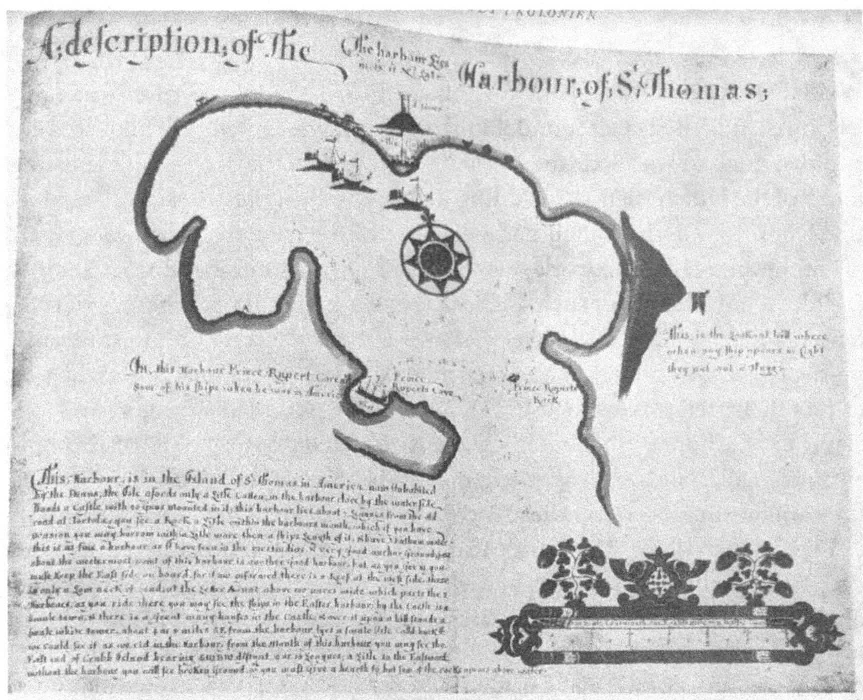

Figure 9.2. Drawing of St. Thomas Harbor circa 1687 by John Jenifer with caption, depicting the taverns along the waterfront, Christiansfort with Trygborg tower, and Skytsborg tower on the hill above (from Johannes Brondsted [editor], *Vore Gamle Tropekolonier*, vol. 2: *Dansk Vestindien*, p. 65 [Westermann, Copenhagen, 1953]). (© The British Library Board)

the hill. Baggaert was a convicted Dutch embezzler who had escaped to Tortola, then St. Thomas.

The Danes initially named St. Thomas's harbor settlement "Tappus," meaning beer hall. The process of developing a pirate expedition at this time always started with a meeting at the all-important beer hall. To entice pirates, a town needed taverns, where pirateers quickly spent their booty on kill-devil rum and prostitutes. Naming a harbor town Tappus at this moment in time was like putting up a neon sign advertising that it was open for pirateering expeditions. The governor boasted of a town in 1681, but it consisted only of four taverns (Bro-Jørgensen 1966:64).

The Danish islands quickly gained a reputation for illicit commerce because neutrality had opened trade to all, good or bad. So what better place for all those Caribbean pirates to go to than the Virgin Islands, now that England, France, and Spain were cracking down on piracy. Soon St. Thomas mirrored the cosmopolitan population of pirate lairs such as Tortuga and Port Royal, and many of the most infamous pirates of this era were dropping anchor there. To add to the illicit activity, the young Danish colony also allowed the operation of the German Brandenburg Company, which was founded on the premise of pirateering. Its warehouse would soon be filled with illicit contraband and attacked by competing pirates (Wild 2019).

Nicholas Esmit, a thirty-year veteran of Tortuga and Port Royal and a known pirate/privateer, became governor of St. Thomas in 1680. He immediately established business with Curaçao, the Dutch pirate lair at the time, and put Baggaert in charge of the militia. He invited pirates to the island, bought their booty, allowed the residents to repair and outfit their ships, and allowed foreign vessels to operate under the Danish flag (Bro-Jørgensen 1966:56, 64, 65). One pirate, Bartholomew Sharp, made famous by the writings of fellow pirate Basil Ringrose (1685) and William Dampier (1937 [1697]), sailed into St. Thomas in 1682. Upon his arrival, Esmit sent men to help careen his ship, bought his cacao, had the plunder unloaded, and wrote that he did not seize the ship to "avoid any unfriendliness with sea robbers" (Westergaard 1917:48–49). The inhabitants then decided the pirates should stay on the island. After Sharp was acquitted of piracy, he retired to St. Thomas, where he lived for many years until imprisoned for a debt to the governor. Under Esmit, even pirates were robbed, as in the case of Thomas Watson and John Campion. The governor gave authorization to come into the harbor, but the ship and all its treasure were confiscated by Carl Baggaert and another wily Dutchman, Jochum Delicaet, under the pretext that they had overstayed their welcome (Westergaard 1917:49–50).

Nicholas Esmit's younger brother, Adolph Esmit, orchestrated a coup in 1682 and took the governorship. Adolph, like his brother, embraced piracy and increased the "island's reputation as a resort for pirates" (Westergaard 1917:50). He infuriated the Leeward Islands' governor William Stapleton by harboring English fugitive indentured servants, debtors, sailors, and multiple English pirates and especially by supporting the French pirate Jean Hamlin. Adolph Esmit had purchased stolen goods from Hamlin and even reoutfitted him with a new pirate ship after Stapleton ordered the burning of his ship *La Trompeuse* in St. Thomas harbor (Westergaard 1917:53). The Danes had no recourse but to arrest and remove Adolph in 1684, replacing him with the distinguished Gabriel Milan. Milan ordered Jochum Delicaet to seize Adolph's ship loaded with treasure as a prize. In a quick reversal of fortune, Milan's head was removed for his pirate activities and for taking a company ship and outfitting it for war against the Spanish. Adolph Esmit was reinstated as governor, as he claimed to know of sunken treasure.

At the close of the seventeenth century, we find pirates such as John (Jean) Martel, Tempest Rogers, and Captain William Kidd coming into the Virgin Islands. When Kidd arrived in 1699, the governor requested that he leave the harbor; however, much of Kidd's treasure ended up in the Brandenburgers' warehouse. British admiral John Benbow tried to retrieve the loot, but it was successfully smuggled out. Kidd's associate Tempest Rogers also visited that year and then retired from active piracy and settled on St. Thomas in 1701 (Bro-Jørgensen 1966:89).

Danish governor John Lorentz in the eighteenth century continued profiting from captured pirate ships and supporting pirateers of many nations under the neutral flag of Denmark. It was nearly impossible to distinguish between pirate and privateer for the next twenty years, as letters of marque were handed out freely in the Virgin Islands (Westergaard 1917). Pirates who received a king's pardon in 1718 for operating off the North American coast either knew or were instructed by governors to go to St. Thomas, where they could receive commissions to go privateering during the War of Spanish Succession (Johnson 1724a).

St. Croix

Privateers and French corsairs continued to be fully embraced by the governors of St. Croix until the French colony was abandoned in 1696. This business included the multitude of pirates working off the coast of St. Croix, who sold their treasure wholesale after seizing it at a literally cutthroat rate. The governors of St. Thomas and St. Croix received a percentage payoff for their collaboration with the pirates, the Brandenburgers, and other merchants, usually Dutch. These go-betweens would take the pirate plunder and smuggle the loot to wherever they could sell it for a substantial profit. A good example of such a transaction involves the pirateer Abraham Macharis, who in 1695 captured the English ship *Phoenix* and sailed it to St. Thomas. When a Brandenburg purchase offer was turned down by the ship's crew, St. Croix's governor Pierre de Begue transferred some of the plunder to St. Croix, where it was sold to a Mr. Borq. The *Phoenix* and 100 barrels of Madeira wine were purchased by Lucas van Beverhoudt on St. Thomas. Borq and Van Beverhoudt paid de Begue his 10 percent value of the plunder. Macharis was put on trial for piracy but probably let go (Highfield 2013:506).

St. Croix suffered with smallpox, malaria, and yellow fever epidemics, and the French Crown continued to lose money on the colony. Therefore, all 1,200 inhabitants of St. Croix were transported in 1696 to the French colony of Saint Domingue, today Haiti (Highfield 2013:513). Within months after their arrival, the French authorities found that nearly two hundred men had left their families to go pirateering, including three of St. Croix's former high-ranking militiamen, who became some of the most infamous of corsairs operating in the Virgin Islands in the era (Highfield 2013:519–520; Johnson 1724a; Labat 1730).

The abandonment of St. Croix by the French made it the perfect pirate lair for the next thirty-seven years, until Denmark purchased and colonized the island in 1733. Not only was no governmental authority present, but the threat of disease deterred military action.

St. John and the British Virgin Islands

St. John Island is within kayak distance of Tortola and a short sail to most British Virgin Islands. After expulsion of the Dutch from Tortola in 1672, England considered itself the owner of the surrounding islands, including St. John. Nonetheless, St. Thomas's Governor Iversen secretly placed settlers on St. John in July 1675 and supplied them with guns and ammunition. They were still there in 1680 and had produced seventy-nine pounds of tobacco (Bro-Jørgensen 1966:64). During the 1680s, the English three times removed trespassers sent by Adolph Esmit, who were perceived to be pirates working in concert with the Danish pirate governor. On one occasion they had to destroy a fort and remove forty men (Westergaard 1917:127). In 1718, under protest by the English, a party of settlers from St. Thomas claimed St. John for Denmark.

The seventeenth century in what is today the British Virgin Islands saw Dutch buccaneers and English planters claiming ownership. By the century's end, the British had finalized their claim. Dookhan (1975), however, makes it very clear that the British Virgins were lawless, with no effective government until well into the eighteenth century. The British islands, including St. John before Danish control, provided the perfect haven for those who were escaping the law and the brutality imposed on the enslaved Africans, indentured servants, and those brought from the prisons and spinning houses of Europe. Inhabitants produced food to supply maritime traffic as well as commercial crops like tobacco. For some, conditions produced "a unique trait in the character of the people. Not content with providing supplies to pirates who called there, the inhabitants soon took to privateering themselves, and this activity was continued so long as the wars of the eighteenth century made it both possible and profitable" (Dookhan 1975:14).

Rediker (2014) provides an example of an escape by those fleeing brutal authority as well as an insight into the food remains that an archaeological pirate site might contain. Medical surgeon Henry Pitman was captured in England and ended up an indentured servant/political rebel enslaved on Barbados in 1686. He gathered a multiethnic crew of fellow political prisoners, indebted prisoners, convicts, and enslaved Africans and escaped with them. At sea they encountered many escapees who had turned pirate, including Native Americans and buccaneers all well versed in surviving on local flora, fish, and shellfish. Such people would have found local resources for survival in the Virgin Islands archipelago while making use of opportunities for smuggling, salvage, provisioning, pirateering, and the like.

Finding the Pirateers, Smugglers, and Refugees

When the Danes took over St. John in 1718, they divided the island into parcels mostly 457 m wide and began a yearly land-list ledger that documented the orientation and occupant of each parcel. Many estates were abandoned over time, while others grew larger as they took over adjacent properties, leaving many of the earlier estates as unaltered time capsules. In collaborative projects of Virgin Islands National Park and the University of Copenhagen's history department (and with the benefit of its translations of Gothic Danish), we have been able to locate many abandoned sites in the park and connect them with individual owners. To do this required converting the land-lists' information (textual only, without maps) to geographic information system (GIS) maps plotting the estate parcels, which were then used to orient the field survey. Danish students tracked down archival data for select research areas that were intensively surveyed, matching archivally deciphered abandonment dates to each site's artifact assemblage. Often sites were encountered that predated the land-lists, but other historical data have provided clues to their ownership history. In this way, we have been able to locate on the landscape all classes of society, from the wealthy pirate smuggler to the poor English indentured servant, the part-time pirate, and the French refugee.

It is usually hard to say for certain that any one settler on St. John was a pirate, but the odds were high during this period. History records that those who survived being an indentured servant, soldier, or sailor had basically three options: (1) go home, which was rare in most circumstances, (2) become an estate overseer, or (3) become a pirateer, the preferred and most profitable choice. If someone escaped prison or slavery, the only option was exile and piracy. Participants in a successful pirateering expedition could spend all their plunder on rum and women, which was most common, settle onto a poor plot of land, or perhaps become an overseer for an absent landowner. Anyone who had profited greatly as a pirate and had not been killed might have the means to quit that risky business and acquire enslaved Africans. As noted by Schmitt (2018) concerning the pirates of Tortuga, piracy was a means by which to obtain the labor and tools needed to start a plantation. Those who became rich as smugglers of pirate loot or as tavern owners profiting from pirates' spending had the means to invest in land in places such as the newly claimed Danish island of St. John, where all were welcomed, land was not taxed, and trade was wide open to the world and unregulated.

These are exactly the types of settlers we are finding on St. John's late seventeenth-century and early eighteenth-century landscape. Many of the poorer dwelling sites are strategically placed: tucked away in small bays that could hide a ship, located at the base of steep cliffs or on steep coastal hilltops with little crop land. Multinational poor settlers, former soldiers, and French refugees, some possibly Huguenot buccaneers, lived on many of these properties in inhospitable locations, good only for maritime purposes.

Other sites are located at maritime choke points that allow observation of shipping traffic where it is busiest and restricted between islands. Such sites also offered the element of surprise in an attack. These sites' material assemblages contain high-status objects and more artifacts, in stark contrast to neighbors, even though the sites have low agricultural potential. Common artifacts recovered include tin-enameled wares, porcelain, period pipe stems, joggled and late seventeenth-century North Staffordshire slipware ceramics, and Rhenish and Westerwald stoneware sherds, plus seventeenth-century Bartmann/witch's bottle fragments.

On some sites the food remains resemble those left behind by the pirates encountered by Henry Pitman and those typical of a Native American site. These remains are largely shellfish (specifically whelk and conch) and fish bone, rather than the more diverse and domesticated animal food remains found on sites devoted to agriculture. Similar food remains of local flora and fauna were found when excavations at Cinnamon Bay, in a separate project, uncovered a seventeenth-century house and artifact remains. Douglas Armstrong of Syracuse University associates the residence with English seaman John Moore (recorded as Jan Mour in Danish) and his wife, Elisabeth Tucker (Elisabeth Tocher), part of a 1680s contingent of Barbadians supported by Adolph Esmit (Armstrong et al. 2005; Knight 1999) for questionable purposes.

Several of St. John's bays and points have English and Dutch names, pointing to individuals who lived there before the Danes claimed the island in 1718. An example is Durloo Bay, named for settler Pieter Durloo's estate. Finding this early site was possible even though it remained occupied throughout the eighteenth century. At Peter Bay, named for Pieter de Buyck and located next to Cinnamon Bay, seventeenth-century artifacts have been recovered. By 1719 de Buyck had an overseer taking care of business at that location.

Like de Buyck, most of the wealthy Dutch merchants such as Lucas van Beverhoudt entrusted their St. John estates to overseers so that they could continue their primary profiteering. Some lived on St. John, such as the aforementioned Captain Jochum Delicaet, whose dwelling was identified. Delicaet, with his involvement in pirate treasure, exemplifies a personal background that probably was common among St. John landowners. Heirs of seventeenth-century tavern owners and kill-devil brewers of St. Thomas harbor have been identified among St. John's landowners as well.

This pioneering archaeological and documentary endeavor has just scratched the surface of this important era of Virgin Islands heritage. It reveals that much information still can be discovered about the early historical period of St. John. It also demonstrates the significance of pirateering as a profession—and on St. Thomas as an administrative system—that operated concurrently with the early plantation economy in the Virgin Islands. The bits of the recorded history found in archival sources in conjunction with archaeological evidence provide a glimpse of the world of the pirateers.

Much more can still be done. Remains of seventeenth-century taverns in St. Thomas are buried under the waterfront street of the downtown area. Skytsborg tower (now called Blackbeard's Castle) still stands, and Iversen's fort and the dungeon where Captain Sharp and others died are preserved. No attempt has been made to locate estates owned by such pirates as Bartholomew Sharp and Tempest Rogers, but it should be possible: St. Thomas's land-list records extend back into the 1600s. Excavations in downtown Christiansted on St. Croix that I directed in 1989 uncovered historic floors dating to the seventeenth century, a meter below the city streets. Thus, it is conceivable that the archaeological record of those evacuated in 1696 is still preserved. Future research, and ultimately the information available to the public, will be informed by the emerging dimensions in our understanding of early European and African presence in these islands.

10

Pirates at Grand Case Bay, St. Martin (French West Indies)

Interpreting Archaeological Evidence from a Late Seventeenth-Century Settlement

Alexandre Coulaud, Nathalie Sellier-Ségard, and Martijn van den Bel

Grand Case Bay is bordered by a long, white sandy beach on the northwestern coast of the island of St. Martin (French West Indies), one of the Leeward Islands of the Eastern Caribbean archipelago (Figure 10.1). This bay is closed in the south by the rocky outcrop called Molly Smith Point and in the north by First Stick Hill, which is 224 m high. The site is located on the southwestern flank of the hill approximately 2 m above sea level, a location protected from the eastern trade winds.

Excavation unit BK 77 (554 m^2) revealed a geological sequence of a local beach affected by marine Holocene incursions as well as colluvial deposits related to destabilization of the hill flanks, creating smooth slopes. Today the bare substratum of the flank contrasts with the hollow part enriched by colluvial deposits. These deposits buried the archaeological material presented here.

It was the construction of a villa that prompted an archaeological survey, conducted by the Institut National de Recherches Archéologiques Préventives (Inrap: the National Institute of Compliance Archaeology). in 2014 (Briand 2014). It yielded a few historic objects mixed with abundant pre-Columbian ceramics pertaining to an American Indian habitation site. The pre-Columbian site was already known through other archaeological investigations and dated to about AD 1000 (Haviser 1988; Romon 2012; Sellier-Ségard and Samuelian 2016; Serrand 2013; Stouvenot and Hénocq 1999).

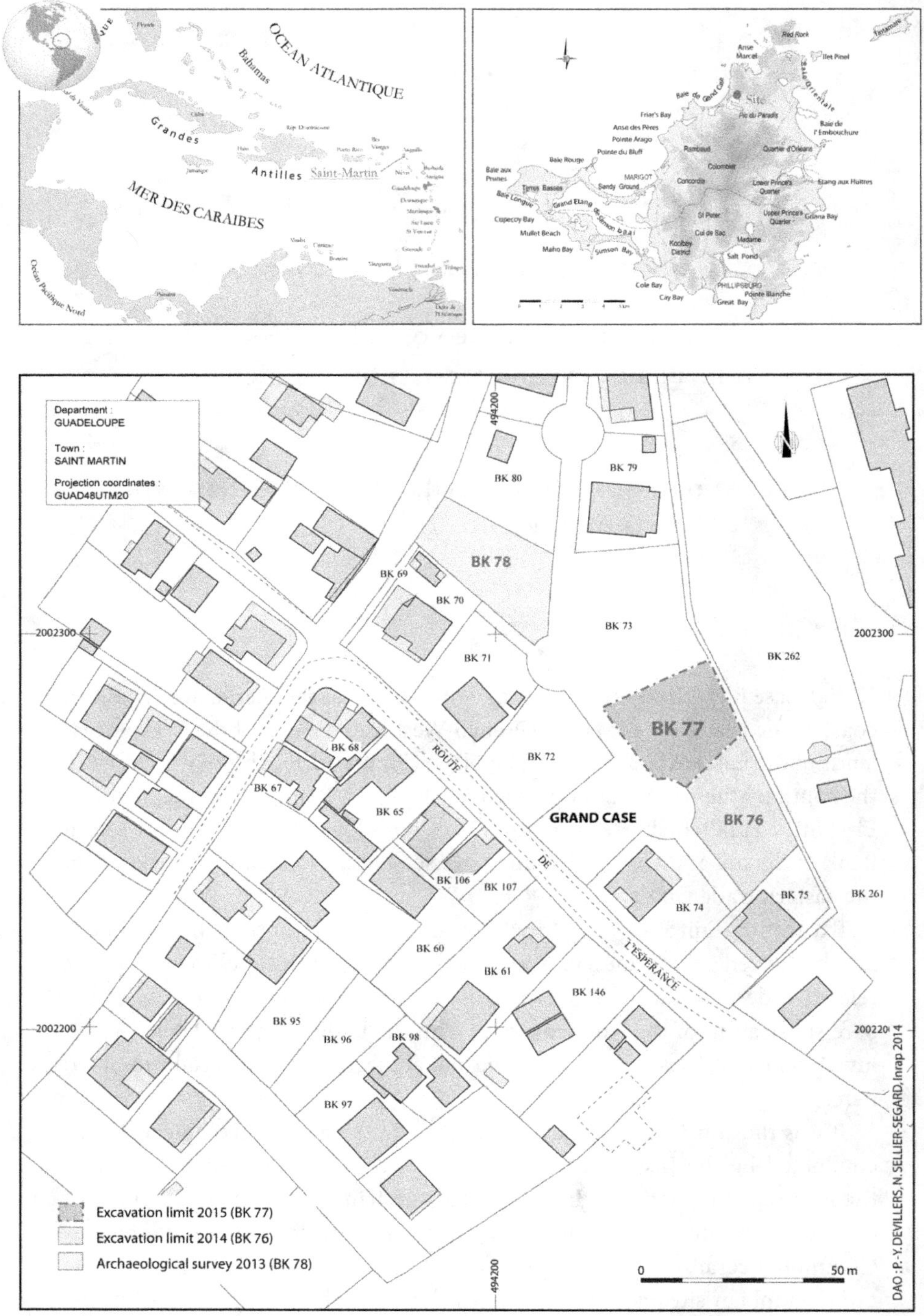

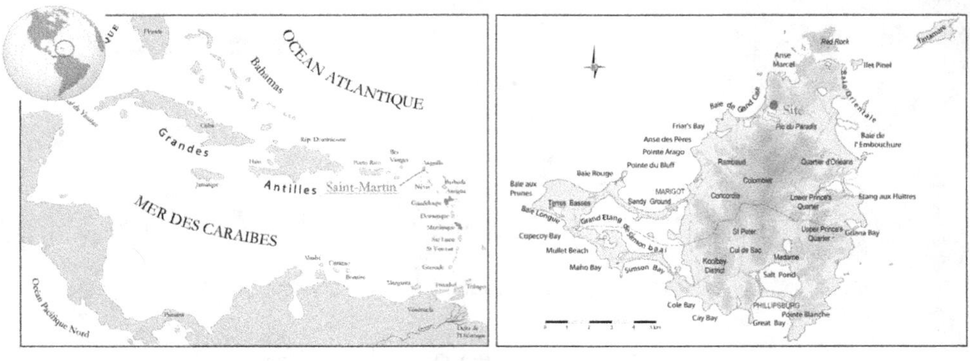

Figure 10.1. Map showing the location of the archaeological excavations at Grand Case Bay. (P.-Y. Devillers and Nathalie Sellier-Ségard, Inrap)

During major excavations in 2014, large features identified as lime pits (Figure 10.2) and traces of wooden foundations from rectangular buildings adjacent to the lime pits were found. These light, elevated structures were probably related to the lime activity. A fragment of a wood post was preserved in a posthole and identified as a local red wood, known in the French Antilles as *bois savonette* (*Lonchocarpus* sp.) A sample of this wood was radiocarbon dated and provided a calibrated date between AD 1436 and 1522. Despite the absence of stratigraphy, the chronology of the historic occupation is based on the identification of the artifacts (ceramics, glass, clay pipes, metallic objects, faunal ecofacts, and so forth) found in the features but also as intrusive material in the pre-Columbian midden or waste areas. Based on these, the principal period of occupation is ascribed to the second half of the seventeenth century.

During this century, St. Martin was first occupied by French colonists from St. Christopher who had settled there, perhaps in 1629 after the attack of Fadrique de Toledo. The French and Dutch reoccupied the island a year later. The French settled near Marigot and were led by Claude de Beulayne (Germain 2007). The Dutch West Indies Company [WIC] Chamber of Amsterdam under the command of Jan Claesz van Campen settled the southern part of St. Martin, due to the presence of a major salt pond located on this part of the island. The Spanish attacked in 1633, however, and dominated the southern part of the island until they abandoned it in the late 1640s (Wright 1934–1935: Chapter 4). The Dutch and French eventually divided the island between them in 1648, as stipulated in the famous Treaty of Concordia following the Treaty of Munster. The Dutch kept the southern part, while the French claimed the northern part.

Under French rule, the governor of St. Christophe, Robert Longvilliers de Poincy, grew tobacco and raised cattle on his estate until his death in 1660 (Archives Nationales d'Outre-Mer 1660). Sugar was also produced on the island, but these plantations were destroyed first by the English during the second Anglo-Dutch War (1665–1667) and then again by the Dutch during the Franco-Dutch War (1672–1678), when St. Martin was occupied by the English. The French part was totally destroyed by the Dutch fleet of Jacob Binckes in 1676. During the Nine Years' War (1688–1697), the English sent all French inhabitants to St. Christopher. They only returned after the Peace of Ryswick in 1697. A scant four years later, during the War of Spanish Succession (1701–1714), the French were again driven off the island, only to return again after the Peace of Utrecht (Parisis and Parisis 1994:9–10). Turmoil and skirmishes between the English and French continued throughout the eighteenth cen-

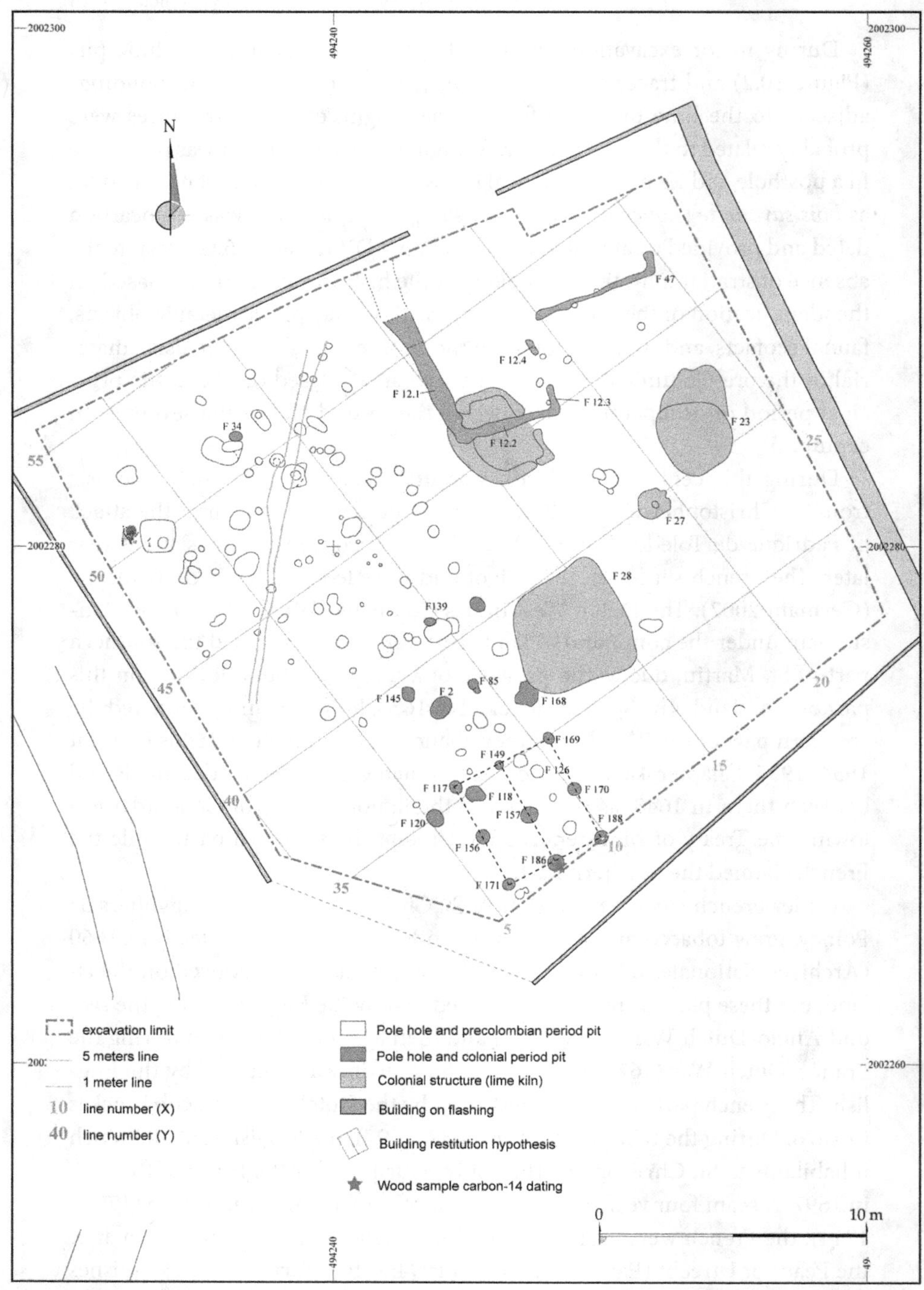

Figure 10.2. Plan showing the spatial organization of features attributed to the colonial period. (P.-Y. Devillers and Nathalie Sellier-Ségard, Inrap)

tury and are evident in the archaeological record. The cultural attribution of the archaeological material is presented here.

The Archaeological Evidence

Ceramics

The ceramic assemblage consists of 248 fragments corresponding to about a hundred individual vessels (MNI, minimum number of individual vessels as determined from the sherds) and shows great variety in type and manufacture (Figure 10.3). It consists mainly of bottles (jugs), fine ware, and utilitarian ware. The grayware is represented by six fragments: one attributed to a bellarmine stoneware jug, one to another unknown bottle type, two to a blue-glazed stoneware from Westerwald with a white medallion, and two from a stoneware beer mug.

Also found was a domestic jug with a tubular spout with a green glaze, dated to the middle of the seventeenth century and probably produced in Sadirac near Bordeaux. The remnants of at least one platter imported from Toulouse (Giroussens?) reveal the usage of another vessel from the port La Lune in Bordeaux (Lassure 2005).

The English ceramic wares are represented by a yellow-brownish cup of slipware (1580–1795) typical of the production centers of Staffordshire (Godden 1966).

Other fragments have been attributed to lead-glazed wares but not ascribed to a particular geographic area or precise time frame. However, we recorded brown glazed wares with an orange paste, most certainly produced in the Netherlands.

Tablewares are well represented, including fragments of a blue faience platter that can be attributed to a Portuguese production center near Coimbra in 1650–1675 (Calado 2003; Casimiro 2013:357–361). Another Iberian specimen was represented by a tin-glazed faience fragment showing blue floral or vegetal decoration executed in a coarse manner. One faience fragment showed a motif with four blue spots corresponding to a type of *milles fleurs* from Delft in the Netherlands. Chinese export porcelain is represented by only one cup fragment revealing blue foliated branches or *rinceaux de fleurs* (floral scrolls) on the interior.

The assemblage also includes common ceramics (made by hand and with the wheel). The culinary vessels or marmites (traditional "pot-belly"-shaped crockery casserole vessels found in France) can be associated with local pro-

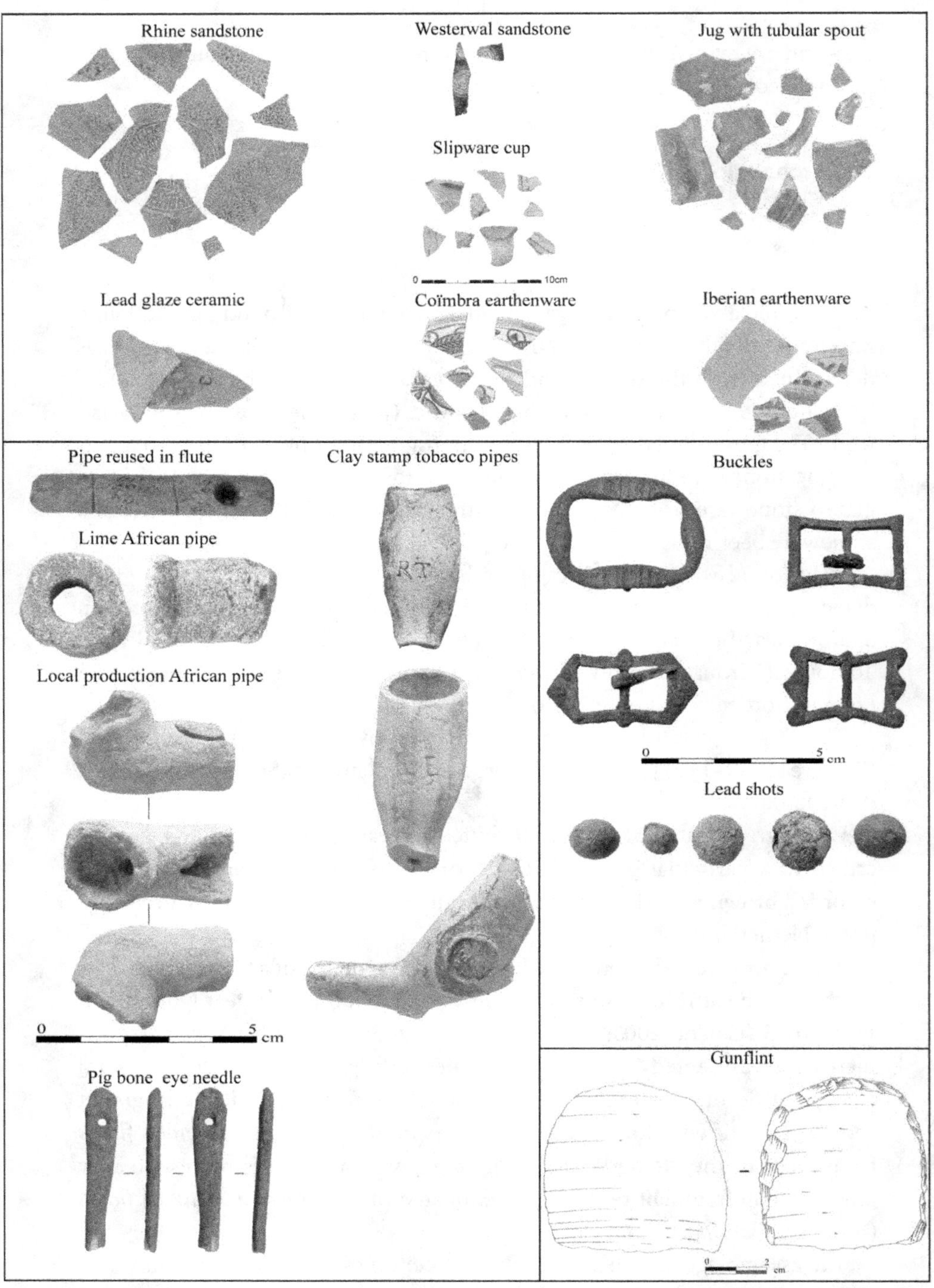

Figure 10.3. Sample of archaeological material found on the site. (Nathalie Sellier-Ségard, P. Bertholet, Noémie Tomadini, Alexandre Coulaud, and F. Casagrande, Inrap)

duction by the inhabitants. This assemblage can be dated to the second half of the seventeenth century and attributed to domestic activities.

The assemblage covers a long period between 1650 and 1720. Despite the fragmentary nature of the ceramics, the edges show little erosion, and the surfaces are not altered by erosion or wear. This suggests that the site was abandoned quickly. Besides one small fragment of a Dutch roof tile, the excavation did not yield any architectural terra-cotta material. The wooden structures at the site were possibly covered with shake shingles or palm fronds.

Clay Pipes

The excavations yielded many fragments of clay tobacco pipes weighing about 84 grams. In total 283 fragments were uncovered, representing 234 individual pipes. The excavators recorded 248 stem fragments and 35 bowls: 15 and 6 specimens, respectively, showed some decoration. The majority of the clay pipes were made of white clay (one was made of limestone).

The origins of the pipes varied. The majority are of European origin, but at least four elements are of local manufacture, attributed to the second half of the seventeenth century and the first half of the eighteenth century. Two areas of production can be clearly identified: England and Holland, particularly Bristol and Gouda. Two locally made pipes can undoubtedly be attributed to an African pipe tradition, for the movable stems are made out of wood or ceramics and appeared in the Americas at the beginning in the eighteenth century (Daviau 2008).

Glass

The excavations recovered 103 fragments of glass (weighing 900 grams) representing at least 24 individual vessels. The majority can be attributed to bottles (87 percent), but there were also a few fragments of jars and small bottles or flacons.

Square bottles made of bluish glass (n = 19) correspond to liquor bottles. One cylindrical and bluish specimen with thin walls was also found. It was attributed to French production originating in the woodlands of Grésigne, situated between the regions of Languedoc and Hérault. This type of bottle was produced during the late seventeenth century and beginning of the eighteenth century (Pajot 2004:34–52).

Two greenish blue flacons also correspond to oven production fueled with wood. These small vessels generally have a medicinal or alimentary content. Various comparisons could be made with similar objects found in North America from the late seventeenth century. However, their usage in the Caribbean is generally linked to sites dated to the eighteenth century.

Finally, a base fragment resembling the morphology of an onion-type alcohol bottle was made of opaque dark green blown glass. Its globular shape suggests French origin in the seventeenth century (De Putter 2014). However, the nonsystematic production of blown glass during the seventeenth and eighteenth centuries makes it difficult to assign it to a more precise period.

Metal Objects and Gunflints

The metal assemblage is rather small: 160 fragments representing 132 objects. The metal artifacts represent objects from daily life. Many wrought-iron nails with a square cross-section and a flat head reveal the presence of wood construction and carpentry on the site.

Culinary activity is characterized by the presence of the rim, body, and feet fragments of cast-iron marmites or cauldrons, rather classic elements during the colonial period in the Caribbean. A tin haft fragment of undetermined cutlery with a quadrangular cross-section is also attributed to culinary activity. Multiple fragments of thin, perforated plates made of a copper alloy can be interpreted as pieces of the blade of a sugar skimmer but also as metal graters for grating manioc tubers with a hand mill (van den Bel 2020).

Metal elements related to clothing include a pin with a spherical head made of a copper alloy. Four copper-alloy buckles are also part of this group. One two-piece shoe buckle, of which the chape is missing, has an oval-shaped frame showing a rectangular internal space and can be dated to 1690–1720 (Whitehead 1996). The frame of another buckle with a double chape, which features acute angles, was common between 1570 and 1700.

Two other buckles with double trapezoidal shape have cast decorations and can be dated between 1620 and 1680 (Whitehead 1996), corresponding to English manufacturing. The first is characterized by a triangular-shaped chape (Fox and Barton 1986; Moore 2000; White 2005, 2009), whereas the second has a clover-shaped chape (Rivers-Cofield 2011). The shape of the first buckle is generally associated with waist belts but also with spur belts (White 2005, 2009). The second is usually associated with spurs and can be found in England as well as in North America.

Weaponry is represented by five spherical bullets made of cast lead that appear to have been made in a bivalve mold. Considering their calibers, at least two bullets belong to a rifle and two others to a pistol. The latter, because of their small size, could correspond to buckshot bullets (many of which are loaded in the barrel of a rifle). This shot is commonly used to hunt for small game and poultry.

This type of shot is also used with specific firearms such as blunderbusses and modified muskets, notably when fighting in close combat, in order to get a higher mortality rate during naval battles. Many examples of this type of firearm and shot in great quantities have been found in the shipwrecks of the *Queen Anne's Revenge* and *Whydah Gally* (Clifford and Perry 2000; Lusardi 2006; and Chapter 2 in this volume).

Finally, a fragment of a half pair of iron scissors as well as an iron hoe represent tools related to the domestic and pastoral domain. A gunspall gunflint was also recorded and can be associated to the lead bullets already mentioned and weaponry equipped with flint pans. This type of gunflint is common during the whole seventeenth century until these flints were replaced by more efficient prismatic flints at the beginning of the eighteenth century (White 1975).

Faunal Ecofacts

The faunal remains recovered from the colonial surfaces yielded 30 taxa from 41 individual animals. Domesticated species include cattle, pigs, goats, and farmyard poultry (roosters, ducks), which were fed, slaughtered, and consumed on the site. In addition, the inhabitants of Grand Case Bay also hunted and fished in the surrounding area for birds and fish. The occurrence of turkey (*Meleagris gallopavo*) bones today represents the oldest archaeozoological appearance of this species. This bird, however, which originated in North America, has been attested at Hispaniola since the beginning of the sixteenth century (Tomadini et al. 2023). This discovery brings into question the origins of this particular bird: was it imported directly from North America or exported to Europe and shipped to St. Martin? In fact, this question can also be asked for the other farmyard poultry.

One worked fibula bone from a pig (*Sus scrofa domesticus*) was completely polished and shows a perforation at the proximal end. The general shape of this object corresponds to a sewing needle. This bone tool may have served in the fabrication or reparation of fishnets as well as ship sails and ropes (splices).

A Pirate's Lair?

The geographical and topographical position of the Grand Case Bay site offers a protected anchorage and watering port for ships along the coast of a barely populated Caribbean island during the colonial period. It must also be noted that the study of a colonial habitation site situated about 10 m behind the coastline is today a rare feature in the French Antilles.

This excavation reveals the first colonial settlement known at the northwestern part of the island of St. Martin: ephemeral structures of light wooden construction, elevated on stilts covered with wooden shingles or other thatch.

This occupation drew freely from the nearby forest and the abundant shell material left by the pre-Columbian population for commercial lime production. The site dates from the second half of the seventeenth to the beginning of the eighteenth century. During this turbulent period, the island of St. Martin was coveted by Spain, France, the Netherlands, and England.

This is reflected through the variety and different origins of the artifacts from these nations but also from their trading partners or dynastic relationships in Germany and Portugal. All of these colonial powers were present on the island during this period, as they disputed each other's commercial supremacy on the main trade routes of the Caribbean (Bridenbaugh and Bridenbaugh 1972: Part II; Israel 1989: Chapter 7).

These different artifacts may be important in the identity and status of the inhabitants of the Grand Case Bay site. Indeed, light or makeshift dwelling constructions appear to be inconsistent with the diversity and richness of particular artifacts. We can certainly question the identity of this population, who may seem somehow marginal considering their structures on the beach. The hypothesis proposed here is that this population can be identified as freebooters or buccaneers.

During the seventeenth century, pirates, buccaneers, and other outlaws generally located themselves up rivers and in hidden bays out of sight and away from densely populated regions but still close to commercial trade routes in order to watch out for possible prizes (Porcher 2020). These ports were used to get fresh water and provisions but also to maintain and repair their ships. When caulking or refitting the hull, the vessels needed to be careened in order to be cleaned and repaired, notably to get rid of the marine worms, barnacles, and weed that grew rapidly on their hulls in tropical waters, reducing the speed of the vessel (Coulaud and Sellier-Ségard 2019).

During such hull repairs, the crew would construct a temporary settlement on the beach or near the vessel, consisting of houses made of perishable material. These activities are described by Defoe (2010a) and Oexmelin (2017). The production of lime was part of these repairs. Lime was used in lieu of pitch or tar, which are usually used for caulking.

Although this interpretation needs to be verified, the disparate archaeological assemblage supports this premise. For instance, one part of a regular domestic household assemblage of colonial artifacts found at a habitation site is usually of high status (fine ceramic wares, glass, buckles), but that is not the case at this site. Instead, the diverse composition of the assemblage is better compared to the assemblages excavated at pirate shipwrecks such as *Queen Anne's Revenge*, *Whydah Gally*, *Quedagh Merchant*, *Great Ranger*, *Speaker*, *Fi-*

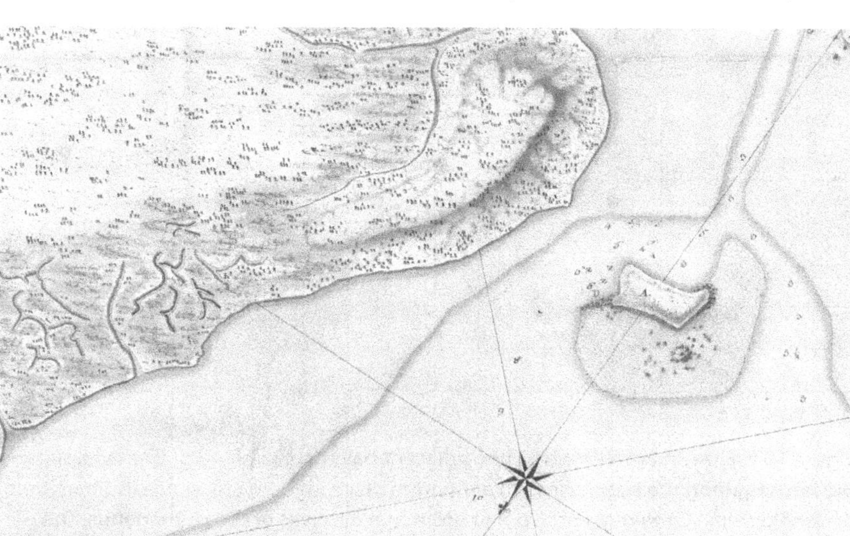

Figure 10.4. Detail of the map entitled *Plan du Port Sainte Marie* drawn by Sieur Sornay, 1733. The text for D mentions "a jetty where the outlaws careen." (Bibliothèque Nationale de France, Paris, Département des Cartes et Plans: FR-BnF DCP, GE SH 18 PF 217 DIV 8 P 2/1)

ery Dragon, and, to a lesser extent, terrestrial sites frequented by freebooters, such as Port Royal in Jamaica.

Sieur Robert, king's officer at Madagascar, provides a description of the arrival of French pirates in 1730 after they had captured a Portuguese ship, which they took to a hidden bay on the island of Sainte-Marie, and made their village there (Figure 10.4):

> indeed when they arrived, they all made a private house on the ground for lodging. They hoisted from every house a colored silk flag and each was marked in a particular way to know them. Each of them took a Black woman to serve them as a woman. . . .
>
> . . . d'ailleurs lors qu'ils y arriverent ils y firent tous chacun une case a terre pour se loger en particulier. Sur les cases ils arborerent a toutes une banderolle en soye de couleur et sur chacune une marque particulliere pour les connoistre ils y prirent tous chacun une negresse pour leur servir de femme. (Service Historique de la Défense n.d.:n.p.)

The archives and imagery from the beginning of the seventeenth century reveal light constructions situated near the mooring place in the Lesser Antil-

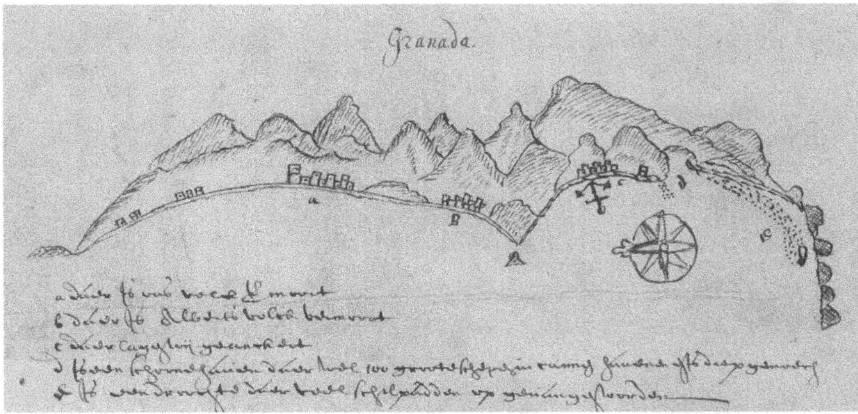

Figure 10.5. Drawing representing two adjacent bays on the island of Grenada, showing houses along the beach close to a mooring place, ca. 1630, facsimile in *Great Atlas of the West India Company, Part I*, p. 111. (National Archives of the Netherlands, The Hague, Foreign Map Collection, Leupe [VEL], 1584–1813 [1865], NL-HaNA 4.VEL 574) The key to the letters reads: a: Our people were murdered there; b: Albert's people were murdered there; c: We were anchored there; d: Is a good harbor where about 100 ships can harbor, for it is very deep; e: Is a sandbank where many turtles can be caught. This drawing is believed to be a copy of a colored drawing found in the journal of Jesse de Forest (ca. 1625), representing Caracas Bay at the southern tip of St. Vincent. (National Archives of the Netherlands, The Hague, Foreign Map Collection, Leupe [VEL], GB-BL Ms 179b, f. 23; van den Bel 2015: Figure k)

les (St. Vincent, Grenada) created by freebooters or buccaneers (Figure 10.5). The anonymous journal relating the voyage of Captain Charles Fleury in 1618 to Brazil, the Guianas, and the Caribbean reveals a rather long stay at Martinique in order to supply the crew (Moreau 2016). Interestingly, the crew members lived in relative peace with the American Indian population. This situation suggests that European makeshift installations in the periphery of their colonies were possible and that they left material traces.

However, as suggested by Porcher (2019), piracy itself has not been the subject of specific research in the Antillean archipelago. His archival research focusing on pirate activity near the Guadeloupe archipelago (Basse-Terre, Grand-Terre, La Désirade, Marie-Galante, Les Saintes, Saint-Barthélemy, and Saint-Martin) during the period 1719 to 1726 has revealed 135 known pirate attacks, of which nearly 87 percent were registered for the Lesser Antilles and the rest for Santo Domingo.

Numerous pirates cruised off La Deseada (La Désirade), Marie-Galante, and Dominica, such as Charles Vane, Edward Teach, Thomas Dulaien, and Bartholomew Roberts (Defoe 2010a; Porcher 2019, 2020). Dominica appears

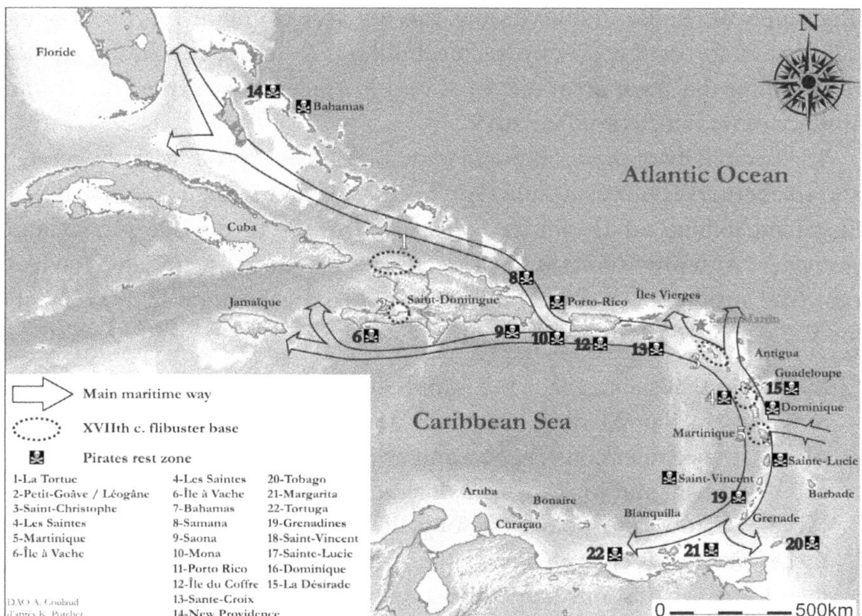

Figure 10.6. Map of the filibusters' bases and pirates' release areas on the Caribbean Sea on the basis of historical sources. (Alexandre Coulaud, Inrap, from Porcher 2019, 2020)

to be a hiding place for these outlaws as well as, to a lesser extent, the Grenadines (Porcher 2019) and La Désirade (Defoe 2010a). The space between Dominica, La Désirade, and Les Saintes becomes an important area of predation. Bartholomew Roberts was hiding at Cariacou in the Grenadines and escaped justice by evading a ship of the French Royal Navy. The Lesser Antilles are dispersed islands situated at different distances and separated by neutral (naval) zones or belonging to different European nations (Porcher 2019). This is also true for the island of St. Martin, which is isolated from the larger French colonies and not densely populated, making it a favored place for refuge and interlopers (Figure 10.6).

The French Antilles also played a role in the emergence of freebooters during the seventeenth century. The local authorities encouraged attacking ships that belonged to rival nations. The Golden Age of Piracy, however, also finds its origins in the Treaty of Utrecht (1713), when French privateers were banned and sailors were thus forced to find a legal but usually less profitable profession (Porcher 2019). The outlaws could most often rely upon the support of the local population, in order to sell their booty and contraband and obtain provisions. The defense of national territories was difficult to assure.

The supply of regular military troops was not very common, but it was often hard to call for swift action by the local militia. A similar conclusion can be reported for the situation at sea. Civil vessels needed to be armed due to the absence of war ships (Porcher 2019).

The complicity of the local population, interlopers or not, with the pirates and freebooters is unmistakable (Porcher 2020). Archival sources reveal that illegal inhabitants of Dominica constructed ovens to provide pirates and smugglers with provisions, as the island is close to the main circuit of navigation. The ensign of the vessel *Bailleul* described the situation in 1717 as follows:

> the barges that sail between the islands also go to St. Lucia, St. Vincent, St. Croix, to Karabacou [Cariacou?], and other Grenadines. At these islands, they gather construction and firewood, to go fishing for turtles and other fish, and look for goats or *cabritos*, pigs, *marrons* [runaway cattle], parrots, and poultry among the savage Caribs. And because there are a few Frenchmen and other people dwelling upon the aforementioned islands, our barges transport all that is needed to do some commerce with them. And because they go there, as do the outlaws, and because they are well received, they take provisions they need, for which they pay handsomely. They go there to careen their ships and find what is necessary to them, what cannot be denied to these inhabitants because they would be looted if they refused them something. (Archives Nationales d'Outre-Mer 1717b)

The geographical position of St. Martin was favorable for predators such as pirates, freebooters, and privateers. The island is situated at the point of return to Europe for ships coming from Martinique and Guadeloupe:

> the French part of this island [St. Martin], which is of great importance to the King, as the ships from the island of Martinique and Guadeloupe must pass this island in order to start the homebound voyage and could serve them as a refuge in order to get some fresh water, refreshments, wood, or other things. (Archives Nationales d'Outre-Mer 1717a)

The geographical, historical, and archaeological data all make a compelling case for the presence of illegal activity.

Acknowledgments

We would like to thank Kevin Porcher for the references on the *Bailleul*.

11

Mysterious Tortuga Island, Republic of Haiti

Laurent Pavlidis

Readers devoted to the archaeology of piracy will no doubt be surprised to read about history rather than archaeology in the following pages. This is the result of a paradox. Although it is one of the most famous freebooter sites in the West Indies, Turtle Island or Île de la Tortue has never been the object of an archaeological excavation (Figure 11.1). Only an archaeological reconnaissance provides a glimpse of the island's potential to reveal information about the lives of pirates. Our team had seriously considered visiting the island during two research expeditions to Haiti to evaluate the possibility of conducting an archaeological study. But the remoteness of Turtle Island from the forts that we were studying at the time in the bay of Saint-Louis-du-Sud did not allow us to go there. However, our archival research on all the fortifications of the colonial period of the Republic of Haiti led to the compilation of a documentary file specific to the fortifications of Turtle Island, which shows quite precisely the nature of the fortifications to be researched and studied.

Before discussing the fortifications and related documentary sources, a word should be said about the people who called Turtle Island home. Anyone approaching the question of buccaneering soon comes up against the myth of piracy (Moreau 2006:293–336). Without retelling the entire history of the freebooter myth, let us specify that the first popular image that emerges is a community of free men who shaped their own rules of life. It is undeniable that a wind of freedom reigned among freebooters, but it is also advisable to view them in a nuanced way. The freebooters of the Île de la Tortue depended on a governor who was attached to the king of France. Jean Le Vasseur established himself on the island of Saint-Christophe, where he commanded a militia. When he seized the island of Tortuga in 1640, he was an engineer and

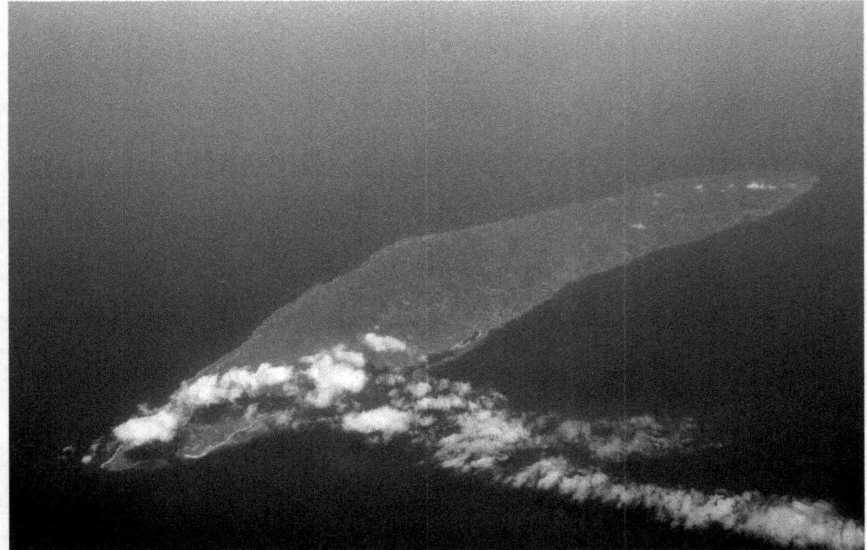

Figure 11.1. Île de la Tortue. (Courtesy Rafaelle Castera)

governor of the king, Louis XIII. The first French fortifications on La Tortue were therefore built on behalf of the king.

This was also the case for the fortifications begun in 1667, the year of French engineer François Blondel's stay on the island. Blondel answered minister Jean-Baptiste Colbert's order to develop fortifications for all the French possessions in the West Indies. As an engineer of the king, Blondel was famous in the mid-seventeenth century. He not only planned fortifications for the colonies but also was involved in the design of public squares in Paris. The fortifications described here correspond well to works of the great freebooter period. They were intended for those who served France by harrying its enemies and later suppressing their compatriots when their freebooting ways jeopardized France's political goals in Europe.

The Historical Approach

Before the French settled on La Tortue, the island was already a refuge and trading place for French, English, and Dutch ships involved in the hide and skin trade. England and France fought for control of the island until Le Vasseur captured it in 1640, before the English could establish a fort there (Dutertre 1667:171). He then visited the island in order to determine the places that needed fortifications (Exquemelin 2005:77).

> He noticed that it was inaccessible from all sides, except from the south, where he thought it would be good to build a fort in the most convenient place in the world, because it did not need great expense, being naturally fortified. This place was on a mountain about 600 paces away from the roadstead from where it could be commanded. On this mountain there was a rock of about 25 or 30 square steps in size, and about four to five *toises* in height [7–9 m], very flat above. Mr. Le Vasseur had a house built on this place to make it his home. (Exquemelin 2005:78; all translations are mine unless otherwise noted)

This fort, known as Fort de la Roche, is sometimes also called Fort Le Vasseur. A contemporary drawing of the fort is the basis for this general description (Figure 11.2).

In the center is the rock that gave the fort its name. According to the drawing, the enclosure has a regular quadrangular plan, flanked to the south by two bastions. The entrance is in the right bastion. There is a small redan on the west curtain wall. Two large buildings stand against the curtain walls. A round building (a dovecote?) is also represented. But is the view accurate? Moreau de Saint-Méry (1797:733) indicates that the fort was "a kind of irregular pentagon." Dutertre (1667) is mute on the layout of the enclosure. But Exquemelin (1684) reports that the fort, which had fallen into ruins through negligence, was restored after the assassination of Le Vasseur by his replace-

Figure 11.2. Fort la Roche (from Oexmelin 2017).

ment, the Chevalier de Fontenay, who added two bastions. Thus, the view represents not the initial state of the fort but its second state after 1643. According to Moreau de Saint-Méry (1797), the surrounding walls were made of dry stone, except in the part facing the sea, where they appear to have been masonry or mortared with a kind of soggy clay.

The central rock, with a diameter of about 36 feet (nearly 11 m), is tall according to the drawing. Exquemelin (2005:78) describes it as 4 to 5 *toises* high (7 to 9 m), while Moreau de Saint-Méry estimates (1797:733) 20 to 25 feet (6 to 7.5 m) and Dutertre (1667:171) 30 feet (9 m). The author of the drawing of the fort represents Le Vasseur's house as being built of wood atop a stone foundation. Moreau de Saint-Méry and Dutertre do not give any indications of the construction materials used in the house. They all agree that it was reached by first ascending a staircase cut halfway up the rock and then an iron ladder that could be withdrawn as needed and maybe every night. They also agree that a spring within the fort itself provided Le Vasseur and his men with the water they needed. Moreau de Saint-Méry (1797:733) estimates that the fortified site could shelter up to 200 men, while Dutertre (1667:171) gives the figure of 300 to 400 men. Moreau de Saint-Méry states that the entrance was to the southeast, which is confirmed by the drawing. But did he rely on the drawing to establish his description or did he visit the site? It is possible that he went there, because he gives the width of the enclosure door as 6 feet (1.8 m), which neither the drawing nor other written sources allow us to determine.

The island was attacked in vain in 1643 by the Spaniards, who lost more than 200 men, according to Exquemelin (2005:79). The inhabitants, who had all withdrawn to the fort, made a sortie and managed to throw the enemy back to the sea.

The Spaniards attacked again in 1654. As they disembarked, the few remaining inhabitants took refuge in the fort. After occupying the island, the Spaniards blazed a path to a nearby mountain top and placed a gun battery there that commanded the fort. Unable to resist, the besieged French had no other solution than to negotiate surrender before the Spaniards decided to massacre them all. Spain was again master of the island, occupying it until the French recaptured it in 1656 (Exquemelin 2005:86–88). The Spaniards repaired the fort, according to Exquemelin (2005:86). But the engineer Blondel, who visited the island in April 1667, claims that it was the Spaniards who razed it. Blondel also specifies that this fortification was useless after the recapture of the island by the French except for "some rather weak batteries erected on the seaside" (Thésée 2008a:291).

Blondel had been in the West Indies since the end of 1666, charged with

Figure 11.3. Basse Terre harbor. (Courtesy Rafaelle Castera)

surveying the French islands and proposing possible means of fortifying them (Goguet 1987; Thésée 2008b). The commission letter sent to him by Colbert in July 1666 specified that "by following in concert with the Governors and Commanders of Icelles [*sic*], he resolves and remains in agreement on the most advantageous places and locations to build forts whose size and stature is in proportion to the merit and consideration of the places and the importance of their situation." Colbert's orders became even more precise: the fortifications must first ensure the protection of the ships and all that concerns the navy. They must then be used to contain "the people from within and the enemies coming from outside" and, finally, to avoid causing great expenses for guarding and conserving future fortresses (Thésée 2008b: 231).

As Le Vasseur did in his time, Blondel began his work by inspecting the island to determine the best places to fortify. He visited Fort de la Roche, agreeing that it was a beautiful place and that the fort was built with good masonry, which Moreau de Saint-Méry would later contradict (Thésée 2008a: 291). But he adds that the fort had little effect on the roadstead, being too far away and too high. As a result, he looked for another site that was a little lower and closer to the roadstead of Basse-Terre (Figure 11.3).

Le Vasseur reports on the need to fortify the island, which offered few advantages to its inhabitants. But many French had settled on the neighboring large island and many freebooters and privateers found a useful refuge there in their incessant war against the Spanish. Finally, it was ideally positioned "above the two largest islands of the Spanish domination, which are Cuba and Santo Domingo, and opposite the great landing of the Caicos Islands, so that ships cannot pass between these islands or land without being seen from the Turtle" (Thésée 2008a:294).

Thus, for Blondel and his king, interest in the island was above all strategic. The same argument would be put forward a century later for the nearby Môle Saint-Nicolas, where the engineer proposed a two-step defense of the island. First, it was a question of defending the port:

> it was found appropriate, under the good pleasure of his Majesty, to choose one of the eminences that are on the southern coast of the Tortoise, the closest to the port, and the most convenient for the defense of its entrance and the roadstead, in order to build a good tower seven to eight feet tall, with a small fort in the shape of a *faussebraye* or earthwork around it, where it can have enough space to handle fifteen or twenty other cannon, the whole built and arranged so that the eminences cannot impede their use and that one can put up considerable resistance to attack, as is particularly explained in the drawings and estimates that were drawn up and how it was depicted in a drawing. (Thésée 2008a:294)

But Blondel knew that they had installed a battery on the heights that dominated Fort de la Roche during the previous Spanish attack, which caused its loss. He therefore imagined establishing a real defensive system, adding redoubts behind the fort, which would themselves be dominated by a second pentagonal fort with a regular layout. Between the first fort to be built and the roadstead, he constructed a few batteries that would slow down if not prevent a direct attack from the roadstead (Figure 11.4).

The project was approved by Bernard d'Orgeron (who also signed the report and the estimate) and started by Blondel. The estimate that follows the report specifies the plan and dimensions of the fort and its tower more precisely:

> This fort, as it has been laid out on the ground, will occupy two sides of a good tower and an enclosure of parapets with a [bomb] proof [magazine?], made of palisades arranged in the form of a long square, one of whose sides facing the sea will be twenty-four to twenty-five *toises* in length, and nine feet high and twelve feet wide, made of earth mixed with stakes and bundles [*fascine*], covered outside with a wall three or four feet thick with embrasures every fifteen or twenty feet that will expose everything in the harbor and will be flanked by the entire half of

the tower. The other side facing the mountain will be flanked by a pincer [gate] made of a curtain of fifteen *toises* and two half bastions, each five *toises* wide and two *toises* long, and will defend half of the tower. And on the fourth [side] opposite, to the west, which is twelve *toises* long, a half bastion five *toises* wide and two *toises* on the flank will be made. All this outline of sides, curtain walls, and flank will be made of a parapet ten to twelve feet high, of earth crushed between two rows of piles, with battlements for firing cover, and another row of palisades set back from the parapet at a distance of three or four feet and closing off the entire fortification from the outside, which has been traced in such a way on the ground that the east and the west sides serve as a ditch, there being only the one facing the mountain, which it will be necessary to dig out if possible, and to raise the parapet high enough to take away the view from the neighboring eminences of what will happen in the fort. (Thésée 2008a:295)

Blondel then describes the tower more precisely:

The tower should be round on the corner of the fort looking east, founded on a firm base and made of good lime and sand masonry of this kind. The diameter will be six *toises* outside on the first floor and two feet inside. The wall will be seven feet wide and raised with good facing on both sides, of which the inner one will be vertical and the outer one a foot of slope at the height of four feet on the first floor,

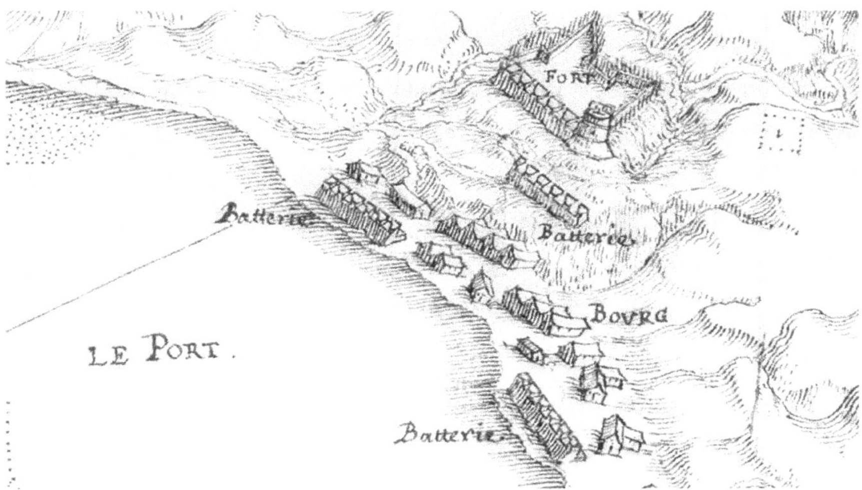

Figure 11.4. Map of fortifications. (Bibliothèque Nationale de France, Paris, Département des Cartes et Plans: GE SH 18 PF 150 DIV 5 P 1)

Figure 11.5. Fort de Blondel. (Bibliothèque Nationale de France, Paris, Département des Cartes et Plans: GE SH 18 PF 150 DIV 5 P 1)

where a surrounding skirt-like belt projecting seven to eight inches will be made; on the top the wall will be raised plumb to the height of seventeen feet on the level, and the plan of the tower on the top where the cannon is to be placed will be at that height. On the inside of the tower, the wall will be raised to four and a half feet, and a foot high and two inches of additional width will be placed around it in the form of a plinth to serve as an impost or pillow for the sight [a banquette or firing-step], which will be a full-circular kiln butt, twenty-two feet in diameter and fifteen and a half feet high, and one and a half feet thick above the key, to reach the height of seven feet above the plane of the tower. The body of the wall and the loins of the vault will be plastered with lime mortar and sand, and the top of the tower will be paved with large, flat stones, if there are any, or made of masonry covered with a few layers of lime mortar and cement to hold water and make it easier to handle the cannon. The thickness of the parapets is to create gutters to channel water away from the fortifications.

Within the fort a cistern and the lodgings for the governors, officers, and soldiers will be built. The vault [or bomb proof] of the tower will be flanked by long battlements four inches wide on the outside and open three feet on the inside; a wall partition will be made that separates it into two parts, one of which can be used as a prison and the other as a store [or magazine] for war munitions. (Figures 11.5 and 11.6)

Blondel began the construction by tracing the footprint of the fort and the tower. We do not know how far the construction had proceeded when he left La Tortue, but the fortification was completed in 1674 (Thésée 2008b:236).

The island then entered a period of decline. A century later, in 1773, Jean-Charles de Baas, governor-general of the islands, came to Turtle Island and found it impoverished by its losses of men and the circumstances of those who were still there. In 1692 La Tortue had seventy men who were capable of bearing arms. There were only half as many the following year. The island was deserted in 1694. Blondell's tower was demolished in 1776 (Moreau de St.-Méry 1797:728, 733).

The decline of the island can be explained in part by its rocky, poor soil and by the attraction of the main island, where there were more French people, especially in Cape Town, Petit-Goâve, Leogane, and especially Port-la-Paix, located a little farther west, on the other side of the straits. The city steadily gained new inhabitants, coming the short distance from La Tortue (Moreau de St.-Méry 1797:728).

Archaeological Perspectives

The two forts of La Tortue have the potential to provide information on the history of the freebooters and the first French settlements in Santo Domingo during the second half of the seventeenth century. The rarity of this sort of site and the various descriptions that survive suggest an evolution of structures, such as the addition of a ditch on the front of Blondell's fort (Figure 11.7).

Figure 11.6. Profile of the fort. (Bibliothèque Nationale de France, Paris, Département des Cartes et Plans:, GE SH 18 PF 150 DIV 5 P 1)

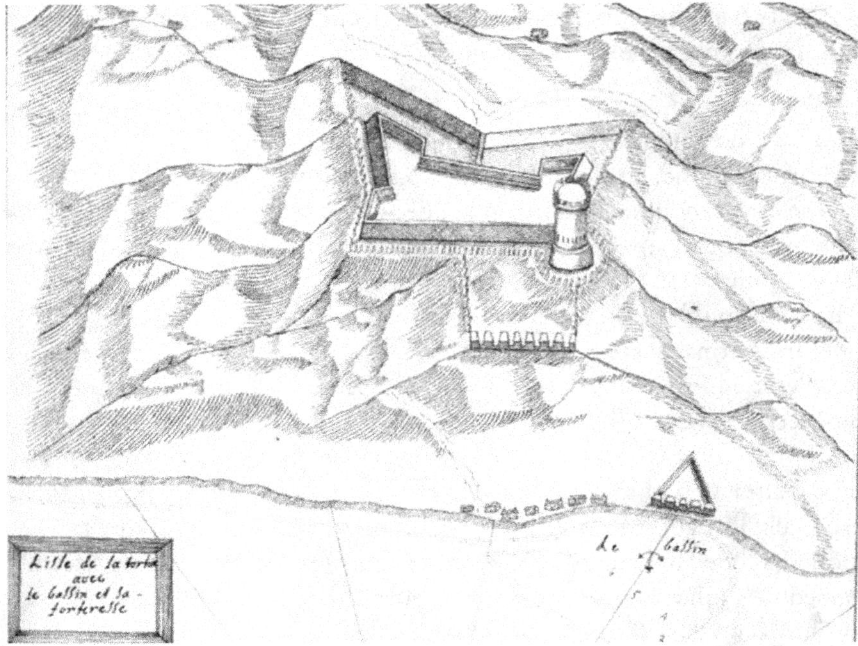

Figure 11.7. Overview of the fort in the latter half of the seventeenth century. (Bibliothèque Nationale de France, Paris, DIV 1 porte 142, 02 fort île de la Tortue 1650–1700)

A Franco-Haitian team composed of eight researchers including the historian Jacques de Cauna and the architect Daniel Elie visited La Tortue in 1987. Their mission was to identify the main sites, including the two forts. They found Fort Le Vasseur: the rock was still in place, and a cursory survey allowed them to detect traces of architecture. They also easily found the fort designed by Blondel. A section of wall, broken slopes, and three guns were still there. The team also spotted a high battery whose ruins are relatively intact. They pleaded for archaeological excavations and published their conclusions in issues 174–175 of the Franco-Haitian journal *Conjonction* in 1987, drawing attention to the fragility and interest of the site (Coustet and de Cauna 1987). To our knowledge, no excavation has been undertaken since that time. The relative isolation of Turtle Island should encourage the resumption of fieldwork. We can only express the hope that an ambitious research program will soon be established. Indeed, the initial survey took place nearly thirty-four years ago. The possible implementation of the project for a huge leisure park dedicated to piracy proposed by the Carnival cruise group could lead to the disappearance of the last vestiges of the great freebooter period.

12

The Pirate of Cotinga Island

The History and Archaeology of a Mysterious Shipwreck in the South of Brazil

Geraldo J. S. Hostin

This chapter is a summary of an archaeological report of findings from November 2000 to January 2020. My research started over twenty-five years ago, when historian Jorge Alberto Canale called my attention to the fascinating description of an unknown pirate who had lost his vessel in 1718 at Cotinga Island, near Paranaguá, a village in the south of Brazil.

History

The major source available in Portuguese at that time was Santos (1951 [1850]:118–119; all translations are mine unless otherwise noted), which depicted a remarkable piracy episode of 1718. The story began with a French merchantman arriving at Paranaguá Bay, pursued by an unknown French pirate coming from the high seas. The powerless locals, expecting to be victimized next, gathered at the local church to pray for the intercession of their patron saint, Our Lady the Virgin of the Rosary:

> Suddenly a wind grew with such intensity, becoming a hurricane, so strong that it did not give the pirates time to avoid imminent danger to their vessel, so that it hit a submerged rock that hides in that place and, breaking apart, the corsair soon descended into the depths on 9 March 1718.

This interesting narrative shows the unprotected state of the isolated coastal villages in the south of Brazil in the early eighteenth century (Figure

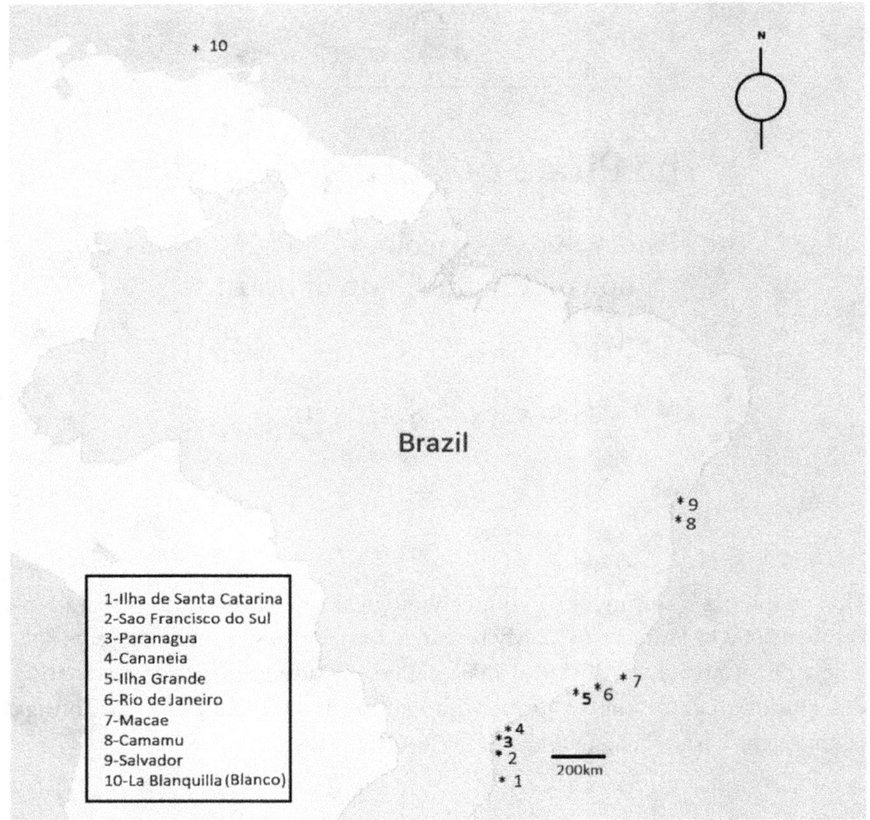

Figure 12.1. The main ports mentioned in this chapter. (section of Nautical Chart 19001). (Courtesy of Marinha do Brasil, Diretoria de Hidrografia e Navegação)

12.1). These places were populated by people of European, American Indian, and mixed heritage and a few Africans, mostly Catholics, who extracted a living from agriculture, fishing, and prospecting (Santos 1951:24, 89–90, 114–118) (Figure 12.2). The story of the miracle was not Santos's invention: the king of Portugal, writing to a government officer in 1726, highlighted the threat of piracy in those locations and noted his belief that the Virgin Mary protected Paranaguá from the raiders in 1718 (Biblioteca Digital Unesp 1896:V18:230).

Pires Pardinho

At the time my research started, this pirate was popularly known as "Bolorot." However, sources showed that this was an error: Bolorot, whose correct name was Charles Tresse Cheville de Valeraut, captain of *Saint-Esprit* of Saint-Malo,

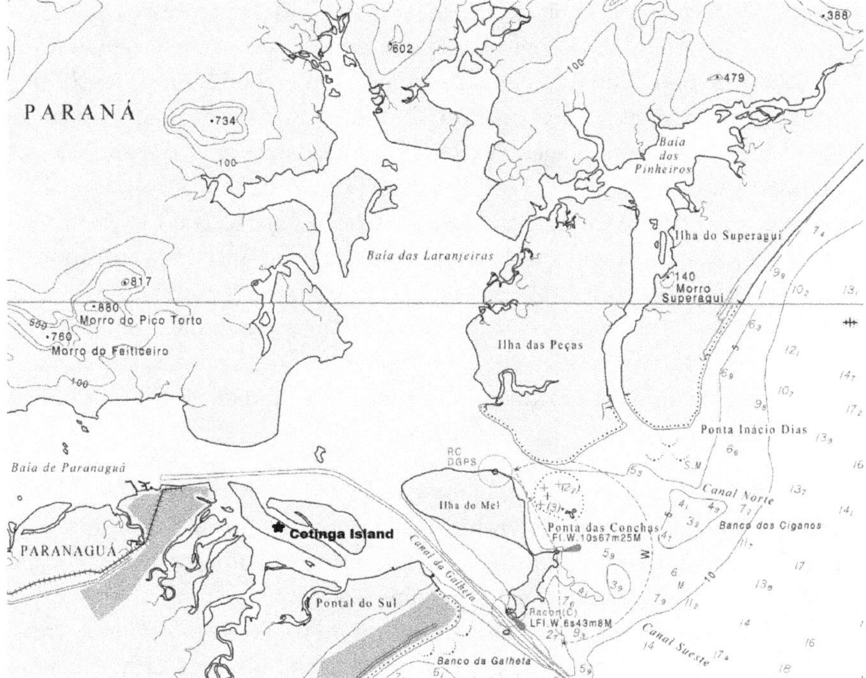

Figure 12.2. The port of Paranaguá and Cananéia (section of Nautical Chart 23200). (Courtesy of Marinha do Brasil, Diretoria de Hidrografia e Navegação)

was only an active smuggler in the south of Brazil from 1721 until his arrest in Paranaguá around 1727 (Arquivo Histórico Ultramarino 1720). Bolorot was not the answer to my questions, so more investigation was needed. Eventually I found an essential piece of evidence in 2000; a 1720 letter from a provincial judge, Raphael Pires Pardinho, to the king of Portugal (Arquivo Histórico Ultramarino 1720:Cx.3/Doc.242[2]). Here is the transcript of the first part:

> In March 1718 a French merchant vessel from Saint-Malo of 18 guns and 67 people took refreshments at this harbor of Pernagua, and its captain was called João Bocachi. A pirate at the island of Cananéia, who had previously been navigating off the coast at full sail, was informed about this ship and its importance. He was guided by some Portuguese among the crew of over 200 persons and, armed with 22 cannon and 10 swivel guns, entered this port chasing the merchantman, which escaped to the inner part of the Island of Cotinga, which faces a river near the village. The pirate ship was arrogantly decorated with flags of skulls and bones of white cloth on black wool. From the ensign staff another

> flag was flown, made of black silk. In its center was the figure of a naked man with a cutlass in his right hand, and his left one held a decapitated head by the hair. As the raider sailed after the merchantman [Bocachi's ship], a thunderstorm fell on him, and after two anchors thrown to hold the pirate ship dragged, its stern hit a hidden rock at the said isle, sinking soon. A few raiders still fled on a brigantine that accompanied it, and others were imprisoned and sent from here to Rio de Janeiro, and many died inside the hull, who had descended into the wardroom to save a chest that, it is alleged, held over 200,000 cruzados in silver coins, bars and objects, gold coins, dust and nuggets, stolen along the Coast of Indies of Castile, where they had committed crimes, and Brazil, where they had been for a long time, and the ballast the sunken vessel carried on board was all iron and steel.

Unfortunately, the name of the pirate is absent in this letter. The "lucky" merchant ship almost captured by him was *Le François* (a.k.a. *Sainte Rose).* Its captain's proper name was not Bocachi, but François Poldecoeur Du Bocage (Archives Départamentales d'Ille-et-Vilaine 1718a).

Pardinho's depictions of the anonymous pirate ship's size, armament, crew, and curious flag were signs of a raider, likely coming from the Caribbean area, particularly Nassau in the Bahamas, which was infested by a new generation of sea thieves in those years (Woodard 2007:1). However, there was a problem: the raider at Cotinga was probably French, and most of the marauders from that place were English (Fox 2013:7–8). A diagram in Rediker (1981:212) shows that a French raider, Olivier Levasseur, stood out in the years 1716–1717. In May 1717 he arrived at Nassau with a new ship of twenty guns and 250 tons (Woodard 2007:194–195). Its description resembled Pardinho's. His name disappears from the registers from August of that year until June 1718, when a British man-of-war spotted him at La Blanquilla Isle (National Archives of the United Kingdom 1718). Intriguingly, his powerful vessel and about a hundred of the crew were missing, so he might be a theoretical fit. The following discussion examines what happened during that intervening ten to eleven months.

Pirates of the Caribbean

Levasseur, also known as La Buse (a French nickname, after a type of hawk), was born in Calais (Brooks 2018:338) and possibly received his training in the naval disciplines during the War of Spanish Succession (1701–1715), which involved many European countries and produced successful raiders like him (Pennell 2001:44). After the war, many of these sailors formerly employed as privateers were left unemployed. Improvements in Atlantic maritime trade after 1715, along with the wealth brought aboard ships, did little to keep them from the lure of piracy. Sea robberies increased at an alarming rate in the Caribbean as a lucrative and clandestine business network was established within the European colonies. The British case is noteworthy: by taking advantage of the derelict state of the Bahamas and inefficient lord proprietors, English pirates made Nassau in the Bahamas their major base, created a loose association, elected their leaders by vote, and, thus organized, became a powerful threat to the maritime commerce in the New World and Africa after 1716 (Pennell 2001:95, 111; Wilde-Ramsing and Carnes-McNaughton 2018:30–31; Woodard 2007:1–9). One of their leaders was Benjamin Hornigold, of the "Flying Gang of New Providence."

Levasseur's crew were mostly French, but he frequently joined forces with the English based in Nassau to attack vessels of opportunity (Woodard 2007:144, 151). He first appeared in 1716, commanding *Le Postillon*, a sloop possibly seized during a mutiny. According to Abijah Savage, master of the sloop *Bonetta* of Antigua, on November 9, 1716, between St. Thomas and St. Croix, he was "overhauled and plundered by two sloops, one called the *Mary Anne*, commanded by Samuel Bellamy an Englishman, and the other, the *Postillon*, by Louis de Boure, a Frenchman" (British History Online 1717–1718:29:211–232).

La Buse's piratical attacks continued and, as mentioned, in May 1717 he had a new command. One Captain John Frost reported the encounter near the coast of New Jersey on July 4 with a "pirate of 20 cannons, 250 tons, 170 men of all nations, led by a Monsieur Laboar," who, after threatening him, looted his cargo of rum. The raider said at parting that he was going to meet a consort ship of 20 guns (*Boston News-Letter*, July 15–22, 1717). As noted, after July his name disappears from the official registers for almost twelve months.

The Mysterious Pirate

The sources in this section, from the Colonial and National Archives of France, were accessed with the valuable help of the late scholar and writer Jacques Gasser, with whom I exchanged documents, who used these same sources in his book (Cally and Gasser 2029).[1] He theorized that La Buse could be the pirate of Cotinga and wanted to find more clues in the Portuguese and Brazilian archives. I was able to find a few more pieces of information from these sources.

During the second half of 1717, an efficient sea robber was plundering French boats around the Gulf of St. Lawrence and at the Grand Banks of Newfoundland. One of the first to inform the maritime authorities was Captain

Christophe Briard, master of *L'Adroite*, who detailed that he was robbed by one Dubourg and his second in command Henry Lebreton, on board *La Louise de Rosfort* (*sic*) near the coast of Canada, who took sailors from his ship (Archives Départementales du Calvados 1718). Captain Guillaume Pestel, commanding *Le Saint Antoine*, reported an encounter on August 1 with a ship named *La Louise de La Rochelle*, crewed by about a hundred men and captained by one Dubourg. They robbed the ship's supplies. Before releasing him, the bandit mentioned plans to get a hundred more seamen, "join an English vessel of thirty cannons, and sail to Brazil" (Archives Nationales de France 1718a:B3 241).

The fishing boat *La Marie* suffered the same fate while navigating Newfoundland waters in the middle of August. It was attacked by Dubourg, master of *La Louise*, "a pirate ship of 20 guns and 160 men," who again let them know of his plans to attack Brazil. The raiders robbed the ship's supplies and "press-ganged" many sailors, two of whom escaped at the Island of Margarita. Both later heard that *La Louise* had sunk somewhere off the Brazilian coast (Archives Nationales de France 1718a:B3/C-11618:92).

And the raids continued. The fishing boat *Le Daniel* was unfortunate enough to meet what was possibly *La Louise* a second time on August 12. The rogues told the master of the captured boat that they had already robbed more than seventeen boats and ships, particularly one merchantman from Britain, carrying 50,000 piastres. To scare the master away, the pirate captain threatened to fire on his boat and cut his throat if he saw him again. According to one witness, the raider's vessel was of "Flushing [Flessingaise] manufacture painted in green and had a figure in front [figurehead], 26 cannon, and was crewed by 200 men, most of them French" (Archives Nationales de France 1718a:B3/C-10227, ff. 67–68). The next victims continued to report attacks by *La Louise* in September. They had to relinquish more seamen to the thieves, plus their cargos, arms, and food. Dubourg was undoubtedly getting ready for a longer voyage to Brazil (Archives du Ministère de la Marine 1718).

According to a purchase document of the admiralty of La Rochelle, *La Louise* was a 150-ton frigate (Archives Départementales de la Charente-Maritime 1718). This vessel was stolen at Dominica on Ash Wednesday, February 10, 1717, and the ship's surgeon, a Dr. Gaschet, had to remain on board (Archives Nationales de France 1718b). A frigate was undoubtedly a premium for a sea robber, because it was a relatively low-tonnage, well-armed, full-rigged ship built for speed and maneuverability and able to sail efficiently on key wind points. The drawing of a frigate of the late seventeenth century shown here (Figure 12.3) possibly shared many features with *La Louise*, whose figurehead might have depicted a woman or girl.

Figure 12.3. A frigate from the end of the seventeenth century. (Bibliothèque Nationale de France, Paris, Département Estampes et Photographie, IC-10-FT 4)

"Dubourg" sounds like "de Boure," the alias of Captain Levasseur (La Buse) when in command of *Le Postillon*. Dubourg could well be Levasseur, still in disguise. Consequently, *La Louise* may be the ship lost at Cotinga Island, Brazil.

A Disastrous Voyage

Taking advantage of the trade winds, at the end of November or early December 1717, an unidentified ship followed by a brigantine appeared on the northeast Brazilian coast, off the Cape of Santo Agostinho (Pernambuco) (Arquivo Histórico Ultramarino 1718:Cx.17/3573–3574). The viceroy, the Marquis of Angeja, soon received the news. From the capital of Salvador,[2] he ordered his sailors and soldiers to watch the adjoining shoreline, as the city was an important port. Unbeknownst to him, the marauders, now known to be French, had wisely avoided the region and later sailed south. Angeja sent off the frigate *Nossa Senhora da Palma e São Pedro* on February 9, 1718, to search for them, under strict instructions to sink the enemy with artillery without further communication (Biblioteca Nacional do Brasil 1939:43:91, 1942:97:140–141).

The bandits carried out at least ten murderous attacks on boats during January 1718 and captured many seamen, who were probably press-ganged into piracy (Arquivo Histórico Ultramarino 1718:Cx. 17/3573–3574; Biblioteca Nacional do Brasil 1942:97:140–141). The example of one slaver coming from Angola to Rio is worth mentioning. After robbing its sails and valuables, and a cargo of 240 slaves, the pirates broke its pumps and forced 50 prisoners taken from earlier incursions to join those already on board, setting them adrift on a leaking boat. Yet those unfortunate seamen survived the ordeal, reached the next port of Macaé, and warned the authorities (Biblioteca Nacional do Brasil 1942:97:132–133).

The raiders anchored off Santa Ana (Santana) Isle near Macaé, on their way to Rio de Janeiro, the port from which galleons and boats loaded with gold departed. They ordered all Africans ashore to get wood, without knowing that Antônio de Brito Freire de Meneses, the ever vigilant governor of Rio, was ready and had dispatched an armed ship to intercept them. Seeing the oncoming warship, the bandits abandoned all the Africans on that island and fled with the Portuguese "at their heels." The warship only gave up after being damaged by rough seas (Arquivo Histórico Ultramarino 1718:Cx. 17/3573–3574).

Sailing south, both vessels arrived at Ilha Grande at the end of January 1718.[3] However, the location was a terrible choice. Crew members deserted, and the authorities reported the capture of a boat with ten thieves who attempted to ransack some canoes (Arquivo Histórico Ultramarino 1718:Cx. 17/3573–3574; Arquivo Nacional 1718a:29–30; Archives Nationales de France 1718a:B3 251). Two deserters, Pierre Porda and Adrien Lamoinne (le Moine) escaped the pirate ship off Paraty in a small canoe. Arriving at Ilha Grande, they begged Pierre des Vaux, the captain of *Princesse de Parme*, which was taking water and supplies there, to give them shelter onboard. They told him that the pirates had taken them by force from their Honfleur ship *L'Adroite* off Newfoundland, Canada (Archives Départementales d'Ille-et-Vilaine 1718b).

Jacques Gasser called my attention to this episode in des Vaux's declaration, which I would later obtain from the St. Malo archives.

As we know, Dubourg had taken sailors from *L'Adroite* in Canada. The discussion so far has established that the pirate in Brazil was Louis Dubourg and his ship the frigate *La Louise*. But was Dubourg the pirate's real name?

Locals sighted *La Louise*, followed by a brigantine sailing down south to Ilha dos Porcos in early February 1718. *La Louise* had a broken spar and forward mast, possibly damaged by those rough seas off Santana Island. The captain had sent ashore fifty people with carpenters to find wood to fix the damage, unaware of an imminent army assault ordered by Meneses (Arquivo

Nacional 1718a:29–30). The attack did not eventuate, but a local militia, under the command of a magistrate from the adjacent town of Ubatuba, took the initiative. When the escorting brigantine came close to shore, possibly near a place called Shark Cove, they seized the boat after killing fifteen to twenty raiders. Unfortunately, the sound of battle alerted the pirates on *La Louise*, who quickly appeared on canoes to assist their companions. The Brazilians abandoned their prize when they ran out of ammunition (Arquivo Nacional 1718a:34–35).

By the end of February the enemy had departed farther south. Meneses suspected they would go toward the isolated villages of Paranaguá, São Francisco, and Santa Catarina, disguising themselves as innocent merchantmen (Arquivo Nacional 1718a:19–23, 29–35). He was almost right: Dubourg sailed down to Cananéia, a paradise isle, and did business with its habitants, who sold them a dugout canoe. This hidden port would be the last for many in the crew. What took place in Cananéia and later Paranaguá encouraged the colonial authorities to send Pardinho on an inquiry (Arquivo Nacional 1718a:17–18). As noted, his account of what occurred on March 9, 1718, at Cotinga is remarkable. Another man witnessed those events firsthand and almost became the victim himself.

A Close Call

Captain François Poldecoeur Du Bocage describes his experiences rather succinctly, without naming the sea robber (Archives Départamentales d'Ille-et-Vilaine 1718a). On March 8 he saw the ship with a brigantine entering Paranaguá Bay. The next day they came for him, and *Le François* fled, chased by the bandits. However, "around three o'clock in the afternoon, fortunately, arose such a furious gale that the pirate ship perished, and their brigantine touched a sandbank." Du Bocage goes on to say that while it was sinking, the brigantine's mast became entangled with those of the large vessel: they were both going to the depths. The boat's crew swiftly cut the masts and riggings, freeing it. Survivors were picked up, and the brigantine fled with *Le François* in pursuit but was not caught.

The news from Cotinga later appeared in Europe in a message sent to the French maritime authorities by one Monsieur Marin in 1718. He described how an unknown pirate ship displayed three different flags, one for each mast, in sequence. The last, meaning "no quarter," was of black cloth with a painted skeleton in the middle, further adorned with images of scattered bones and crossed cutlasses. This is a curious variation of the classic "memento mori" theme. Together with the first flag (ensign) previously reported by Pardinho, it expressed the raiders' ethos of terrorism and violence (Figure 12.4). Marin also portrayed two captains, one from France who had debauched several Canadians on board, and an Englishman, who repeatedly tried to remove him, possibly invoking the famous Pirate Code, because the French captain often opposed his cruelties to kidnapped crews (Archives Nationales de France 1718a:B3 251). So two outlaws coexisted: the Frenchman, who could recruit many men into piracy; and the Englishman, a criminal without conscience who committed heinous crimes at sea.

Sailing Back North

After leaving Paranaguá, the brigantine, crowded with the surviving raiders, sailed down to the neighboring village of São Francisco do Sul. Armed with six handguns out of the eighteen to twenty that remained, they took a boat loaded with cassava flour and returned to their refuge at Cananéia, where they got shelter, food, water, and firewood then sailed back north (Arquivo Nacional 1718a:18–23, 34–35). In early April the viceroy in Salvador received news of a raider, identified as French, operating off the shores of Bahia again. Disinformation was the norm; nobody knew whether he was the same bandit of previous months or not. They had reasons to be worried: galleons from India carrying precious goods, slavers, and merchantmen from the Mina Coast in Africa were about to arrive at Salvador (Biblioteca Nacional do Brasil 1939:43:107–109, 114, 1942:55:21–30).

Still, answering a May 18, 1718, letter from the viceroy, the governor of Rio, Meneses, offered him reassuring information. News that "the pirate brigantine was sailing those seas accompanied by a larger vessel was false, as the latter sank off Cotinga Island, Paranaguá, on 8th March 1718 [*sic*], while trying to sack the village and a French merchantman and only 80 men survived" (Arquivo Nacional 1718a:34–35). The bandits seized a small merchant ship near Salvador on May 13 (Biblioteca Nacional do Brasil 1939:43:121–122). They were last noticed around that time when guards at a fortress in Salvador spotted two vessels sailing north after a rainfall (Biblioteca Nacional do Brasil 1942:55:29–30). Those events did not go unnoticed in England: the *Weekly Journal and British Gazette* (London), on October 4, 1718, reported that Olivier Levasseur (La Buse) had captured many prizes off the coast of Brazil in May.

End of the Voyage

While navigating off La Blanquilla Island, on June 13, 1718 (logged date), the commanding officer of HMS *Scarborough*, Francis Hume, saw unusual activity on the western part of the island involving a large vessel and a sloop, both

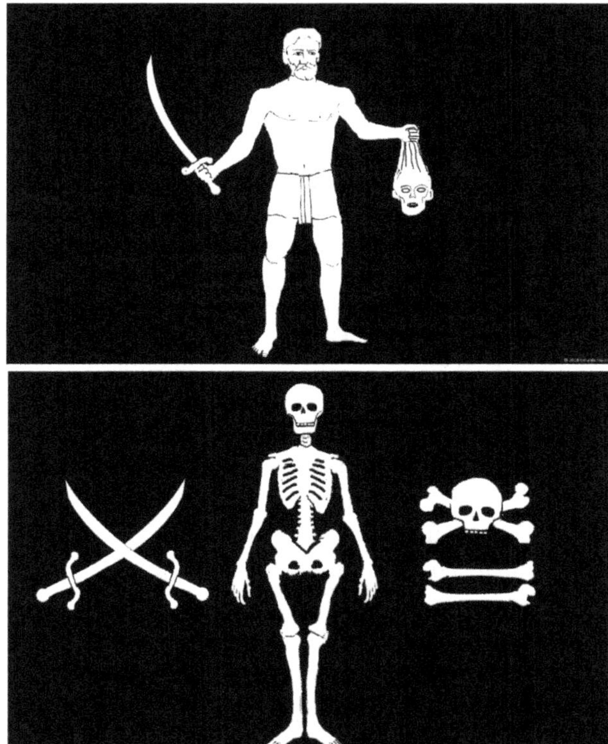

Figure 12.4. The flags used by the pirates. Artwork by the author. (© All rights reserved)

at anchor. As he approached, the sloop named *Boneeta* escaped, abandoning *Blanco*, a Brazilian six-gun ship, which he notes in his log: "Had been taken in her way home by Capt. L. Bour the pirate and his crew of about 80 Men." About seventeen rogues could not leave *Blanco* in time and were captured (National Archives of the United Kingdom 1718). A Boston newspaper also reported the occurrence and noted that "la Bouss" was on his way back from Brazil and that his abandoned vessel was Portuguese, loaded with tobacco and sugar (*Boston News-Letter*, July 28, 1718). The High Court of Admiralty also reported that after "Lewis Le Bour" and crew had taken the sloop *Boneeta*, they put some goods on board and left, armed with muskets, cutlasses, and pistols, "with a considerable quantity of gold and silver" (National Archives of the United Kingdom 1718). As noted, Louis Bour (Boure) was Levasseur's nickname when commanding *Le Postillon* in 1716.

In conclusion, all data make a compelling case that the pirate captain at Cotinga Island was Olivier Levasseur (a.k.a. La Buse, Laboar, Dubourg, de Boure, Le Bour, Le Bouss) and his ship was the frigate *La Louise*.

Archaeology

A few days after the sinking at Cotinga, *La Louise* was resting on the bottom upright, with the tips of its masts sticking out of the water. Tidal currents later rolled it to one side. The hulk ended up at abrupt depths on the seaside area of the island and close to a hazardous submerged rock.

Judge Pardinho, helped by a mulatto diver, started the first recovery of a few artifacts from the wreckage, including a loaded swivel gun, in 1720 and reported the operation to the king, saying that a large-scale operation was necessary (Arquivo Histórico Ultramarino 1720:Cx. 3/Doc. 242[2]). The colonial administration in 1722 offered anyone industrious enough to carry out an undersea job half the money in a "treasure chest," which was supposedly held inside the wardroom by chains from starboard to port. João de Araújo, who had salvage experience, took up the offer in 1730. Although his skin divers salvaged a substantial number of items from constantly murky waters in 1731, the expected fabulous fortune eluded them. One diver also died during the dangerous enterprise (Arquivo Histórico Ultramarino 1731:Cx. 3/Doc. 273[1], Cx. 9/Doc. 960[1]).

The First List of Objects

Government officers were meticulous in writing the findings of the 1731 diving expedition. Many of the artifacts recorded are no different from those found on board an early eighteenth-century merchantman for a good reason. Pirates were mostly seamen who became felons, so their objects reflected the existing maritime culture and society. Artifacts in former pirate ships cannot be studied without the accompanying historical record (Konstam 2003:12–15; Wilde-Ramsing and Carnes-McNaughton 2018:14–15, 142–143). Here is an excerpt from the original listing and a quick assessment (Arquivo Histórico Ultramarino 1731: Cx. 9/Doc. 960[1]).

1. Gold objects, dust, a pocket watch, foreign coins, and so forth: 0.464 kilograms of gold.
2. Items put on auction in Paranaguá: 242,550 *réis*.
3. Silver from Brazil, Spain, and Portugal, two broken watches, and so forth: total 229.65 kilograms of silver.
4. Cannon and ammunition: about 26 kilograms of musket lead shot, two iron pieces of ordnance said to be the 8-pound caliber, two minor iron guns each 1.5 *palmo* long (about 33 cm), 220 artillery shot, about 132 chain shot, 29 bar shot, 65 grenades, 4 blunderbuss bronze barrels, and lots of corroded muskets and pistol barrels.

5. Other articles: a bronze bell weighing 18 "libras," 63 little ceramic medicine jars of different colors, 4 pewter syringes.
6. From a Black man, considered a slave of the pirates, found on land when their ship sank: 90,000 *réis*. The guns that the Black man had on him were sold in Paranaguá: 12,800 *réis*.

Many of the gold objects were stolen, and the quantities of precious metals recovered by the divers, although significant, were not exactly a fortune. Perhaps the shipwreck at Paranaguá did not occur too quickly, and Levasseur could save most of his treasure. As the British Admiralty stated, he still had lots of gold and silver when he escaped at La Blanquilla. The large numbers of firearms, grenades, cannon, and ammunition found in the shipwreck typify other pirate ships in archaeological sites. Such weapons, including swivel guns, are used for boarding. The idea is to capture a relatively intact prize (Sandler 2017:149; Wilde-Ramsing and Carnes-McNaughton 2018:111, 119–120). The bell, which could help identify the vessel, was probably sold, but it is still worth searching for. Jars, mortars and pestles, syringes, and mercury were tools and medicine that Dr. Gaschet would have used to treat sick people on board. The case of a man of African ancestry, caught bearing arms on Cotinga Island, is interesting. He had been in hiding for a long time after the shipwreck and might have been an actual pirate. The authorities considered him a slave of the raiders and treated him as one (Arquivo Histórico Ultramarino 1731:Cx. 9/Doc. 960[1]). As bad as this was, execution as a sea robber would have been a far worse fate.

The 1963–1971 Expeditions

Spanish commercial diver Juan Miralles located a wreck on July 29, 1963, which was identified as a pirate vessel. He was part of an expedition headed by history enthusiasts Roberto De Aquino Lordy and Fernando Guerra Bittencourt. This eight-year venture was approved and partially financed by regional authorities, the Brazilian navy, and the Instituto do Patrimônio Histórico e Artístico Nacional (IPHAN). Unfortunately, it was more a salvage operation than archaeology. The salvors depicted the hulk as half-destroyed, split in two and resting on its starboard side under a thick layer of mud and silt. Supported from a barge, the diver uncovered the remains with an airlift or a suction dredge. Divers with aqualungs discovered exposed items, which Miralles, in hard-hat gear, collected (Lordy 1982; *Última Hora*, October 19, 1963). Soon many deteriorated objects appeared, including iron guns. The conservation of these weapons posed a challenge: Acir Bezerra, the diver who worked at the site in the first year, advised that one piece of ordnance encountered decomposed quickly when dry. As a result, preservation techniques were improved. Interestingly, he said that a swivel gun still had black powder inside (Acir Bezerra, personal communication, 2020). A similar situation occurred with another big gun given to a police academy, still loaded with a charge of lead shot in a cloth bag (*Diário do Paraná*, June 7, 1973). There were roman numerals next to the touchhole in almost all fourteen guns salvaged in 1963 (Acir Bezerra, personal communication, 2020). One cannon found that year measured 2 m long and weighed about 500 kilograms. It exhibited the letters "290 HP" at the rear (*Última Hora*, August 21, 1963). A 12- or 18-pounder Swedish gun 2 m long and weighing 800 kilograms was donated to Ipiranga Museum in São Paulo (*Folha de São Paulo* September 4, 1964). Except for one swivel gun, all pieces of ordnance discovered are iron smoothbore muzzle-loading.

Despite sensational headlines promising a big treasure, the explorers found nothing. But they recovered interesting items and offered a few to museums. This is a provisional list based on newspapers and one journal article by Lordy (1982): two anchors, one about 3 m (a bower, clear sign of a large craft) and another about 0.9 m; twenty-nine iron cannon (of different sizes, some possibly used as ballast); one bronze swivel gun; a 15-kilogram bronze bell; a statuette of the Virgin Mary; one golden coin dated 1714 (moidore); a signet ring; lead paste; one pewter tankard with lid; an image of Christ from a crucifix without arms; a Jamaican totem; three dividers; one gold medal of Saint Ignatius of Loyola; a bronze candlestick; one grindstone; and a large clay container. Lordy also mentions an assemblage of other objects but provides no numbers: cannon round projectiles, lead shot, cutlery with ivory and bone handles, fragments of swords, carabiners, blunderbusses, pistols, silver coins, scissors, Dutch pipes in a box and others of Indigenous origin, faience and tin dishes, a few perfume and rum bottles, pulleys, and pieces of the hull. Although the sinking of the ship claimed about a hundred lives, a lower human jaw was the only human remain reportedly found. It is possible that bodies washed ashore and were buried in an unknown location (*Jornal do Brasil*, March 17, 1966; Lordy 1982; *Última Hora*, September 16, 1963, November 1, 1962, November 26, 1963).

Preliminary Artifact Study

Artifact analysis is still extremely limited because the items from the shipwreck are hard to find and identify. Many are dispersed among private museums and collectors, and so far there is a lack of written registers of the findings. These constant obstacles are the aftereffects of the 1963 project conducted on the wreck site, which, although legal, was not archaeological by modern stan-

Figure 12.5. The objects described (*from top left, clockwise*): gold moidore, cannon, pipe, commemorative postcard, and original statuette (photos by the author). (Courtesy of the Instituto Histórico e Geográfico do Paraná, Curitiba, Brazil)

dards. Of the items recovered, a few have been located and proved to originate from the site by careful examination of museum records, contemporary photos, and reports from newspapers and interviews. These verified objects are three cannon, a gold coin, two pipes, one divider, one expanding shot, and an image of the Virgin Mary. The following section provides a preliminary evaluation of four of them, by functional category (Figure 12.5).

Weapons

One gun, very eroded, is at the entrance of the Instituto Histórico e Geográfico do Paraná (IHGPR) in Curitiba, Brazil. The inner diameter is about 8–9 cm, possibly a 4-pounder (Blackmore 1976). The length overall is 1.58 m. Outside diameter is about 25 cm at the back and at the muzzle 13 cm, with no markings/ciphers. The barrel ornaments have nearly corroded away. The trunnion hoops are very decayed. This cannon is a Finnbanker type, easily identifiable by the shape of the weapon and the larger number of reinforcement rings and possibly cast in Sweden between 1675 and 1700 (Blackmore 1976:150; Wilde-Ramsing Ewen 2012:123). One similar gun, yet to be inspected, is at the IHGPR museum in Paranaguá. Another larger cannon is at the Ipiranga Museum in São Paulo.

Everyday Items

An unknown number of clay pipes, some in fragments, are now in museums and private hands (*Última Hora*, October 7, 1971). Acir Bezerra received one as a gift for his work. It is Dutch, and the mark in the heel appears to be "Dordtse Maagd" rather than "Job op Mesthoop," dated 1710–1719 (Bert van der Lingen, personal communication, 2020; see also Duco 1987:27; and Meulen 2003). The length of the remaining stem is 15.4 cm, the height of the bowl 5 cm, and the diameter 1.75 cm. It shows signs of use (burn marks in the bowl). Another pipe with a longer stem is at the Museu Paranaense (Curitiba), which also owns an expanding shot and a divider from the wreck.

Currency

I tracked down one moidore (gold coin) retrieved during the 1963 expedition (Lordy 1982). Its picture was supplied by the IHGPR for analysis. It is dated 1714 and was struck in Rio. It weighs 10.75 grams: 0.917 fine gold, 29.60 mm in diameter, value 4000 *réis* (Pimentel 1962).

Religious Objects

Divers found a statuette of the Virgin and Child in an ammunition box in 1963 (Acir Bezerra, personal communication, 2020). This unusual discovery in a pirate ship became a significant event for the finders, as they already knew the traditional story of the 1718 miracle (*Última Hora*, November 27, 1963). Unsurprisingly, that statuette is now strongly associated with the shipwreck. It is called Nossa Senhora das Vitórias da Cotinga (Our Lady of Victories of Cotinga). Commemorating 250 years of the incident in 1968, the Brazilian government printed stamps and postcards showing this image. It is a ceramic object (height 12 cm, diameter at base 3.2 cm), with a few marine concretions. The country of origin is unknown. This iconography is a common Catholic representation of Our Lady Queen of Heaven (Roten 2019). The child is making a gesture of blessing. The piece was possibly donated to the Notre Dame Cathedral Museum in Paris (*Diário do Paraná*, November 17, 1971).

Is the 1963 Shipwreck *La Louise*?

This wreck site, like Blackbeard's *Queen Anne's Revenge*, has not provided key objects or marks that could immediately identify it. Here are some points to consider, based on the documentary evidence.

1. The position of the wreckage found by salvors in 1963 matches Pardinho's depictions, close to a dangerous underwater rock (Ponta da Cruz). The remains were also in abrupt depths of around 15 m, and the hulk was leaning on one side (*Última Hora*, November 1, 1962).
2. Pirate ships were always heavily armed. The work during the 1963–1971 period exposed many weapons and ammunition.

3. All pieces analyzed so far are within the expected date.
4. There is no record of a similar vessel lost at the same location.
5. Except for cannon, the last exploration produced relatively few artifacts, clear signs of previous disturbance and salvage.

The data gathered so far eliminate the hypothesis of another vessel, so the shipwreck is most likely *La Louise*.

Conclusion

This study connects the dots by drawing on freshly uncovered documentary evidence, especially from the Portuguese and Brazilian archives, and thus recreates a more complete and reliable picture of an earlier event of piracy in Brazil. It properly identifies Olivier Levasseur (La Buse) and the frigate *La Louise* as the mysterious pirate of Cotinga Island and his ship. These new data should correct the errors often seen on websites and in books in Brazil.

From a historical perspective, the bandits who raised havoc in Brazil were initially successful because they attacked by surprise on a fast ship. Being a step ahead of their persecutors was not too difficult, as the Portuguese had only one good warship to patrol a large stretch of coast from Rio to Salvador, leaving most of the Brazilian coastline uncovered and the locals to fend for themselves (Arquivo Nacional 1718b:C85, letter, June 27, 1719; Biblioteca Nacional do Brasil 1942:97:184–185). His raids highlighted the weakness in Brazil's defenses and paved the way for other sea robbers, many of them his associates, in the following years (Arquivo Nacional 1718a:24–25). As for Levasseur, he was back to "business" in Africa and the Indian Ocean in 1719. He would end up executed for piracy on the island of Réunion, on July 7, 1730 (Brooks 2018:338–340). Contrary to what some modern tales and ideologically motivated theories about pirates would want us to believe (see Pennell 2001), this report simply confirms their general attributes as self-interested outlaws who took part in an essentially vicious and parasitical activity. They brought financial and material losses and terror to those outside their business network, particularly the "common folk," already burdened by colonial powers. As a product of their time, pirates also profited from the slave trade. They lived in a shadowy, dangerous, and violent world, which was well represented by the flags they proudly displayed, a reality far from "romantic" or "revolutionary."

The loss of archaeological evidence from *La Louise*'s remains was significant for the study of piracy because this vessel was in action for more than one year, unlike other famous pirate ships lost and found.

Although this report expands and strengthens the previous identification of the shipwreck, further underwater archaeology investigations are advised to get direct proof of identity, such as marks or inscriptions on objects. Yet this is not advisable, given the costs and risks involved. It is wiser to track down and work with the pieces already found in the 1963 expedition.

Assessing the present condition of the shipwreck is essential for its preservation, so an on-site survey and mapping by high-resolution, multibeam side-scan or sector scan sonar imagery, combined with sampling and photography, is recommended. It is paramount to ensure that the wreckage remains undisturbed by changing the long-lasting perception of it as a treasure trove, which is a major cause of its disastrous condition. I hope that this initial study helps to dispel myths and disinformation and enhances the shipwreck's cultural and historical importance.

Acknowledgments

Thanks to Jean Soulat, John de Bry, and Christophe Polet, members of the group Archéologie de la Piraterie des XVIIe–XVIIIe Siècles, for all help possible; Baylus Brooks, Colin Woodard, Ben Thweatt, and my colleague Pierre Brial from Réunion, for documents and data concerning La Buse's life; and Professor Ernani Straube of the IHGPR. My heartfelt thanks to the former diver Colonel Acir Bezerra for providing essential information and to Kate Birch from Tasmania, Braden Miller, and my wife, Denise Hostin, for the corrections to this text.

Notes

1 All these references and links were kindly passed on to me by Gasser by email.
2 São Salvador da Bahia de Todos os Santos, now Salvador in the state of Bahia, northern Brazil.
3 "Ilha" means island in Portuguese.

13

Buccaneers and Harpooners of the Miskito Coast

Lynn B. Harris

The Danish frigates *Christianus Quintus* and *Fredericus Quartus*, carrying 671 enslaved Africans and a mutinous crew and running critically low on food supplies, arrived serendipitously at a bay in Costa Rica in 1710. The reported location was Punta Carreta (believed to be renamed Cahuita or Coaita Point on nineteenth-century maps), instead of the intended destination of St. Thomas, West Indies (Figure 13.1). At that time, this circum-Caribbean coastline was an economically contested area characterized by changing alliances and hostilities between the native Miskito Indians, Africans, and Creoles (Miskito-Africans referred to as Zambos) and Spanish and English stakeholders (Harris 2020; Transatlantic Slave Voyages Database).

Caribbean and Central American buccaneers exploited these ethnic and economic tensions, serving as go-betweens in transactions and perhaps even conspiring, facilitating, or staging ship-wrecking and salvage operations with captains and crew who were possible beneficiaries of the event. It was geographically convenient to situate camps in remote locales with rich fishing grounds and treacherous reefs well known to turtle harpooners, who were valued participants in their buccaneering expeditions. Turtle harpooners are mentioned a few times in the voyage narrative of the two ships, both at the unintended stopover at the island of Santa Catalina and upon arrival on the southern Costa Rica shoreline at a time when slaves were sought-after commodities in the Matina Valley, at Porto Bello in Panama, and at lucrative redistribution centers in Jamaica. Even if a shipwreck or stranding occurred accidentally, news spread rapidly. This appeared to be the case with the two Danish ships, both deliberately destroyed by their crews three days after arrival, becoming a centerpiece for intrigue and suspicion surrounding the postwrecking events and the illegal capture of slaves destined for the Danish

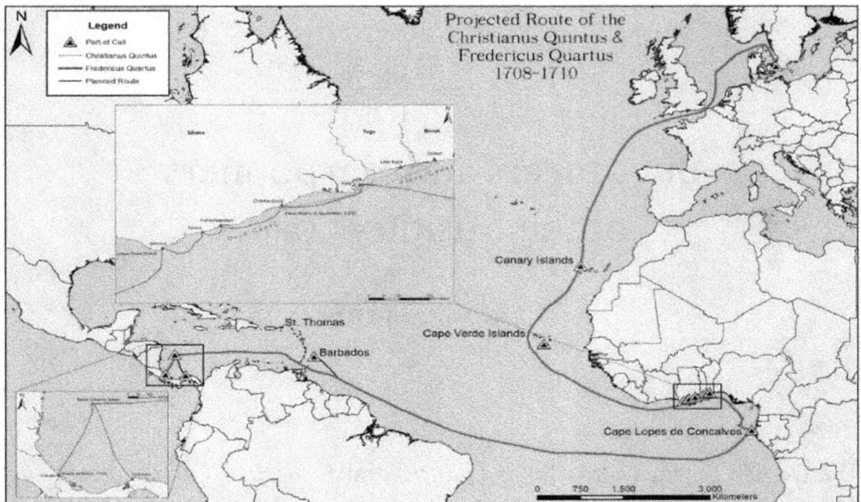

Figure 13.1. Projected route of the voyage of the Danish frigates *Christianus Quintus* and *Fredericus Quartus* (1708–1710). (Courtesy of the Program of Maritime Studies, East Carolina University)

outpost at St. Thomas. More understanding of buccaneers and harpooners as interveners in the slave trade network contributes toward expanding the framework of Atlantic world themes (Lohse 2002, 2005a, 2005b, 2014; Nørregård 1948).

Contested Landscape

Pirates, privateers, and explorers repeatedly stressed the dependence of European ships on the skills of Miskito harpooners while voyaging in Central America and the West Indies for survival and lucrative commerce. Explorer William Dampier (1906 [1697]:39) explains: "Their Chief employment in their own country is to strike fish, turtle and manatee . . . so that when we careen our ships we choose commonly places where there is plenty of turtle or manatee to strike." Alexandre Exquemelin (1969 [1684]:92–93, 220), a French buccaneer and surgeon who voyaged on ships to the Miskito coastline, notes:

> Through the frequent Converse and Familiarity with [*sic*] these *Indians* have with the Pirats [*sic*], they sometimes go to sea with them, and remain among them for whole years, without returning home. From whence it cometh, that many of them speak *English* and *French*, and some of the Pirats their *Indian* language. They are very dexterous at darting with the Javelin, whereby they are very useful to the Pirats,

> towards the victualling of their ships, by the fishery of Tortoises, and Manitas [manatees]. . . . For [four] of those *Indians* is alone sufficient to victual a vessel of a 100 persons. (Figure 13.2)

Turtle and manatee trade goods and consumption patterns led to a variety of encounters between native Indians, Europeans, Africans, and Creole inhabitants (Harris 2021). Crawford and Márquez-Pérez (2016) highlight that turtle hunting was a central part of the making of the early modern Atlantic world. McKillop (1985) blends historical narratives, archaeological data, and ethnographic accounts to reconstruct the prehistoric and lesser-known colonial exploitation of manatees in circum-Caribbean areas. Clearly, by the mid-eighteenth century, distinctive maritime commerce in turtle and manatee products existed, especially among English-speaking inhabitants from the Cayman Islands and Jamaica to outposts of Costa Rica, Nicaragua, and the Colombian islands (McKillop 1985). These connections occurred within the setting of a contested landscape where new Creole societies emerged within engagements with pirates.

Draper (2017) illustrates how these earlier studies remain poorly known but also why they should be more widely appreciated. Her study examines the role of timber and green sea turtle acquired in the coastal areas of early English Barbados and Jamaica, respectively. She found that available surpluses of these off-island resources were essential for urban and capitalist development in the English West Indies. In the case of Jamaica, the harvesting of green turtles from surrounding ecosystems allowed for the rise of Port Royal as a critical entrepôt for piracy and smuggling. Her work suggests but does not fully develop the implications of the centrality of turtle hunting for provisioning the enterprises that provided the start-up capital necessary for commercial

Figure 13.2. *Spearing Green Turtle on the Mosquito Coast* (W. Trummbull, 1874). (Art and Picture Collection, New York Public Library, https://digitalcollections.nypl.org/items/510d47e1-08f7-a3d9-e040-e00a18064a99)

agriculture, sugar mills, and the purchase of enslaved labor in Jamaica. Offen (2020) reflects upon the ways in which human exploitation of the green sea turtle subsidized developments across the colonial Caribbean. This demonstrates the importance of marine resource exploitation to Jamaica, specifically how the green sea turtle provisioned other important Caribbean port cities and east-bound Atlantic vessels of multiple nations. It enabled mobile seafarers to successfully attack Spanish ports throughout the circum-Caribbean.

Miskito Harpooners aboard Pirate Ships

By the end of the seventeenth century, pirates prowling the Caribbean coastline and island had established lucrative and convenient contact with Miskito Indians, whose tools and hunting and fishing skills were in much demand to support them during their covert operations. They had "extraordinary good eyes, and will descry a sail at sea farther, and see anything better, than we" (Dampier 1906 [1697]:8). Along with English privateers and traders, they not only exchanged quantities of meat but also were known to hire or capture Miskito Indians to serve aboard their ships with possessions such as canoes and fishing gear. It is unclear whether hunters always joined the crew of a vessel willingly. This may have varied at certain times or locations. Esquemelin (1969 [1684]:72) describes turtle hunters taken as prisoners: "once captured, these men have to provide turtle for the rovers as long as they remain on the island. Should the rovers intend to cruise along the coast where the turtles abound, they take the fishermen along with them. The poor fellows may be compelled to stay away from their families for four or five years, with no news as to whether they are dead or alive."

It is evident from pirate codes that enslaved Africans were awarded as prizes or confiscated as penalties in a variety of situations, especially for loss of limbs in battle. For example, loss of a right arm: 600 pieces of eight or six slaves, loss of a left arm: 500 pieces of eight or five slaves. The injured individual was given the choice of a slave or financial compensation (Esquemelin 1969 [1684]:71, 171). No doubt these disabilities would necessitate assistance in daily tasks, and slaves accommodated these setbacks inherent in a buccaneer lifestyle. As Rediker (2004:74) explains, it was a sort of welfare system to increase recruitment and loyalty among buccaneers.

Long Ben

A tantalizing entry in several sources notes that the notorious pirate Long Ben or Ben Avery engaged with two unnamed Danish ships of twenty-six guns each on the island of Princes. He "fell in with them, fought, took, plundered, and burnt them, and that was the end of their Unhappy Voyage." The Portuguese Principe Island (off the coast of Africa) was known to be the only other island apart from São Tomé where Dutch and Danish ships provisioned ships with supplies and fresh water. The two islands were a major transit point for ships engaged in the slave trade. This was the first stopover where captains anchored to replenish supplies on their trip to the West Indies. Here they ordered crew to carry the sick ashore for the "benefit of air and likewise fresh water" (M. W. 1699:212).

Ben Avery in other accounts was noted for his extortion of supplies from the São Tomé governor. This was becoming prevalent after 1697 with the suppression of piracy attacks not only on the high seas but in port cities with high volumes of seaborne commerce. Further research into the digital documents of the Danish archives suggests that the ship destroyed by Long Ben was *Kron Printzen*, voyaging in convoy with *Christianus Quintus* in September 1705. They were heading to St. Thomas in the West Indies, only two years prior to the fatal voyage of the *Christianus Quintus* in convoy with *Fredericus Quartus* (wrecked in Costa Rica). *Kron Printzen* was carrying 200 elephant tusks and 860 slaves at the time it was burned (Rigsarkivet Arkivalieonline 1671–1754; M. W 1699: 212).

Long Ben, whose given name was Henry Avery or Every, was an English pirate with several aliases, such as Jack Avery and John Every (Figure 13.3). He started his career like other pirates, serving on British Royal Navy ships. When the War of Spanish Succession ended in 1714, many privateers like Avery became pirates or slavers. Privateer bases like Nassau in the Bahamas became pirate bases, with at least twenty pirate captains acknowledging it as a home base. The island of Prince similarly was a known pirate base. After Long Ben's discharge from the navy, again like many other British sailors, he entered the Atlantic slave trade and disappeared from official records. He was believed to be illegally slave trading during the 1690s on a ship called *Fancy* with 46 guns and 121 crew under the protection of the governor of the Bahamas, Cadwallender Jones. After this service, Long Ben buccaneered in the Caribbean Sea and captained a freighter in Central America, giving him knowledge and connections in the West Indies and Miskito Coast at roughly the time when the next two Danish Slave ships were conducting a disastrous 1708–1710 voyage in the area (Burgess 2008).

Avery was likely familiar with mainland pirate lairs located at Belize, Cape Gracias a Dios, and Bluefields near small plantations. In the early decades of the 1700s buccaneers enlisted the help of Miskito Zambos, who provided canoes and turtle meat and partnered or served as go-betweens on slave raids

Figure 13.3. Captain Henry Avery (Long Ben). A woodcut from *A General History of the Pyrates* (Johnson 1724a). (Wikimedia Commons)

into Spanish settlements and inland communities traveling up the rivers. In return, the Miskito accomplices received guns, ammunitions, and a variety of other goods. Like Avery, English men served as captains of coastal trade vessels, logwood cutters, goods traders, and sugar plantation workers or owners in Costa Rica, becoming intimately familiar with coves or river mouths where ships could load and unload covertly. Slaves from shipwrecks or stolen from plantations were one of the most valuable commodities desired by the British in Jamaica. While most of this labor was provided by slaves imported directly from Africa, Miskito Zambos, shipwrecked Africans, and Miskito Indians from the Central American mainland were also sold in Jamaican slave markets, particularly prior to 1740, while Jamaican sugar estates were still in the formative stages of development. Sometimes the Central American captors kept the women and children and sold the men. Historians speculate that the Miskito women immersed Afro Miskito offspring in their local culture, according to the matrilocal customs, with mothers, daughters, and sisters maintaining cultural continuity in the absence of men, who were often gone for long periods conducting seasonal turtle hunts or serving on British ships, or when the men were of a non-Miskito culture. Children were considered fully Miskito, not Creole, despite African or European heritage (Esquemelin 1969 [1684]:225).

Miskito Zambo Raiding

Buccaneer M. W. (1699) wrote a lengthy account of the Miskito Zambo slave-raiding activities. He mentions two separate shipwrecks in the early 1600s that contributed African labor from shipwrecked slaves. His report details how Miskito Zambos created political structures and identified as a distinct ethnic group, settling in the Miskito territory extending along the coast from Cape Cameron, in Honduras, to the Rio Grande and in Nicaragua. They conducted intertribal raids, stealing women from polygynous family units, brutally killing men and children, and taking mementos from their victims (M. W. 1699:291).

By 1699 Miskito raids had reached into Costa Rica, to the cacao plantations established by the Spaniards at Matina. Raiders stole slaves and commodities, including cocoa nuts and turtle shell, primarily traded to Jamaicans. M. W. reported that a Miskito king named Jeremy, a sixty-year-old six-foot man of dark brown complexion with hair hanging down to his shoulders and a voice like a bear, was crowned by his brother in Jamaica and thus had many "courteous" dealings with the British. He was known to "possess several islands of the West Indies, particularly that of Providence (since called St. Catalina by the Spaniards) which is situated at 13 degrees 10 n. latitude lying east of Cap Gracios de Dios." King Jeremy was contracted to supply men to "hunt Negroes" and to "give them [the crew] rum for the voyage home." Clearly, Miskito raiding by the early decades of the eighteenth-century was heavily influenced by the market provided by Jamaica and by Jamaicans and European residents on the Miskito Coast. Santa Catalina Island was a strategic locale in the planning process (M. W. 1699:288, 295).

Despite Miskito matrilineal status, literature also suggests that Miskito Zambos identified strongly with the English in dress, language, and customs, claiming to be distinct from the neighboring "wild Indian[s]" in their association with the English. They readily imitated the buccaneers, sought English affiliation, and "acknowledge the King of England for their sovereign, learn our language, and take the Governor of Jamaica to be one of the greatest Princes in the World" (Dampier 1906 [1697]:17). In the early nineteenth century it was frequently stated that the Miskito desired foreign trade goods to live in the "right English Gentleman Fashion" (Roberts 1827:113, 132). The English tried to create and foster this British identity in a variety of ways. One example was taking a young Miskito boy, paddling his canoe, aboard a buccaneer's ships and giving him the English name John Gret, intending to "breed him amongst the English" (Dampier 1906 [1697]:181).

The relationship between English buccaneers and the Miskito Zambos grew increasingly productive economically. They provided the buccaneers with local trade goods, turtles being one of the most lucrative. M. W. writes in detail about the abundance of three sorts of "large tortoises," hawksbill, logger head, and green turtle. The green turtle had the best meat, the hawksbill the best shell, and the logger head the best oil. The most important commodity was the manatee or sea cow, a 500- or 600-pound creature that resembled a cow without horns, with a white, pleasant-tasting meat that sailors believed cured pox scurvy (M. W. 1699:298).

In return, the Miskito Zambos received steady access to European arms for more effective hunting, raiding, and protection against neighboring tribes. English privateers working through the Providence Island Company (an English chartered company founded in 1629 by a group of Puritans in order to establish the Providence Island colony on Providence Island and the Mosquito Coast, then Nicaragua), for example, made informal alliances with the Miskito. Holm (1978) suggests that—unalike the Spanish, who viewed the Miskito as a threat—the English approached them with greater diplomacy as an ally against their enemy, Spain. Promoting pidgin Coast English was one means to promote closer discourse. In the years that followed the dissolution of the Providence Island Company, small numbers of European settlers, escaped slaves, ship crew, and shipwrecked sailors settled in several centers along the Santa Catalina and Providence Islands coast, many of them intermarrying with the local tribes of Indians. Their offspring later participated in the military and administrative affairs of the Miskito kingdom.

Wives, Kings, and English Gentlemen

Another cultural facilitating mechanism for trade was marriage between British men and Miskito women (Holm 1978:28). Esquemelin (1969 [1684]:249) explains:

> When any Pirates arrive there, everyone has the liberty to buy for himself an Indian woman, at the price of a knife, or any old wood-bill or hatchet. By this contract the woman is obliged to remain in the custody of the Pirate all the time he stayeth there. She serves him in the meanwhile, and brings him victuals of all sorts, that the country affords. The Pirate moreover has liberty to go when he pleases, either to hunt, or fish, or about any other divertisements of his pleasure; but withal is not to commit any hostility, or depredation upon the inhabitants, seeing the Indians bring him in all that he stands in need of, or that he

> desires. . . . If any Pirate marries an Indian Woman, she is bound to do with him, in all things, as if he were an Indian born man.

In contrast, Dampier (1906 [1697]:8) found that relationships between the French and Miskito women were not quite as cordial, noting that "they do not love the French" and citing Sir Hans Sloane: "The French they mortally hate for their wanton behaviour towards their wives." It seems clear, nonetheless, that on occasion both French and English pirates stayed on the Miskito Coast with local women. M. W. (1699:288) comments on "Thomas Arks and Joshua Thomas, who were Capt. Wright's crew, who, with 150 French and English Buccaneers, . . . chose rather to live here, than return home, and venture to take a trial for piracy, and now have 40 wild Indian slaves and harlots to attend them leading a slothful and heathenish life since." He is referring to the crew who deserted Captain William Wright (fl. 1675–1682), an English privateer in the French service who later became a buccaneer raiding Spanish towns, including Segovia, in present Nicaragua.

King Jeremy of Santa Catalina was not the only Miskito ruler recognized by the British. Close connections and alliances with local communities were a strategic influence. These relationships served both parties. They gave allied Miskito groups a façade of power and prestige by crowning Miskito leaders as kings (or chiefs), governors, generals, and admirals. Helms (1983:76–77) contends that the kings and other titles were simply to create British go-betweens or "puppets," whereas Olien (1998) suggests otherwise. Olien notes a long-standing traditional line of succession from the eldest son of a primary wife and that the choice of kings was closely controlled by the Miskito. He concedes that the structure of this leadership was likely influenced by Africans as well as by British protagonists as they entered the Miskito stage. History provides interesting details about English recognition of the leaders and validation of British prestige, including several kings who visited England or received commissions from the governor of Jamaica and the English representative in Belize. English was a prestige language, and followers expected leaders to become fluent.

Although the amount of influence exerted by the English on the Miskito coastline varied over time and space, the argument of Helms (1983) seems pertinent. This strategy of cultivating allegiance and fostering a growing comradery with the English served buccaneers well: Miskito men subsequently joined English raids of Spanish communities. During Jeremy's reign, this escalated. Pertinent to this study are the raids to the south, along the coast of Costa Rica, around the Matina Valley, especially at cacao harvest time. The Miskoto Indians started to sell their captives of both sexes and all ages as slaves to Jamaican traders and became further involved in the return of fugitive slaves. Raiding expeditions extended farther south along the southern coast of Costa Rica, inland into its southern mountains, and in the Bocas del Toro area of what is today Panama. Between 1710 and 1722, more than two thousand persons were said to have been taken as slaves from the Valley of Matina and the Island of Tojair (Olien 1998:198–199).

There are contrasting scholarly paradigms regarding the dynamics of the socioeconomic relationships with British buccaneers and the balance of power, especially regarding consumption, raiding, war tactics, and political structure. These vary from the very traditional argument about the native Miskito Indians as "British puppets" lured by the temptations of European rum and consumer goods to a diametrically opposite view of the Miskito's strategic exploitation or opportunistic utilization of the European relationship to gain leverage against local neighbors and former enemies, whether it was arms, wealth, or political control of land in a changing geopolitical environment in central coastal Caribbean areas (Mendiola 2018). Other factors to consider are the long history of warfare tactics and ethnic tensions that existed prior to alliances with the buccaneers; unanticipated peopling of the landscape by ethnicities other than Europeans (such as shipwrecked or smuggled slaves); and, perhaps most significantly, the emergence of new Creole identities of all protagonists. This was no longer a simplistic colonial European and native Indian alliance, but rather communities that considered themselves neither one nor the other.

Miskito and Pirate Allies as Inland Raiders

Pirates frequently seized ships voyaging or anchoring in small bays between Panama and Costa Rica. More blatantly, cargos of goods requested and shipped to planters were intercepted and stolen from ships docking in larger Central American ports like Porto Bello intended for destinations like the Matina Valley. Porto Bello had become heavily fortified in response by 1670, and pirates diverted their attention to smaller ports like Puerto Viejo. Pirates also made incursions into agricultural areas, knowing the cycle of crop seasons and when laborers were likely to be working the fields. These raids were destructive and involved burning housing and crops as well as stealing both slaves and free laborers. Zambos joined the pirates or worked independently. They used a variety of strategies, including posting lookouts at high spots like the extinct volcano at Tortuguero or a mountain range to view smoke from settlements in valleys, a fleet of ships in the ocean, or canoes in the river. They often knew the people in a village, having conducted daylight trading with the group prior to a raid. Raiding frequently took place at night with a full moon, burning plots, crops, and homes or flushing out individuals hiding in coastal caves. One form of torture to terrify enemies or glean information was to build a fire under a prisoner trussed up on a barbecue. Other psychological warfare tactics included advancing on the enemy while making a great deal of noise, like hitting trees, drumming, fluting, and shrieking (Rojas 2012:114–116).

Miskito knowledge of the coastal and river valley landscape, as well as skills at sea or in the rivers in large canoes were exceptionally useful to the raiding strategies. Retaliation against the raiders was challenging, as the groups lived in scattered settlements in the forests and on the coast. The raids drove up the price of cacao, creating difficulties in agricultural development in Costa Rica. Raided goods from haciendas and natural resources from Costa Rica like logwood, dye, sarsaparilla, turtle meat, and shells were shipped usually to Jamaica in small boats often too old and unreliable for Atlantic crossings or recycled from prior Atlantic trade uses. Especially between 1655 and 1685, Jamaica was an English Caribbean emporium and middle market until larger vessels took the goods to European markets and likewise stored goods desired by Spanish Caribbean colonies. Other mechanisms for transporting goods were locally built and used smaller flat-bottomed dugout canoes, highly praised by buccaneers and ideal for navigating the rapids and shoals of inland rivers. These could also be built up as larger models from mahogany and cedar, with extra planking on the sides of the hull to carry extra cargo. In addition, the canoes were used for warfare and raiding, easily carrying high volumes of goods. They were known to carry six thousand tons of freight and more than thirty men.

The illustrious Dutch buccaneer Lorencillo (Laurens) Cornelis Boudewijn de Graaf raided and ravaged the Matina Valley for three months in 1687, killing Spanish landowners. Miskito Zambos, many from Honduras and Nicaragua, allied with the British again in 1690 and in 1705, attacking the Matina Valley. In all the raids, taking prisoners alive was extremely valuable. Slaves from Central America were sold to the colonies in the eighteenth century, including Charleston, South Carolina, and New York. It is estimated that two thousand people were captured from the Matina Valley and Island of Tojar between 1710 and 1722 (Rojas 2012:114-116). An attack on the Matina Valley in 1724 involved five hundred armed Miskito Zambos who took as prisoners twelve slaves and twenty-one freemen and seized ninety-seven metric tons of cacao that they loaded onto boats and took to Nicaragua and Honduras (Macleod 2010: 361, 362, 366, 338). Inland slave raids continued beyond the turn of the seventeenth century, expanding to the southern mountains and

Bocas del Toro area. Some were exchanged for goods or became socialized and assimilated into the Miskito community. Pirates exploited this dynamic and pitted groups against each other, competing for trade (Helms 1983:194).

A Case Study: Cahuita Shipwrecks and Memory

Palmer's (1993) oral history emphasizes material culture reminiscent of pirate ships in childhood memories of the descendants of William Smith, reputed to be the first Afro-Caribbean turtle hunter to settle permanently in the town of Cahuita, within the province of Limón. Anchor chains feature prominently: the sound of chains reeling out of trees, where pirates ran them through holes in the trucks and cinched them up with turnbuckles. There are classic tales of pirate treasure buried on the shore, which instead yielded old documents. From this early period until contemporary times, locals have assumed that the two old shipwrecks in Cahuita Bay (now protected in Cahuita National Park) were integrally connected to stories of piracy and continue to advertise the sites to tourist snorkeling expeditions as such.

Selles Johnson, Smith's grandson, speculated that the ships were hiding in Puerto Vargas, just south of Cahuita. Upon coming around the point, they saw smoke from an English vessel patrolling the area and tried to go around the point to hide before wrecking on the reef (Palmer 1993:28). Whether or not Johnson's story is true, it does correspond to historical events. Local legends surrounding Cahuita and the larger Caribbean coastline clearly reflect a deep relationship with the Golden Age of Pirates. Johnson not only provided historical background for his pirate argument but discussed a wreck at Cahuita Point. As a child, he free-dived on the wreck and found all sorts of objects, besides the large cannon on the seabed (Palmer 1993:19–20).

A Maritime Studies underwater archaeology team from East Carolina University (ECU) gathered further information from 2013 to 2017, focusing on the two shipwrecks and community connections to the ocean (Harris et al. 2015, 2016). In addition to the Afro-Caribbean stories about pirates, there are also tales of slave ships, even further back in time.

Research into the perceptions and memory of the local population reveals a trend toward believing that the two wrecked ships either belonged to pirates or engaged in the slave trade (Table 13.1). Underwater archaeological investigations yielded evidence of two shipwreck sites in question in the Cahuita National Park. The ECU team with local collaborators mapped the sites in detail, in addition to revealing a rich surface scatter of artifacts ranging from the seventeenth to the twentieth centuries extending from the wreck carrying a brick cargo (Brick Site) to the shore in the vicinity of a historic turtle-hunting

Table 13.1. Perceptions of the identity of Cahuita National Park shipwrecks

Tourist Agency	Perceptions	Quotations
Costa Rica Guide	(no thoughts)	"If the corals, lobsters and clams don't hold your attention, there are also two sunken ships to explore. They are well known and in shallow water so the likelihood of treasure is low, but the exposed cannon insinuate they are protecting something secret."
OSA Travel	18th-c. slave ship	"A shipwreck located at the mouth of the Perezoso River was used to transport slaves in the 18th century."
Tierra Verde Adventuras	18th-c. slave ship	"A shipwreck located at the mouth of the Perezoso River was used to transport slaves in the 18th century."
Manuel Antonio Park	18th-c. slave ship	"The remains of the slave ship that sank in the second half of the 18th century comprise the most valuable cultural feature of the park. The shipwreck can be seen at the mouth of the Perezoso River."
Cahuita National Park	18th-c. slave ship	"One common attraction is the shipwreck near the mouth of river Perezoso. The ship used to carry and transport slaves in the 18th century."
Viva Tropical	1700s Spanish galleon	"Within the nearly 600 acres in the national park are two shipwrecks. The premier attraction is the Spanish galleon from the 1700s, a scant six meters below the water's surface."
Costa Rica Tourism	18th-c. slave ship	"The remains of the slave ship that sank in the second half of the 18th century comprise the most valuable cultural feature of the park. The shipwreck can be seen at the mouth of the Perezoso River."
Tripatini.com	18th-c. slave ship (bound for Limón)	"Another attraction outside the reef is a shipwreck from the 18th century—a slave shipbound for Limón that didn't make it. The broken up ship, complete with cannon, now sits conveniently in about 20 feet of water at the mouth of the Perezoso River, covered in crustaceans and other marine life."
Select Costa Rica	18th-c. slave ship	"The remains of the slave ship that sank in the second half of the 18th century comprise the most valuable cultural feature of the park. The shipwreck can be seen at the mouth of the Perezoso River."
Costa Rica Paradise Adventure Tours	French and Spanish pirate ships	"There are two shipwrecks in the bay off the north side of Punta Cahuita that are believed to be Spanish and French pirate wrecks."

(*continued*)

Table 13.1—*Continued*

Tourist Agency	Perceptions	Quotations
Rough Guide	French and Spanish pirate ships	"Two shipwrecks in the bay on the north side of Punta Cahuita are believed to be pirate wrecks, one Spanish and one French."
Sustainable Tourism	Slave or pirate ships	"The wrecks of two ships, possibly slave or pirate ships, are located at the edge of the reef."
Transportation Costa Rica	French and Spanish pirate ships	"There are two shipwrecks in the bay off the north side of Punta Cahuita that are believed to be Spanish and French pirate wrecks."
CRS-Tours	18th-c. Spanish galleon	"The second one is part of Cahuita National Park and shelter, a 242 HA coral reef and an 18th c. Spanish galleon whose guns are now home to corals and fish."
Caribbean Beat	18th-c. Spanish galleon	"Just offshore lies the wreck of a shipwrecked 18th century galleon, a fascinating throwback to the region's more turbulent era of slavery and piracy."
Costa Rica Scuba	1700s Spanish galleon	"The more spectacular shipwreck is a Spanish galleon from the 1700s, only 6 meters below the surface."
YourTravelMap.com	18th-c. shipwreck	"Another attraction at the outside reef is a shipwreck from the 18th century. The wreck is equipped with cannon and 6 meters below the surface."
CentralAmerica.com	(no thoughts)	"Besides the remains of beautiful coral, there are two old shipwrecks about seven meters below the surface, both with visible ballast and cannon; one wreck has two cannon, and the second, a more exposed site, has 13."
Costa Rica Bureau	18th-c. slave ships	"The most interesting feature of the park is a shipwreck located on the north of the mouth of the river Perezoso, which sank in the 18th century and was used to transport slaves."

community (Figure 13.4). Extensive underwater archaeological surveys of the foreshore and reef areas near the Cannon and Anchor Site resulted in the identification of artifacts, large quantities of turtle shell, and cut bamboo likely used for turtle stockades and cabins at the water's edge. These artifacts represent the history and use of Punta Cahuita and community engagement with the wreck over the past three hundred years (Borrelli and Harris 2016; Harris and Richards 2015; Harris et al. 2016).

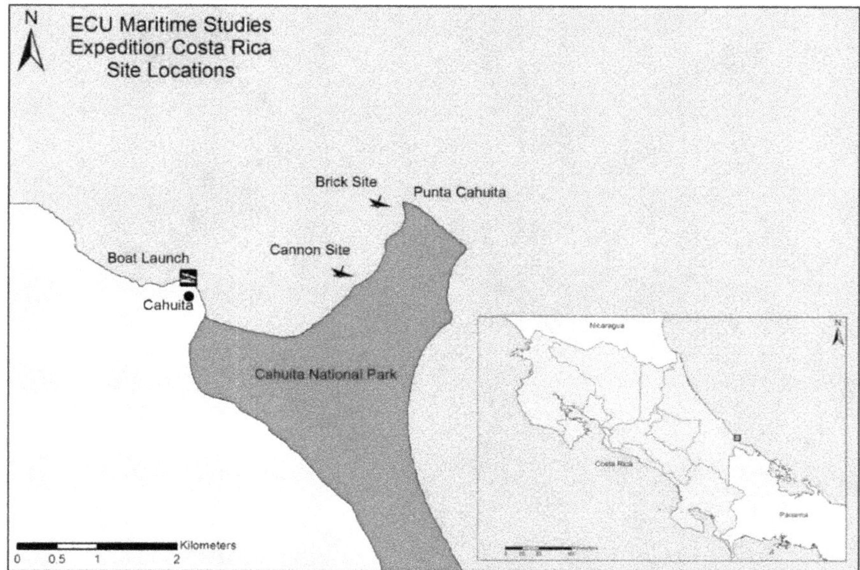

Figure 13.4. Location of the shipwreck sites in Cahuita National Park. (Courtesy of the Program of Maritime Studies, East Carolina University)

Historical and archaeological evidence suggests that these two sites may be the two Danish frigates carrying supercargos of slaves, bricks, and ivory, arriving serendipitously at highly contested Costa Rica coastline in 1710. When the two ships approached land, the crew encountered a heavy storm, forcing an unanticipated landing. Jamaican fishermen piloted the captains to a bay where the ships anchored and were days later destroyed by a mutinous crew (Harris 2020; Harris and Richards 2015).

The unexpected arrival of hundreds of slaves subsequently led to opportunistic captures or assimilation into local protective or exploitive communities. Turtle harpooners and Caribbean buccaneers, like Long Ben and Miskito King Jeremy, served as intermediaries, informants, beneficiaries, and facilitators of strategic action along the slave trade voyage routes and at replenishing island depots. They played an important part in the narrative's historic fabric that deserves further investigations. Turtle harpooning, slave trading, raiding, and buccaneering are intricately intertwined themes along the circum-Caribbean Central American coastline during the eighteenth century.

PIRACY IN
THE INDIAN OCEAN

14

Pirate Lairs in Ambodifototra Bay (Sainte-Marie Island, Madagascar)?

Traces of Fortifications and Camps in Archives and Archaeological Remains

John de Bry and Jean Soulat

The east coast of Madagascar was frequented by Europeans at the beginning the sixteenth century: first the Portuguese, followed by the Dutch, followed by the English and the French. They came initially as traders, but a new category of foreigners had appeared by the end of the seventeenth century: pirates. The zenith of piracy occurred between 1680 and 1720. The eastern coast of Africa served as their primary base of operations. Their main port of refuge was the northeast of Madagascar, in particular the bay of Antongil, Foulpointe, and Sainte-Marie Island (Île de Sainte-Marie).

There they formed a cosmopolitan group with a variety of social backgrounds, including nobles, former sailors of the British and French royal navies, and merchant sailors, but they were primarily English. Their physical presence in these places answered strategic imperatives, as their location made it possible to monitor shipping on their way to or from India. The pirates based in these areas quickly formed a coalition of shared interests with the local Malagasy population, especially the Betsimisaraka, who occupied the shores of the northeast coast of Madagascar and in particular Sainte-Marie Island. The bay of Ambodifototra on Sainte-Marie Island appears in historical sources as a pirate's lair between the 1690s and 1730s. It was the seat of piracy in the Indian Ocean (Figure 14.1).

It should be emphasized that no terrestrial investigation of prehistoric, colonial, or pirate occupations has been carried out on Sainte-Marie Island. However, the area has been the subject of underwater investigations. These

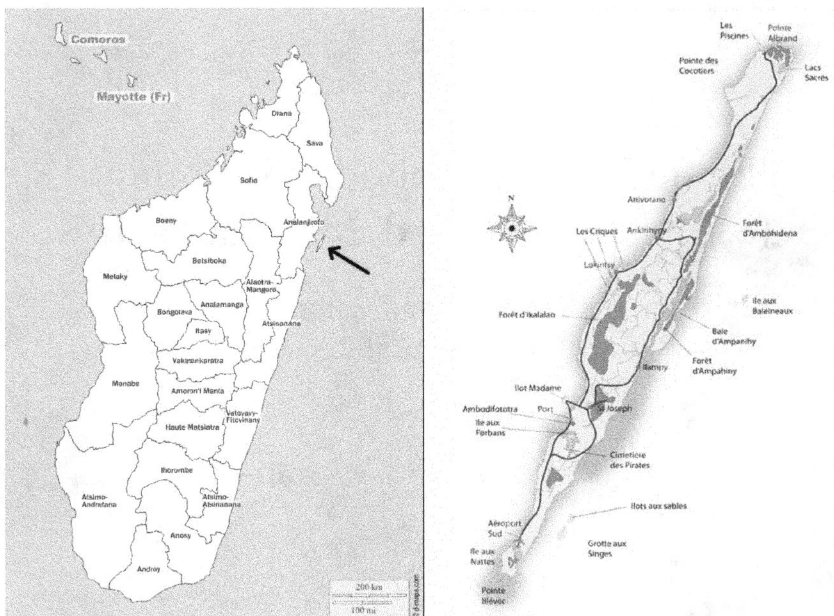

Figure 14.1. Location of Ambodifototra Bay, Sainte-Marie Island, Madagascar.

have revealed the first evidence of the presence of these *forbans* (rascals or scoundrels) through the investigation of their shipwrecks. These vessels seem to have been purposefully scuttled to create a barrier to defend the bay against the navies of France and Britain.

Between 2000 and 2015 a wreck presumed to be the ship of the pirate captain William Condon (alias Christopher Condent), the *Fiery Dragon*, was investigated (de Bry 2006; de Bry and Roling 2016). The ship was allegedly scuttled by the crew in February 1721 in the bay. Two archaeological projects using controversial excavation methods were carried out in 2010 and 2015 in the area. A possible second wreck, probably Asian and dating to the same time, was found atop a portion of the *Fiery Dragon*, but this hypothesis remains to be confirmed. In addition to the wooden structural remains of the supposed wreck of the *Fiery Dragon*, a large number of objects have been recovered. These include more than two thousand fragments of Chinese porcelain, thirteen gold coins of various origins, and other objects of European origin. The assemblage is dated between the end of the seventeenth century and the year 1721, based on an analysis of coins and porcelain.

Another wreck known as the "channel wreck," which may be either the *Mocha Frigate* or *Great Mohammed* (the ship of the pirate Robert Culliford), has also been discovered and only partially excavated. Finally, the *Adventure*

Galley, the ship of pirate William Kidd, was also reportedly found, but no information related to this discovery has been detailed in the available reports. In total, two or even four wrecks might have been discovered by the American team. However, a United Nations Educational, Scientific and Cultural Organization (UNESCO) team led by Michel L'Hour came in 2015 to verify the identification and authentication of these discoveries. The UNESCO report clearly contradicts the identification of these wrecks, but the debate remains open for the *Fiery Dragon*, which could also be another ship recovered by the pirates of Condon. UNESCO nevertheless recommends further research.

No new investigations have been carried out on these sites since 2015. In spite of great interest in the remains discovered, an in-depth multidisciplinary scientific work remains to be undertaken to positively identify these wrecked vessels in order to place them in the historical context of the bay and maritime trade to Asia in the eighteenth century. Obviously, the investigations in this field will have to continue within the framework of an international collaborative archaeological program associating the authorities and Malagasy archaeologists.

The Occupation of the Bay of Ambodifototra by the French Royal Navy and Later by Pirates

In addition to the study of these wrecks, it is important to try to identify the vestiges of the land occupations left by the French colonists and by the pirates. Accounts and plans dated between the second half of the seventeenth century and early eighteenth century clearly show that the bay of Ambodifototra was occupied by the French Royal Navy as early as the 1650s. It was an outpost of Fort Dauphin, which is located on the opposite shore on the large island. The area was occupied by the French from its construction in 1640 until 1674, when the French abandoned all of its installations. Several conflicts took place between the French of Sainte-Marie Island and the Malagasy native peoples, notably in 1656 (Froidevaux 1896:7). With the progressive abandonment of Fort Dauphin by the French, the outpost of Sainte-Marie was deserted by French troops in 1669 (Saint-Yves and Fournier 1898:210–213). It is known that the French built defensive installations on the site, including a fort that they later abandoned. The first pirates began to land on Sainte-Marie Island and particularly in the bay of Ambodifototra in the 1680s. They occupied the area until 1720–1730.

Several dated and undated plans in French present the bay as an attractive area with resources of wood, coral, and water for the supply of passing ships. One plan in particular explains how to set up an elaborate defensive system and shows the plan of a typical fort of the second half of the seventeenth century, similar to the plan of Fort Dauphin, built around 1660. When the French left the area, did they leave behind any installations and facilities? It is difficult to say.

It is known that pirates occupied the area from 1680 to 1690. Whether or not they incorporated the French defensive constructions into their own defensive scheme after they invaded the island, the pirates also set up a system of protection for the bay that included buildings, camps, careening areas, fortified houses, and defensive installations (forts, bastions, batteries, and fortifications). The defensive occupation of the bay would have been developed from 1691 under the impetus of the English pirate Adam Baldridge. The plans and maps found in the archives provide precise information on the location of these installations. Sainte-Marie Island was a strategic stopping point to control ships passing through on the route to India but also to provide supplies. The study of the wreck of the supposed *Fiery Dragon* is therefore part of this phenomenon of settlement and provisioning in the bay.

To date, no archaeological investigation has been carried out on the colonial land remains of the bay in connection with the occupation of the French Royal Navy and then the settlements of these pirates. This innovative approach in the archaeology of piracy could allow a better understanding of their way of life, the exploitation of raw materials, and the method of construction of these settlements. Through archaeology and the study of material culture, it is essential to try to measure the impact of the native populations on the pirate settlements, determine the balance between the two cultures, and perhaps perceive a certain acculturation between the two communities.

Development of a Four-Year Research Program

The international team of Franco-American researchers who lead the Archéologie de la Piraterie des XVIIe–XVIIIe Siècles (Archaeology of Piracy in the 17th and 18th Centuries: ADLP) program (http://archeologiedelapiraterie.fr/en) set up a four-year archaeological project in this area with the aim of recovering the remains linked to the pirate occupation of the island. Based on the evidence unearthed in 2022, the following three years (2023–2025) of archaeological excavation will examine the defensive installations and reexamine the supposed wreck of the *Fiery Dragon*, the wreck best informed by previous operations.

The research design calls first for the targeted zones to be the subject of aerial, pedestrian, and underwater reconnaissance. These will be coupled with digital mapping campaigns: LiDAR (light detection and ranging), UAVs (unmanned aerial vehicles), ROV (remotely operated vehicles), and GIS (geographic information system). Depending on the results obtained, sounding and excavation campaigns will be set up, both on land and underwater. In parallel with the field investigations, general analysis of the collected objects will be conducted, thus linking the new investigations with those carried out between 2000 and 2015. A database will be created to inventory all the artifacts collected. Because of the varied research carried out, the team will be divided into a terrestrial group (study of terrestrial remains), underwater group (study of wrecks), and artifact group (study of artifact assemblages).

Presentation of the Archaeological Mission (2022)

The goal of the four-year project to explore the bay of Ambodifototra and the 2022 mission is to highlight the archaeological remains related to the pirate occupation between the 1680s and 1730s.

The STM 2022 archaeological mission took place between May 9 and 26, 2022. Its first objective was a terrestrial archaeological reconnaissance of Ambodifototra Bay. Lacking authorization, no work was conducted on the wreck of the alleged *Fiery Dragon*.

The first week was devoted to a large aerial survey using a drone equipped with LiDAR in order to identify potential terrestrial remains. Six zones were tested, notably the Aiguade (zone 3), the Île aux Forbans (zone 4), and the Fort de la Possession (zone 6) (Figure 14.2). The data are currently being processed to create an accurate digital map of these archaeological elements. The other two weeks were used to initiate the field survey in the areas tested by the LiDAR. Several surveys and test pits were conducted, notably at the Aiguade (zone 3), on the Île aux Forbans (zone 4), and at the bottom of the ramparts of the Fort de la Possession (zone 6). At the same time, the inventory and prestudy of the museum's collections were carried out with more than 3,500 ceramic/porcelain shards, 120 metal objects, 100 glass remains, and 100 faunal remains.

Franco-Malagasy archaeologists made up the team, accompanied by archaeology students from the universities of Antananarivo and Tamatave. The mission was directed by Jean Soulat (Laboratoire LandArc, Craham—Unité Mixte de Recherche for Centre National de la Recherche Scientifique [CNRS] 6273, University of Caen Normandie), Chantal Radimilahy (Institut de Civilisations Musée d'Art et d'Archéologie [ICMAA]), Bako Nirina Rasoarifetra (ICMAA—International Council of Museums), and professor emeritus Jean-Aimé Rakotoarisoa (ICMAA). The drone equipped with the LiDAR box was directed by Isabelle Le Tellier (Air d'Eco Drone). French field archaeologists

Figure 14.2. Drone flight plan for the LiDAR of two areas of Ambodifototra Bay, Sainte-Marie Island, Madagascar. (Courtesy of Benoit Duverneuil, La Condamine Exploration)

were present to supervise the surveys under the direction of Alexandre Coulaud (Inrap Guyane, Nouvelle-Aquitaine Outre-Mers). In conjunction with the field mission, a team was dedicated to the inventory and study of the artifacts kept at the Reine Bétia Museum on Îlot Madame. Finally, Malagasy students participated in the fieldwork and study phases at the museum and in the training workshops.

The Study of the Defensive Installations of Ambodifototra Bay

A particularly important map of the bay of Ambodifototra was found, preserved at the Bibliothèque Nationale de France (Division 8 of portfolio 217 of the Hydrographic Service of the Navy devoted to Sainte-Marie Island). This undated plan gives an inventory of the land and sea fortifications protecting the bay of Ambodifototra and clearly explains how to most effectively defend it in the event of an attack (Figure 14.3). It also specifies the importance of local resources (wood, water, and coral to make lime). This plan was clearly drawn up by the French Royal Navy, because it uses the military cartographic codifications (color and shape) and its legend is in French. Although undated, it appears to have been drawn made the end of the seventeenth century and the beginning of the eighteenth century, but an earlier date (the second half of the seventeenth century) is possible. The plan obviously predates the 1730s when compared to the plans dated to that period, which present a project for a Vauban fort. This map (47 by 65 cm [500 *toises*]) is titled "Plan du Port Sainte-Marie." The graphic quality of the plan, the coastline, the reliefs, and the detailed legends provide reliable information on the state of the bay during the time in question. The author indicates that his plan is "made from memory, but within a few *toises*, more or less, it represents exactly."

The map shows not only a fort on the hill but many fortifications around the bay, referred to as a "port." It also indicates that a chain to Île aux Cayes (Îlot Madame) to the north blocked the entrance to the bay. The shape of this fort with flanking bastions obviously raises questions because it is typical of the forts built between 1640 and 1650 by the European colonists in the Caribbean (Île de la Tortue, Fort de la Roche) and in the Indian Ocean (Fort Dauphin, Madagascar, and Fort Frederik Hendrik, Mauritius) (Figure 14.4).

The current Fort de la Possession is located on the site of this fort project and presents a primitive form characteristic of these seventeenth-century forts that can be distinguished in particular through to aerial drone shots and LiDAR (Figure 14.5). However, the archives stipulate that the fort was founded by the lieutenant (named Saulnier) of a frigate in 1750.[1] This raises the question of a possibly earlier foundation of this fort during the second half of the seventeenth century, perhaps made of perishable material with a stone foundation. Obviously, a fort of this type during the second half of the seventeenth century and its durability could thus coincide with the presence of pirates from the 1690s onward or even be reoccupied by these forbidding men. In the 1750s, well after the departure of the pirates and in connection with the return of the French Royal Navy and the East India Company to the

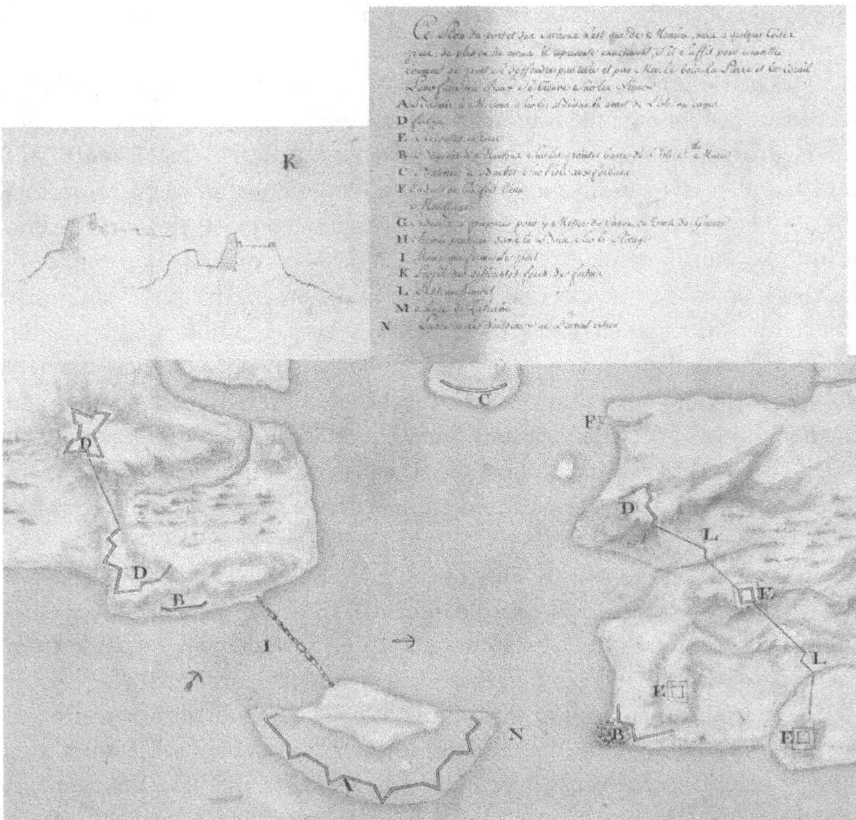

Figure 14.3. Extract from the map of the port of Sainte-Marie Island (anonymous) from the beginning of the eighteenth century (the north is on the left of the map). (Bibliothèque Nationale de France, Paris, GE SH 18 PF 217 DIV 8 P 3 D)

bay, the fort could very well have been rebuilt and developed, with the French archives retaining information only on this new phase of construction.[2]

The French plans of the nineteenth century show the evolution of the occupations of 1819.[3] Only the 1847 plan mentions the fort on the hill, known as Fort de la Possession (commemorating France's possession), while the other plans mention the presence of a "monument, mât de pavillon" (monument, flagpole) or the "Pierre de la Prise de Possession" (Stone of Possession) as early as 1819. The buildings and the present fort were built at this period, possibly on a preexisting fortification, leveled or partially rebuilt.

Îlot Madame, located at the mouth in the Bay of Pirates, has also been inhabited and fortified since the end of the seventeenth century. A 1829 plan mentions two defensive batteries (the island and the mainland).[4] Îlot Ma-

Figure 14.4. Plan of Fort Dauphin drawn by Étienne de Flacourt between 1650 and 1659. (Bibliothèque Nationale de France, Paris, GE DD-2987 [8411])

Figure 14.5. View of the current northeast flanking bastion of Fort de la Possession, Sainte-Marie Island. (Courtesy of Isabelle Le Tellier and Éric Yény)

dame houses buildings of the French prison between 1825 and 1848 (Maillard 2014).

Was there a fortification before 1691 in the bay of Sainte-Marie Island? The French settlement of Fort Dauphin in southern Madagscar,[5] installed on the site of an old Portuguese fort of the sixteenth century, was abandoned around 1674. However, the place was still frequented by many ships, many of which were involved in piracy. At that time, there was a link with Sainte-Marie Island and its outpost, the bay of Antongil, through the slave trade with Île Bourbon (today La Réunion).

Rogozinski (2000:58, 62) provides some clues to the origin of the pirate settlement in the bay of Sainte-Marie. Adam Baldridge, coming from Jamaica, arrived in Madagascar in the 1690s and installed the first fort in 1691, which

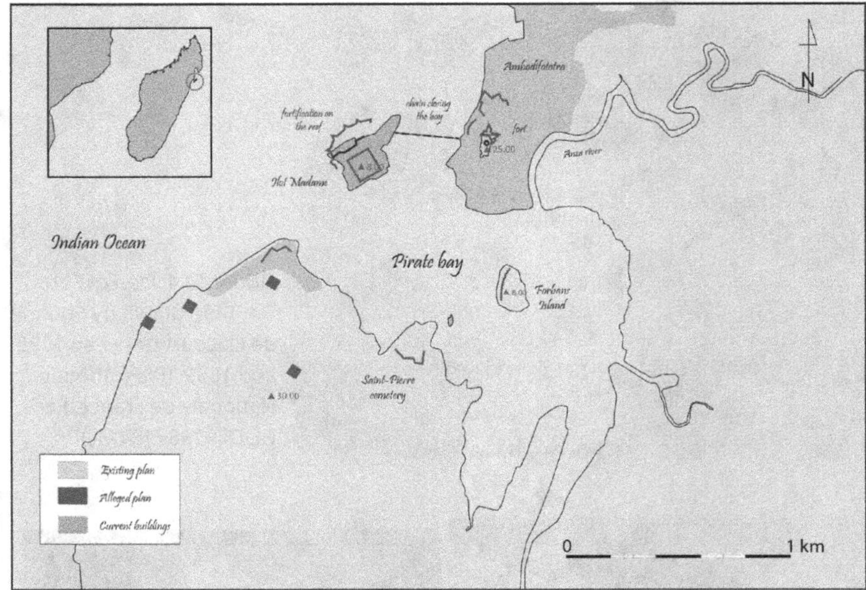

Figure 14.6. Plan of the bay of Sainte-Marie with the supposed late seventeenth-century or eighteenth-century fortifications. (© Nicolas Morelle)

could have housed twenty-two cannon (Collectif 2017:10). He settled in this isolated port of Madagascar in order to make his trade prosper and establish a trading post. Baldridge built his house on the "Isle of Pirates" (Île Madame) and added warehouses and a fortification with six cannon recovered from the *Batchelor's Delight* in 1693. The occupation of Sainte-Marie Island allowed pirates not only to be strategically placed to control ships passing through on coming back from India but also to refuel in abundance and make port calls (Rogozinski 2000:55; Figure 14.6).[6]

When pirates settled and fortified the bay area,[7] probably on the remains of French fortifications, what were their relations with the Malagasy? Do these fortifications testify to a local adaptation or to pure mimicry of Western fortifications, especially if they follow the French model? The defense being essentially turned toward the sea, with a chain barring the bay, suggests that the pirates sought first to protect themselves from attacks coming from the sea, by other pirates or by Western powers. The native Antavaratra populations were in conflict over the control of the trading centers. What was the position of the pirates in relation to local conflicts?[8] Is it necessary to analyze the fortified ensemble of the roadstead only in the global framework of the Indian Ocean or also from a more local perspective? Indeed, John Blacon's deposition in 1698 reports that the fort was used to defend against the native peoples.[9]

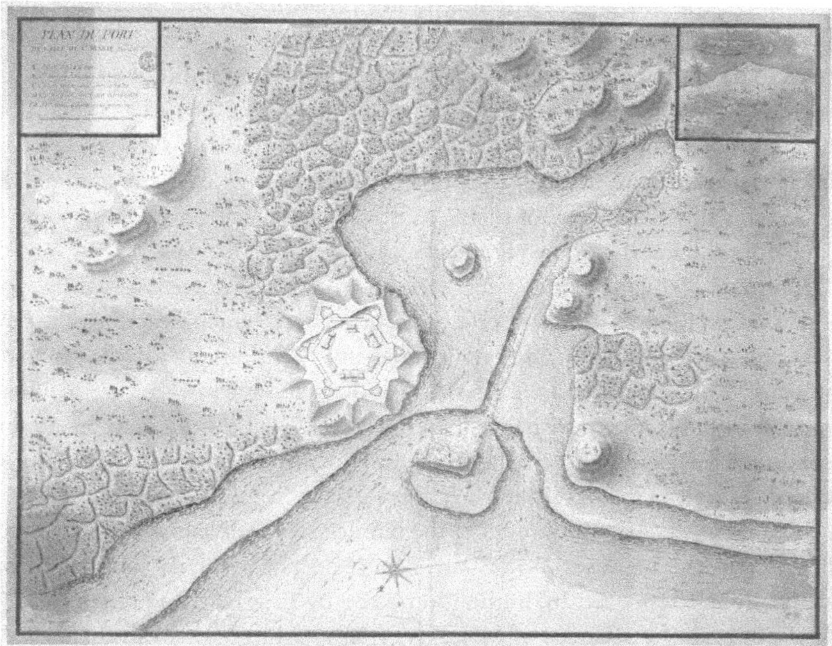

Figure 14.7. Map of the port of Sainte-Marie Island, Madagascar, 1733. (Bibliothèque Nationale de France, Paris, GE SH 18 PF 217 DIV 8 P 2/1)

A construction plan published by the French Royal Navy in 1733 representing a monumental star-shaped fort, worthy of Vauban's great citadels, mentions the desire to create a fortified complex on the hill to the north, controlling the entrance to the Bay of Pirates (Figure 14.7). Compared to the current remains and other sources and plans available, this plan appears fanciful and shows a willingness to promote the representation of the power that controls or seeks to control the island and thus the nearby trade route. Indeed, following the marriage between Reine Bétia and Corporal Jean Onésine Filet (known as "La Bigorne"), Sainte-Marie Island was ceded to France by the treaty of July 30, 1750, and returned to the French East India Company for control of the maritime routes of the Indian Ocean and the Red Sea. The island was already occupied by the French and became a colony around 1820, with the rise of Port-Louis (Blanchard 1872:598). A penal colony was temporarily installed in the Ambodifototra region between 1825 and 1848 (Maillard 2014).

Two other plans probably from the first half of the eighteenth century or even the beginning of the nineteenth century attract our attention. A first plan of the Port of Sainte Marie does not locate the fortifications but indicates where the "forbans carènent" (pirates careen) with the nearby location of two "sunken shipwrecks" just north of Île Madame.[10] A second plan of 1733 seems to be an inventory used for the project plan of the monumental fort, as noted above.[11] It details the relief and the swampy areas as well as the rivers. On these two levels, the area appears virgin: the fortifications do not appear, which casts doubt on the existence of the elements visible on the plan of the figure. Was the occupation of the port of Sainte-Marie provisional or perennial before the middle of the eighteenth century?

The manuscripts provide even more information. We have a manuscript from 1730 written by a former officer, Sieur Robert, which describes the bay of Sainte-Marie in detail. However, it does not mention any fortifications of the place except fortified houses with wooden palisades (were the fortifications of 1691 built of perishable materials?). He reports the facts of piracy near Bourbon Island and the pirates' place of retreat, in the bay of Sainte-Marie,[12] as well as in Fort Dauphin, a former French trading post.

The progressive abandonment of the bay after 1719 explains why the plans of 1730 and the manuscript of Sieur Robert do not precisely indicate these fortifications (destroyed by human hands or by time).[13] The French, under the command of the Count of Maudave, attempted to reestablish themselves at Fort Dauphin in order to make the old trading post a supply base for their Mascarene colonies. It is probably during this period that they planned to create a new fort on the edge of the bay of Sainte-Marie Island. It was not until the nineteenth century that a new fort was erected (or the old one partially taken over), this time on the entire hilltop.

The approach to studying the remains of pirate camps is closely linked to the study of the batteries. Indeed, the remains of camps can be directly associated with the defensive elements of the bay. Written sources inform us about the installation of pirates between the end of the seventeenth and the first third of the eighteenth century. As Sieur Robert's manuscript describes perfectly, "the houses are built on several wooden pillars with direct access by a ladder, while the courtyard is surrounded by a strong palisade made of big stakes and equipped with loopholes in order to install small pieces of cannon," while on "squares on the ground, the scoundrels displayed colored silk banners with their particular mark to get to know them" (Robert 1730:109–111; our translation). It is interesting that this precise description is close to the representation of a fortified house or fort visible on the background of an engraving depicting Henry Avery and his slave published in 1725 in the volumes of Captain Charles Johnson, alias Daniel Defoe (see Figure 13.3). Unfortunately, the archaeological survey carried out in 2022 did not reveal any remains of a camp, which was probably made of perishable material.

Conclusion

The bay of Ambodifototra on Sainte-Marie Island in Madagascar appears in historical sources as a real pirates' den between the 1690s and 1730s, probably the main focus of piracy in the Indian Ocean. However, the area has far from revealed all its secrets. Underwater archaeology has begun to show the first evidence of the presence of these rogues through the remains of ships scuttled with the aim of creating a barrier to forestall the ships of French and British royal navies. In spite of the great interest in the remains discovered thus far, in-depth multidisciplinary work remains to be undertaken to properly identify these wrecks in order to place them in the historical context of the bay.

Apart from these wrecks, the 2022 archaeological project made it possible to focus on the terrestrial remains left by these pirates in connection with work in the archives. The ongoing examination of the plans created through LiDAR and the archaeological study of the ramparts of the Fort de la Possession bring answers on these fortified installations built between the second half of the seventeenth and the beginning of the eighteenth century in connection with the French and pirate presence.

This innovative approach in the archaeology of piracy will provide a better understanding of the illicit lifeways of pirates and their exploitation of raw materials and the mode of construction of their forts, batteries, and camps.

Thanks to archaeology and the study of material culture, it will be possible to measure the impact of the native populations on the pirate presence and the acculturative forces that existed between these two communities.

Acknowledgments

The authors thank Alexandre Coulaud, Nicolas Morelle, Isabelle Le Tellier, and Chantal Radimilahy for their collaboration on this project.

Notes

1 From a 1775 report: "Notes . . . on the Remains of the Buildings Constructed on This Island [Sainte-Marie] from 1750 to 1758 by Saulnier," Archives Nationales d'Outre-Mer, C5A 5, 27 (Versailles, March 19, 1775), ff. 2–3. Many thanks to Alexandre Audard, PhD candidate, Université Paris Cité.

2 Bibliothèque Nationale de France, Plan FM DFC XVII/MEMOIRES/88/3: Manuscript 6, confirms the creation of the trading post by the French Royal Navy in 1751. The Stone of Possession, imported from Réunion Island, was installed at the top of the hill when the present fort was built. The Île Madame was then defended by a garrison of thirty men sheltered behind a double wooden fence. Because of the brutality of the

French commander of the place, the native peoples rebelled and massacred part of the garrison and the commander in that same year. Had the construction of the fortress already been completed?

3 Bibliothèque Nationale de France, Plan FM DFC XVII/28PFB/103. This 1819 plan is finely crafted and gives many details about the coastline and the relief of the bay and its surroundings.

4 Bibliothèque Nationale de France, Plan FM DFC XVII/28PFB/480, 1829.

5 Robert (1730:85–87). Colbert created the East India Company in 1664 in order to insert himself into the great commercial routes of Asia, facing Dutch and British competitors. In 1642 the French, with Jean de Pronis, settled in Fort Dauphin, which bears the following inscription: "Cave ab incolis" (beware of inhabitants!).

6 The bay of Ambodifototra offered an excellent anchorage, naturally well protected. During this period, Madagascar became a destination of choice for English and other European merchants, as slaves were cheaper than on the African continent and the native peoples were attracted by the demand for firearms and other Western goods.

7 Pirates also settled (perhaps occasionally) in the roadsteads of Antongil and Tintingue in Madagascar.

8 Sieur Robert (1730:109) confirms that the *forbans* did marry the daughters of Malagasy dignitaries and sometimes "reign" over two or three villages.

9 Collectif (2017:10), Blacon Deposition (1698): "Those that used the place [Sainte-Marie] had built a little Stockado Fort with twelve Gunns in it, capable to contain One hundred and fifty men about a Gunshot distant from the Waterside, only to defend themselves from the Natives. In that Fort they had Warehouses where they kept their Goods"; Willock's Deposition (1698?): "There at St. Maries lives one Baldridge, an old Pirate who hath sent to him from New England, especially from New Yorke and Rhode Island, severall Consignments of goods, Liquor of all sorts, stores of cordage, & sailcloth of all sorts and Ammunition with Pitch & Tarr wch he sells to the Pirats at great rates. He has built there a great house wich by its situation being on the top of a great hill is as good as a fort. He has some Guns in it, and all the Country people at his Command for the reigne there as a King" (Willock had never seen the place but was reporting on what the pirates had told him). The rule of this Stockado Fort is very important in the configuration of Sainte-Marie Island as a pirate station. It became an important hub for pirate ships and pirate trade. The names of the pirates and their ships' descriptions and activities are recorded in these primary sources.

10 Bibliothèque Nationale de France, GE SH 18 PF 217 DIV 8 P 5 D.

11 Bibliothèque Nationale de France, GE SH 18 PF 217 DIV 8 P 2 and FM DFC XVII/28PFA/2.

12 Robert (1730:101–110) gives many descriptions of Fort Dauphin, a kind of inventory of fixtures for France, with the aim of occupying this trade counter again.

13 Robert (1730:110) reports two acts of piracy in 1721 linked to the activity of the *forbans* of Sainte-Marie.

15

The *Speaker* (1702) Pirate Shipwreck on the East Side of Mauritius

Review of Archaeological Data and Research Perspectives

Jean Soulat, Yann von Arnim, and Patrick Lizé

The *Speaker*, a 500-ton French frigate under the command of pirate captain John Bowen, ran aground on January 7, 1702, off the east coast of Mauritius. Discovered in 1979 by a French expedition led by Jacques Dumas and Patrick Lizé, the shipwreck lay under 5 m of water. No traces of its wooden structure remained (Lizé 1984, 2006; von Arnim et al. 2019). The archaeological survey made it possible to draw up a site plan and revealed a large quantity of artifacts. A second French mission led by Erick Surcouf was undertaken on the site in 1990. Its purpose was to search the shipwreck in its entirety, but a tropical cyclone or hurricane completely devastated the site shortly after it began, canceling the project.

Today the site still contains its thirty-four guns in situ and three anchors spread over nearly 200 m of ocean floor. However, no scientific investigations have been conducted in more than forty years. The *Speaker* was the first pirate shipwreck authenticated through historical and archaeological research. Despite the incomplete nature of the investigations, 1,746 objects have been recovered and are now kept at the National History Museum in Mahébourg, under the ownership of the Mauritius Museums Council (Soulat et al. 2019:247).

The artifacts collected date from the second half of the seventeenth century and are divided into several functional categories: armament, personal effects, ship furniture, navigation, dishware, and exchange. The material culture of the *Speaker* appears singular in two respects: the cultural and geographical mix of artifacts (England, Spain, Italy, Germany, Egypt, Peru, India, and China) and the predominance of armament on board (cannon, cannonballs, grenades, and musket balls). The artifact assemblage in particular makes it possible to suggest that it is indeed a pirate ship, while the archives, the zone of the sinking, and the number of guns make it possible to confirm its identification as *Speaker*.

As part of a research visit to Mauritius in March 2019, we were able to reexamine the artifact collection and prepare a complete analysis. An archaeological mission to the site was carried out in February 2021 to survey the remains and measure the guns and anchors (Soulat and von Arnim 2019). The results are being processed. Other research is planned to detect the presence of pirates at the Dutch Fort Frederik Hendrik in Vieux Grand Port, Mauritius. The site was excavated between 1997 and 2005 by the University of Amsterdam. Its artifacts may provide insights with those found on the *Speaker*.

Overview of Historical Mauritius

Arab navigators first mapped Mauritius in the fifteenth century. It appeared in 1502 on the Italian Alberto Cantino's planisphere, under the Arabic name "Dina Morare." It is unclear whether ships used it as an anchorage. The island was used for the first time around 1510 as a port of call by the Portuguese, who named it Ilda do Cirné (Swan Island), probably because of the presence of the dodo bird. The Dutch admiral Wybrand van Warwyck renamed the island Mauritius in 1598, in honor of Count Maurice (Moritz) of Nassau, Prince of Orange. It was colonized for the first time in 1638 by the Dutch, who were attracted to its vast tracts of ebony forests. They abandoned the island in 1710 after suffering the effects of several cyclones. Five years later, the French settled there and named it Île de France. When the island was captured by the British in 1810, it was renamed Mauritius. It kept that name following its independence in 1968. During the island's Dutch period, the pirate ship *Speaker* was wrecked on the Mauritian coast. The settlers, few in number at the time, were then living near their governor, Roelof Diodati, in Fort Frederik Hendrik, in the Vieux Grand Port on the southeast coast.

John Bowen and the *Speaker*

Captain John Bowen was born around 1660 in Bermuda. Little is known about his life until 1698, when he had the misfortune of being captured near the coast of North Carolina by French buccaneers under the command of

Captain Julien Forget. Bowen served as pilot for the crew on the way to the island of Sainte-Marie in Madagascar. Becoming captain after Forget's death, Bowen met another pirate, George Booth. Together they captured the *Speaker*, a 500-ton French slave frigate under the command of a Captain Eastlake, in the Methelage River in Madagascar on April 16, 1700 (letter in India Office Library 1700, cited in Defoe 2010b [1724]). After several incidents in the Indian Ocean, the *Speaker* was wrecked by a violent cyclone on January 7, 1702, on the Islet of Rocks, on the east side of Mauritius. On board were 170 pirates, 12 English prisoners, and 30 captive Arabs. The pirates were welcomed by the Dutch colony led by Governor Dioodati, in Fort Frederik Hendrik, located at the Vieux Grand Port on the southeast coast of the island. The pirates negotiated with the colonists and bought a ship, the sloop *Vliegendehart*, in order to leave again for Madagascar two months after the shipwreck.

Location of the Wreck of the *Speaker*

The sinking of the *Speaker* occurred on the coral plateau on the east coast of Mauritius about 2.5 km from the Great South East River, 3.4 km from the Four Sisters, and 1.5 km from the Islet of Rocks, formerly called Swarte Klip by the Dutch. The archaeological site is located outside the lagoon just beyond the reef flat, at a depth varying from 1 to 5 m. As a result, the site is constantly swept by a strong swell, which constitutes a serious handicap to any in-depth study.

Positive identification of the ship whose dispersed remains were found was made possible through the study of official documents (Lizé 1984:130, 2006:98). The documentary evidence comes from the legal depositions of some of the *Speaker*'s victims. For example, carpenter Thomas Towsey stated that several ships of different cultural origin had been looted by pirates. These numerous prizes, which appear to be the work of Bowen and his crew, may explain the diversity of the pieces found at the site. Other records provide information about the size of the *Speaker*, an important element in the identification of a ship. These documents clearly indicate that the *Speaker* was a 500-ton French frigate armed with fifty cannon. Partial underwater excavations revealed thirty-five cannon and three anchors of a size appropriate for a 500-ton ship (Figure 15.1). It appears to have been between 20 and 30 m long. Finally, the island council indicates that the *Speaker* sank near the Swarte Klip, in the same area where the wreck was found. All these factors, the absence of any other shipwreck recorded in this area, and especially the archaeological artifacts (including coins dating from before 1702) allow us to posit that the vessel located is indeed the *Speaker*.

Figure 15.1. View of two cannon of the *Speaker*. (Photo by Yves Halbwachs, 2012)

Archaeological Excavations on the *Speaker*

The wreck of the *Speaker* was discovered by fishermen in the early 1970s. The site was then known as the *Trois Canons* (Three Cannon) because of the guns placed together near one of the two farthest anchors on the reef. An archaeological exploration permit was granted by the minister of education

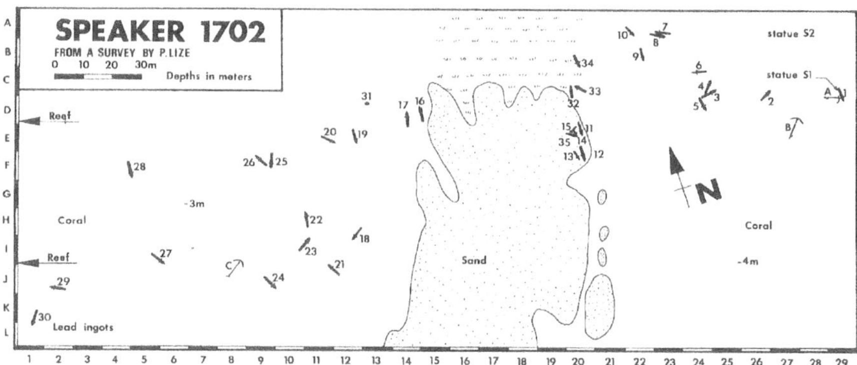

Figure 15.2. Plan of the wreck of the *Speaker* in 1980. (© Patrick Lizé with additions)

and cultural affairs of Mauritius in July 1979 to Jacques Dumas and Patrick Lizé. The main purpose of the first archaeological campaign between September and December 1980 was to inventory the remains of the wreck (ballast, cannon, and anchors) and make a photographic survey in order to draw up a first plan of the wreck. For this, a rudimentary grid was set up with cables and ropes, which made it possible to study the site systematically and to identify thirty-four cannon and three anchors scattered over an area of 300 m by 80 m, approximately 2.5 hectares (Figure 15.2). Although study of the wreck of the *Speaker* has not contributed to knowledge of naval architecture due to the lack of remains of the hull, it did allow the recovery of numerous objects of great diversity, constituting exceptional testimony to piracy in the Indian Ocean at the beginning of the eighteenth century.

A second campaign of archaeological excavations from November 1990 to January 1991 was led by Erick Surcouf and Thierry Proust. This new project planned to continue the excavations of Jacques Dumas, to complete the plan made in 1980, and to complete a report on the *Speaker* and the pirate John Bowen.

The sand basin in the middle of the site was excavated with an air lift. It revealed nothing new. In the end, a very strong swell, caused by the powerful cyclone Bella at the end of January 1991, destroyed the equipment and caused the project to be abandoned. Less than 10 percent of the site had been studied during this work, which recovered only a few additional objects. These two projects were the subject of working notes and a scientific article by Patrick Lizé (1984, republished in 2006). A few books and press articles were published, centering on the life of the famous pirate John Bowen, including a comic strip. Neither a survey report nor an excavation report was ever written, and no in-depth analysis of the collected artifacts was done. The two ar-

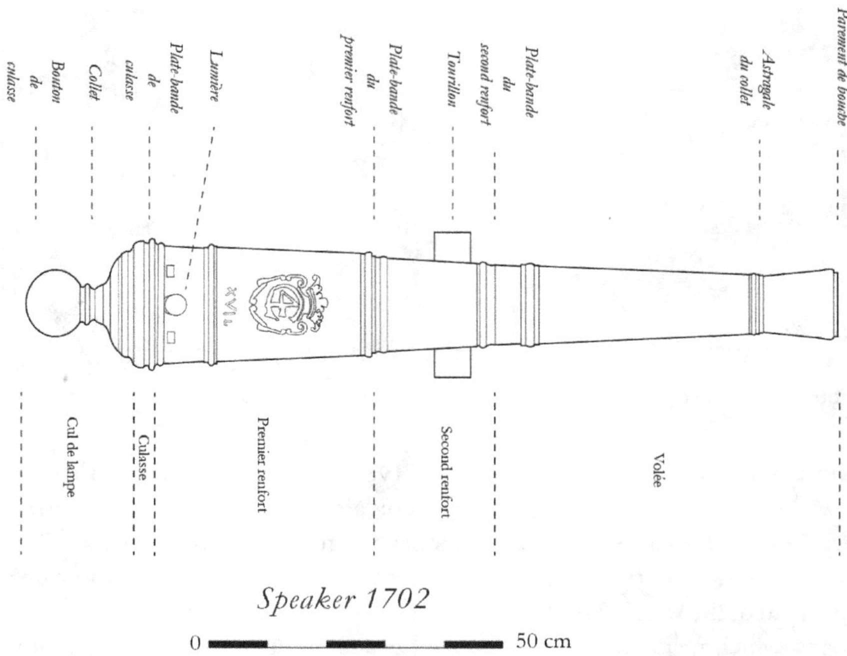

Figure 15.3. The *Speaker*'s bronze cannon, SP-225. (© Alexandre Coulaud)

chaeological campaigns of the *Speaker* wreck have shown that this site, very exposed to swell and storms, is extremely difficult to study.

Because the site is shallow, more or less organized looting of the remains took place between the two excavation campaigns and after 1991. A team of South African divers visited the wreck in 1984 and brought up a bronze cannon, the only one discovered so far. Exported in 1986, this cannon was restored in Cape Town and then resold. It was briefly presented by Lizé (2006:89) and bought by the Mauritius Marine Conservation Society and the Mauritian government and is now part of the collections of the National History Museum in Mahébourg. This 136-kilogram bronze artillery piece is 1.41 m long and appears to be a 4- to 6-pound gun. This cannon is important at several levels because it is identifiable, thanks to the visible cast crest. It is marked with a royal emblem, a crown above a "4" in a "C," which represents the monogram "C4" of Christian IV, king of Norway and Denmark from 1588 to 1648 (Figure 15.3). The king founded the Danish East India Company in 1616, so this cannon probably belonged to a ship of this company captured by Captain John Bowen at the very beginning of the eighteenth century.

Reexamination of the *Speaker*'s Artifacts

The inventory and study of the artifacts carried out in March 2019 at the National History Museum in Mahébourg examined 1,746 objects. They belong to several functional categories: 1,190 armament items (artillery, various ammunition, remains of edged weapons), 63 personal effects (clothing accessories, ornaments, knives, pipes, and so forth), 61 objects of on-board furniture (caulking items, various metal sheets, candlesticks, furniture fittings, remains of a bell, and so forth), and a number of other items, including 7 navigational instruments (compass and portable dial), 98 fragments of glass bottles and flasks, ceramic vessels, and metal caps, 221 beads (which can be categorized both as personal effects and as trade), and 103 objects related to trade and the slave trade (gold and lead ingots, coins, and shackles).

Of the 1,746 objects collected, 1,259 are kept at the Mahébourg National History Museum, the vast majority of which are in storage. Another 147 objects belonging to private collectors were made available for analysis, and 340 objects can no longer be located or were lost due to deterioration. These included cannonballs and cast-iron grenades. The artifacts are made from different materials: 1,378 metal (1,138 lead, 118 iron, 50 copper alloy, 40 silver, 20 gold, and 12 brass), 240 glass, 90 ceramic, 30 stone, and a single item each of bone, hemp, and wood.

The category of weapon-related items contained 1,190 artifacts. Artillery, portable weapons, and ammunition must be distinguished. For artillery, there is a bronze gun that has been reassembled and restored. In the portable armament category we noted a possible wooden remnant from a pistol, a brass saber guard, and a large stone grindstone used as a sharpener for edged weapons. The subcategory of ammunition accounts for 90 percent of the weaponry: 1,072 lead musket balls. Unfortunately, 104 cannonballs and cast-iron grenades were destroyed by corrosion. Not included in the inventory are the 34 cast-iron cannon that remained on the site.

The 63 personal objects are categorized as clothing accessories and elements of adornment or individual utensils such as buttons, brooches and shoe buckles, rings, chain bracelets, a monetiform (money-like) medallion associated with its chain, remains of clay pipes, pins, 2 padlocks, and knives.

The furniture found on board consisted of 61 objects: elements of lead caulking, various lead repair sheets, a fragment of a candlestick leg made of a lead-bearing copper alloy, furniture fittings, 4 small remains belonging to a bell, a fragment of an iron hammer, and remains of rope, in addition to the 3 large iron anchors still on the site. A finely engraved portable brass sundial and 9 brass compasses constitute the 10 navigational instruments.

Figure 15.4. Gold and silver objects from the *Speaker*. (© Jean Soulat)

The galley crockery is represented by 98 artifacts: a copper-alloy spoon, 49 sherds of various ceramics, 22 sherds of Chinese porcelain, 24 fragments of onion bottles and gin bottles in green translucent glass, and 2 glass stoppers. The 221 beads that can be associated with personal effects as well as trade are made of glass or agate with little variety of types.

Finally, 99 artifacts are related to trade, including 34 gold, silver, and copper-alloy coins from about 10 localities, 4 small gold ingots, 42 small and large lead ingots, 17 copper-alloy shackles, and 2 bronze statuettes of divinities from south India (Figure 15.4).

In all, 34 coins were discovered: 8 gold coins, 22 silver coins, and 4 copper-alloy coins. Of these, 23 came from Europe and its colonies, while 11 came from the East (Lizé 2006:96–98; Table 15.1). European coins include 3 Venetian gold ducats minted between 1618 and 1694 (SP-021, SP-022, and SP-165), 12 silver four-(#)and eight-*real* coins minted in Mexico and Peru (SP-087–SP094, SP-274–SP-277), a silver *demi-écu* "*aux palmes*" of Louis XIV minted between 1693 and 1699 (SP-013), 2 silver *leeuwendaalder*, one of which was minted in 1602 in Dordrecht, the Netherlands (SP-112 and SP-113), a silver thaler minted in 1695 in Kremnica, Slovakia (SP-004), 2 English copper-alloy coins: a farthing and a halfpenny from the 1670s (SP-144 and SP-145), and 2 unidentified copper-alloy coin blanks (SP-150–a and b). Among the coins

Table 15.1. Identification of the *Speaker*'s coins

	Europe and its empires	The East
Gold	Venice	Ottoman Empire
	1 ducat Ant. Priuli (1618–1623) [SP-021]	5 dinars (Cairo, Egypt, 1617–1687) [SP-017 to SP0-20, 288]
	1 ducat Al. Contarini (1676–1684) [SP-165]	
	1 ducat Fr. Morosini (1688–1694) [SP-022]	
Silver	Spain	Ottoman Empire
	12 coins of 4 and 8 *reales* (Mexico and Peru) [SP-087 to SP-094 and SP-274 to 277]	2 dirhams (1687–1691, Cairo) [SP-103 and SP-104]
	France	Yemen
	1 *demi-écu "aux palmes"* (1693–1699) [SP-013]	2 dirhams (1697, Al-Khadra) [SP-101 and SP-102]
		1 dirham (1687–1718, Al-Khadra) [SP-105]
	United Provinces of the Netherlands	India
	2 *leeuwendaalder* (one minted in 1602, Dordrecht) [SP-112 and SP-113]	1 Nayak coin (16th–17th century, Tirunelveli?) [SP-106]
	Germany	
	1 thaler (1695, Kremnica) [SP-004]	
Copper alloy	England	
	1 farthing and 1 halfpenny (1670s) [SP-144 and SP-145]	
	Indeterminate	
	2 blank coins [SP-150a and b]	

Copyright J. Jambu.

of the East are 5 Egyptian gold dinars minted in Cairo between 1617 and 1687 (SP-017–SP-20, SP-288), 2 silver dirhams minted in Cairo between 1687 and 1691 (SP-103 and SP-104), 2 silver dirhams minted in Al-Khadra in 1697 (SP-101 and SP-102), another minted in Al-Khadra between 1687 and 1718 (SP-105), and a small Indian silver coin of the Nayaks minted in Tirunelveli (?) in the sixteenth to seventeenth centuries (SP-106). The *Speaker*'s coin assemblage bears many similarities to the assemblage from the wreck of the supposed *Fiery Dragon*, a pirate ship sunk in 1721 in the bay of Ambodifototra, Sainte-Marie Island (Madagascar) (de Bry and Roling 2011). Note that both lots offer coins from the Ottoman Empire but also Venetian gold ducats: 3 on the *Speaker* and 5 on the *Fiery Dragon*.

After detailed analysis, the material culture of the *Speaker* appears typical of the second half of the seventeenth century (Soulat et al. 2019). The objects found on the wreck in particular indicate that it was indeed a pirate ship, while the archives, the area of the wreck, and the number of cannon reveal its identity.

One of the criteria suggesting a connection with piracy is the geographical mix of the artifacts. This combines a strong British influence in connection with the English crew. Objects from Europe (Italy, France, Germany, Austria, Holland, Spain), the Ottoman Empire, India, and China are witnesses to the many prizes taken by Captain John Bowen before the shipwreck. In addition to the 34 coins (23 from Europe and 11 from the East), the crockery bears witness to the prizes and multiculturalism, including a British brass spoon, remains of a British glass bottle and flask (onion-shaped or quadrangular) for alcohol, the remains of Asian storage vases from South China (probably Fujian), sherds of Chinese blue-on-white export porcelain from the city of Jingdezhen (Ching-te Chen), in the province of Jiangxi (southeastern China) in the Kangxi period (1661–1722; Figure 15.5), and fragments of Rhenish stoneware jugs.

The second criterion that can be highlighted is the large quantity of weapons on board, in particular the size of the ammunition (cannonballs, grenades, and musket balls), which clearly indicates that this ship was ready to engage in combat. It is interesting to note that the *Speaker* was not taken by the pirates until April 16, 1700, two years before it ran aground off Mauritius. Thus, the assemblage of objects probably comes from an accumulation of several prizes taken by Bowen's crew between 1700 and 1702.

Research Perspectives

After this reexamination of the artifacts, a team of diving archaeologists under the direction of Jean Soulat and Yann von Arnim returned to the wreck site in December 2020 and January 2021 (Soulat and von Arnim 2019). The aim of this mission was to produce a digital map of the wreck's remains (guns and anchors) using a photogrammetric plan drawn by an ROV (remotely operated vehicle). The plan was also to create a baseline report on the condition of the remains and to produce an inventory and measurements. The results of the 2021 mission are currently being analyzed and are not included here. This work is part of a larger systemic undertaking created in 2019 by Jean Soulat and John de Bry called Archaeology of Piracy Focusing on the Study of Seventeenth- to Eighteenth-Century Pirate Archaeological Sites.

Figure 15.5. Fragment of a Chinese porcelain bowl from the *Speaker*. (© Jean Soulat)

The January 2021 mission experienced calm weather at the wreck site. Yann von Arnim carried out several dives and was able to measure 14 cannon and an anchor located in the eastern part of the wreck site, east of the sandbank that divides the wreck site in half. All the guns were made of iron and measured between 1.8 and 3 m long, giving a first glimpse of the size of the ordnance on board the *Speaker* when it sank on January 7, 1702. Measurement of the cannon located to the west remains a task for a future project.

The heavy swell in the area has so far prevented a large-scale excavation to gather more information in addition to the 1980 and 1990 projects, including the examination of the seabed in search of remains of the ship's wooden structures or additional artifacts.

Nevertheless, new research is planned, but this time on land. Indeed, we know from the archives that the *Speaker*'s pirates visited Fort Frederik Hendrik (Vieux Grand Port) in 1702. This fort was the subject of several archaeological excavation campaigns between 1997 and 2005 by the University of Amsterdam (Floore and Schrire 1997; Floore and Jayasena 2010). A few objects in the archaeological collection present good comparisons with the *Speaker*'s objects, especially faceted agate beads, while the objects have various origins. These artifacts, reposited partly in the Fort Frederik Hendrik Museum and largely in the reserves of the National History Museum in Mahébourg, could be reexamined in order to compare them with the *Speaker*'s objects and perhaps bear witness to the presence of the Bowen pirates. Historically, it is known that the wreck and the fort were linked through the presence of these pirates. It would be enlightening to be able to confirm this link through the archaeological record.

PARTING SHOT

16

Unpacking the Dead Man's Chest

Russell K. Skowronek

More than thirty years ago, the fictional archaeologist Dr. Henry (a.k.a. Indiana) Jones Jr. admonished his students in the film *Indiana Jones and the Last Crusade* (1989) not to accept mythology at face value or expect to find a map with an "X" marking the location of buried treasure. He went on to note that the majority of archaeology takes place in the library. The audience later learned that careful library research did indeed lead to an "X" (the roman numeral for 10), marking the spot where material evidence would transform the mythology associated with the location of the cup used by Jesus at the Last Supper to fact. While this was a fictional tale, Dr. Jones's friendly warning resonates in this book and its companions in this series.

Nearly two decades ago, we called the first book *X Marks the Spot*, a phrase popularly associated with pirates and treasure maps and by then with the character Indiana Jones. The general public, when not equating archaeology with paleontology, often envisions archaeologists hunting for treasure. Of course, archaeologists do find a kind of treasure in that the artifacts contain ephemeral evidence of past lives and societies that gains value when juxtaposed against the totality of the archaeological record. When considered in this light, the fictional archaeologist Indiana Jones was partially correct. In many ways, *X Marks the Spot* did lead to a treasure trove of knowledge about the shadowy world of illicit behavior. As we saw then and see again in this volume, much of that treasure was found in the library. Two decades ago, the idea of exploring the possibility of an archaeology of piracy seemed like a nonsensical fantasy, a mythology tied to popular literature and media and usually associated with treasure hunters like Rick and Marty Lagina of *The Curse of Oak Island* and *not* with academic archaeologists. We hope that this third book will help make such bromides recede from scholarly inquiry.

When Charles Ewen and I sought to identify the factual and not the mythological story of piracy, we recognized that archaeologists extrapolate from normative behaviors and their associated expressions in material culture. Piracy and smuggling were uncharted waters for archaeologists. This required us (and our colleagues) to step outside the realm of popular culture, history, and anthropology to do library work in allied fields, such as economics and sociology. Through meticulous fieldwork, questions arising from these perspectives have produced growing material evidence for illicit behavior. In the third decade of the twenty-first century—almost three hundred years after the end of the so-called Golden Age of Piracy—a growing number of books, journal articles, and popular publications and webpages on piracy in the archaeological record are being penned by American, Australian, Brazilian, English, French, Irish, and Mauritian scholars. Topics have included pirate ships, life, and lairs and their representation in popular culture. But are we closer to a recognizable "pirate pattern" in the absence of documentary evidence? The short answer is "yes" in outline, but there is still much to explore and disentangle until the pattern comes clearly into focus.

Privateers, Pirates, and Smugglers

While praising how the archaeological, ethnographic, documentary, and oral records provide complementary and nonexclusive data for examining the past (Skowronek 2016), I provided an overview of how an archaeology of piracy was multidimensional and should be approached not only through the lens of anthropology and history but from the perspective of other social sciences like economics and sociology. Social disorganization theory provides just this sort of approach. In this approach crime and delinquency flow from interrelated phenomena, including economic status, ethnic diversity, family disruption, residential instability, proximity to urban areas, and population density. When applied to seafaring communities, whether in the Golden Age or in post–Cold War Somalia, we see groups of individuals once well-compensated as privateers or "cold warriors" supported by North Atlantic Treaty Organization (NATO) or the Warsaw Pact nations "beached" without family, far from home, and impoverished. Many who became pirates began their sea careers in legitimate employment, but changing circumstances compelled them to turn to piracy. Simply put, piracy tends to thrive during times of weak rule and in isolated places (Kelleher 2020:3–6). Meanwhile, nearby ports and shipping lanes encourage banditry and other illicit activities such as smuggling as a means of survival.

Wild (Chapter 9 in this book) coined the term "pirateers," noting that for mariners the "distinction between 'pirates' and 'privateers' was usually blurred." They were at times legitimately sailing under a letter of marque for a sovereign nation and sometimes turned to illicit activities for survival. In his discussion of Tortuga Island off the north coast of Hispaniola (Chapter 11) Pavlidis points out that fortifications were expensive to build, staff, and maintain. They were crucial, however, for the protection of imperial claims. In times of "peace," these defensive nodes passed to other caretakers to use for illicit purposes until some nation or power had a renewed need for their use. When there was "no peace beyond the line" (Mattingly 1963), those who engaged in larceny and related activities against sometime enemies were the epitome of a pirateer. This provided plausible deniability, giving cover to nation-states that might support pirates and piracy with a nod and a wink but could never outwardly sanction such activities.

Smuggling is another undocumented illicit activity that can be difficult to recognize in the archaeological record. A century ago, "bootleggers" brought alcohol into the United States by trucks and cars from Canada over frozen Lake St. Clair to Detroit (David Brewer, personal communication, 1983; Haddad 2019). Other "rum runners" ran boatloads of alcohol from Cuba, Bermuda, and the Bahamas to Miami, Savannah, and Charleston. *Tequileros* led mule trains from Mexico across the Rio Grande into deep south Texas, where they met waiting trucks to carry tequila and other alcohol to San Antonio, Corpus Christi, and points north (Hennessy-Fiske 2018). After the Cuban revolution, Cuban cigars were coveted by many in the 1960s, though illegal to possess. Today drugs, art, and other products move clandestinely by sea or overland carried by human "mules."

It is clear that commodities may shift from legal to illicit and back again. What that means is that smuggling may be most visible at synchronic transshipment sites. As communities are diachronically occupied, the presence of material objects might at some moments represent contraband but at other times represent simple legitimate trade. Evidence of smuggling in the archaeological record has received some scholarly attention (for example, Deagan 2016; Ewen and Skowronek 2006; Skowronek 1992), although its relative significance or insignificance in colonial society is debatable. It is evident, however, that with excellent temporal control the presence or absence of certain material items can be revelatory in terms of meaning (Skowronek 2021).

Pirate Ships

Two pirate vessels—the *Whydah* (C. Hamilton 2006) and *Speaker* (Chapter 15; Lizé 2006)—were identified in the twentieth century. The opening decades of the twenty-first century added more pirate-associated shipwreck sites to the list, including the *Queen Anne's Revenge* (Wilde-Ramsing 2006; Wilde-Ramsing and Carnes-McNaughton 2018; Wilde-Ramsing and Ewen 2012;), *Quedagh Merchant* (Hanselmann and Beeker 2016), *Fiery Dragon* (Chapter 14; de Bry 2006; de Bry and Roling 2016), *Ranger* (Gulseth 2016), *La Louise* (Chapter 12), and the Morgan's Island Wreck in Bermuda (Chapter 8). All these sites have appeared in the three volumes of this series. In addition to these and other publications, *Queen Anne's Revenge* and *Quedagh Merchant* have received book-length treatments (Wilde-Ramsing and Carnes-McNaughton 2018; Hanselmann 2019). Based on archaeological evidence corroborated in the documentary record, including the testimony of individuals who were the victims or members of the vessels' crews, these studies have all have made good cases for the identities of the wrecks. The *Fiery Dragon* on Sainte-Marie Island and the Morgan's Island Wreck in Bermuda are still being scrutinized, but researchers are narrowing the possibilities. Nonetheless, these sites have provided a picture of a "normal" pirate ship in the Golden Age.

Pirate ships share several traits: the preferred vessel was shallow drafted, fast, and heavily armed. This gave pirates the ability to overtake and intimidate prey but also outrun naval vessels seeking to intercept and capture them. Simply put, they were the getaway car for pirates. Those identified to date carried twenty to forty guns. In terms of armament, these were the equivalent of a sixth-rate British warship. *La Louise*, lost in 1718 off Brazil, was a twenty-gun frigate with 160 crew members. *Ranger*, lost in Jamaica in 1722, mounted only twenty-four guns. *Quedagh Merchant*, lying in the waters of the Dominican Republic, was armed with thirty guns in 1701. *Whydah*, which sank off Cape Cod in 1717, was a thirty-gun vessel with a complement of 200 men. *Speaker*, lost on Mauritius in 1702, boasted a crew of 170 men and forty guns (Soulat and von Arnim 2022:34, 36–40). *Queen Anne's Revenge* carried forty guns when lost in 1718 at Top Sail inlet (now Beaufort inlet) in North Carolina. *Fiery Dragon* was also said to be armed with forty guns when it was scuttled in 1721 at Sainte-Marie Island in Madagascar.

Guns on these vessels varied in caliber but tended to be small. Six- and four-pound and smaller cannon of iron or brass were common. Some have been identified as being of English, French, or Swedish origin. Round shot and antipersonnel langrage are common. In addition to guns, small arms including muskets and pistols, cutlasses, and grenades are associated with these sites. What is significant is not that these sorts of artifacts were present but rather that they reflect a spectrum of weapons associated with small-scale hand-to-hand fighting. Warships would have carried the same sorts of weapons but also bar and chain shot to cripple vessels and muskets and bayonets for complements of marines (for example, Skowronek and Fischer 2009). Slave ships like the *Whydah* and *La Concorde* (a.k.a. *Queen Anne's Revenge*) needed to protect themselves from attack from within by their human cargo as well as from the sea. Merchant ships carried few guns and smaller crews, as more of them would have cut into profit margins by limiting cargo space and wages (Cragg and Thomin, Chapter 3). Hence, in the absence of national markings (such as a Broad Arrow or guns with royal ciphers: Skowronek and Fischer 2009), identifying pirate ships without a documentary record can be problematic.

Pirate Life

A lengthy description from Chapter 4 of *Treasure Island* (Stevenson 1883: 33–34) was the catalyst for the ongoing investigation of what it means to be a pirate:

> It was like any other seaman's chest on the outside, the initial "B" burned on the top of it with a hot iron, and the corners somewhat smashed and broken as by long, rough usage. . . .
>
> A strong smell of tobacco and tar rose from the interior, but nothing was to be seen on the top except a suit of very good clothes, carefully brushed and folded. They had never been worn, my mother said. Under that, the miscellany began—a quadrant, a tin canikin, several sticks of tobacco, two brace of very handsome pistols, a piece of bar silver, an old Spanish watch and some other trinkets of little value and mostly of foreign make, a pair of compasses mounted with brass, and five or six curious West Indian shells. . . .
>
> . . . Underneath there was an old boat-cloak, whitened with sea-salt on many a harbour-bar . . . the last things in the chest, a bundle tied up in oilcloth, and looking like papers, and a canvas bag that gave forth, at a touch, the jingle of gold.
>
> . . . the coins were of all countries and sizes—doubloons, and louis d'ors, and guineas, and pieces of eight.

Those who served in the navy, in the coast guard, and on merchant vessels (or grew up in such households or reading "sea" novels) are well aware of "working" versus "going ashore" rig. Closets and surplus stores are filled with almost-new dress uniforms. Work clothes were worn until worn out. For example, my father's leather flight jacket from World War II has three sets of new cuffs knitted by my mother in the decades following the war. Beyond "like-new" uniforms, other mementos tucked away in his sea chest included the brass from a three-inch shell cut down to make an ashtray, a solitary dollar bill marked "HAWAII," a Zippo lighter, and a scrapbook of photographs, drawings, and mimeographs from the Aleutian Islands.

The chest of Billy Bones (a.k.a. the Captain) in *Treasure Island* contains a similar mix of personal treasures and keepsakes from his journeys: "a suit of very good clothes, carefully brushed and folded. They had never been worn," a navigator's compass and other objects "of foreign make," and a small purse of silver and gold coins minted in many locations. Jim's mother, Sarah Hawkins, the owner of the Admiral Benbow Inn, recognized the coins and their intrinsic value, saying she would only take what was owed to her.

Our takeaway from the fictional account and the first-person observation (ethnoarchaeology, if you will) is that personal space is a limited and precious commodity at sea. What is found is usually generic and mundane or a keepsake of a special place or incident. While Kinkor (2016) suggests that certain iconography might be indicative of some who became pirates, Soulat and de Bry (2019:89) conclude that there is no pirate material culture: only "object[s] of everyday life used by pirates in particular contexts."

Kenyon (Chapter 2) notes that artifacts found on a wreck can connect that vessel to historic ships. For example, the case has been made since 2006 (for example, Wilde-Ramsing 2006) that the Beaufort inlet wreck was the *Queen Anne's Revenge*, formerly *La Concorde*, a French-owned slave ship. The discovery of a bird-shaped copper-alloy scale weight for gold dust may be associated with the Akan peoples of West Africa. But, as Kenyon notes, once the ship was taken by Blackbeard, the presence of items from the capture of other vessels means that "the interpretation of artifacts, how they came to be on board, and who used them becomes muddied."

Finally, there is the issue of specie. *Treasure Island* (Stevenson 1883:50) once again provides insights. The Captain's papers contain an account book of which ships were taken, what was taken, and their respective value and a table for reducing French, English, and Spanish moneys to a common value. Later, in Ben Gunn's cave, the treasure contained a

> diversity of coinage, but so much larger and so much more varied that I think I never had more pleasure than in sorting them. English, French, Spanish, Portuguese, Georges, and Louises, doubloons and double guineas and moidores and sequins, the pictures of all the kings of Eu-

> rope for the last hundred years, strange Oriental pieces stamped with what looked like wisps of string or bits of spider's web, round pieces and square pieces, and pieces bored through the middle, as if to wear them round your neck—nearly every variety of money in the world must, I think, have found a place in that collection. (Stevenson 1883:286)

We need to remember that into the 1850s Spanish *reales* were legal tender in the United States. Whose picture was struck into the coin was not what mattered: it was the bullion itself (Skowronek 2006:295). International commerce was based on precious metals, not promissory notes. Newsfeeds in April 2021 reported the discovery in a Rhode Island orchard of a Yemeni coin called a *khamsiyat*, minted in 1693 (Davis-Marks 2021). The discoverer, Jim Bailey, suggested that it might have been taken from the *Ganj-i-Sawai* by pirate Henry Every (or Avery) in 1695 (Smith 2021). What is overlooked by those seeking "pirates" is that English and Spanish coins were also found. Having lived on the borders of Canada and Mexico, I have commonly received these base-metal foreign coins in change. Because the intrinsic value exceeded the "face" value of the coin, the United States and other nations ceased minting gold, silver, and copper coins for circulation. Simply put, mixtures of coins do not a pirate make.

Lairs

If "pirate archaeology" has had any success, it has been in the realm of revealing how the landscape is a dynamic participant or contributor to past behavior. Thus, landscape archaeology considers how people constructed and used their surroundings. This approach considers both terrestrial and marine environments. Prevailing winds and currents, proximity to sea-lanes, sightlines both landward and seaward, and resources such as food and potable water are all important aspects of this research. Kelleher (2020:18–19, 284) notes that pirate landscapes go far beyond vessels, including alehouses, ports, safe houses, careening areas, marketplaces, and transshipment locales. Cragg and Thomin (Chapter 3) provide an 1822 report on a pirate landing site in Cuba "near a cart road that led to the mountains." Hidden out of sight was a schooner and a small settlement. The goal was not to be caught and to be able to move captured cargos to marketplaces. Exnicios (2006) reports that a site on Grande Terre Island on Barataria Bay in Louisiana has yielded evidence of Jean Lafitte's establishment, where illicit cargos were lightered into a bateau for transport into New Orleans. This is an excellent example of a transshipment locale.

Kelleher (2020:3) draws on the work of historian Eric J. Hobsbawm (1985), who notes that banditry flourishes among the poorer aspects of society, who live on the margins beyond ordinary social norms. Kelleher (2020:6) points out that piracy flourishes in isolated places during times of weak rule. Ireland's Golden Age of Piracy was at the end of the sixteenth century and beginning of the seventeenth century. Kelleher (2016:179) investigated the "invisible," using cartographic sources and field reconnaissance. She was able to identify places where clandestine operations could occur in a controlled and deliberate manner: locations in Munster with access to both land and sea, including steps, places to moor and unload, and niches for navigational aids to help in the navigation of these vessels.

Boyle (Chapter 7) complements the work of Kelleher. Lundy Island in the Bristol Channel was the focus of illicit activities for five centuries (about 1230–1750). While he wrestles with identifying "pirate material culture," others have noticed that the objects are not inherently pirate-related. The island's use as a settlement for pirates resulted in fortifications not unlike those of Tortuga Island (Pavlidis, Chapter 11) and places like Benson's Cave for hiding human and material cargos.

Illicit activities in the Americas flourished in isolated places far from state-sanctioned communities. Donny Hamilton (2006:26) argues that illicit activities in Port Royal, Jamaica, would be invisible in the archaeological record of this thriving port town if not for the documentary record. But the marginal areas are different.

Several scholars (Finamore 2006; McBride 2006; Harris, Chapter 13) have focused on the Bay of Honduras and Roatán, where logwood harvesting, fishing, turtle harpooning, and ship-wrecking and salvage operations were supplemented with raids on the Spanish mainland colonies or passing vessels to capture African slaves for sale in British colonies. Finamore (2006: 71–72) describes these settlements as being temporary in nature, with wood and thatch construction.

Wild (Chapter 9) and Coulaud et al. (Chapter 10) provide similar observations for the Virgin Islands and St. Martin. Wild notes that sites in the Virgin Islands associated with pirates are

> strategically placed: tucked away in small bays that could hide a ship, located at the base of steep cliffs or on steep coastal hilltops with little crop land . . . in inhospitable locations, good only for maritime purposes.
>
> Other sites are located at maritime choke points that allow observation of shipping traffic where it is busiest and restricted between islands. Such sites also offered the element of surprise in an attack.

Coulaud et al. (Chapter 10) make almost the same observations about the Grand Case Bay site on St. Martin. The site was protected from eastern trade winds and was largely invisible from the sea. They note that it offered a privileged shelter and watering port for ships, where repairs could be made. The site yielded evidence of temporary structures of wood and the manufacture of lime, which was used as a substitute for pitch or tar.

Victor (Chapter 6) situates piracy in seventeenth-century Maine through the comparison of two tavern sites in fishing settlements: one at Pemaquid and the other on Smuttynose Island in the Isles of Shoals. Pemaquid had been the victim of pirate attack, while Smuttynose Island was a "motley, shifting community of fishermen . . . sailors, smugglers, and picaroons" who were known to be friendly toward pirates (Jenness 1875:122–123). Through a detailed analysis of their respective ceramic assemblages, Victor finds that the Smuttynose Island tavern contained a far wider variety of ceramic types and places of manufacture, marking interactions with a broader range of trade routes traversed by more "worldly" sailors.

Recognizing Lairs in Oral History

We will never know the identity or whereabouts of successful pirates and smugglers. They were protected by the physical location of their lairs and sometimes by the surrounding community. In the preface to *X Marks the Spot* (Skowronek and Ewen 2006) we cite MacNeill's (1958:61) interviews with people living on the Outer Banks of North Carolina, where stories about William Teach (Blackbeard) were still told: "He was a respectable pirate and a good neighbor when he was around the community." Blackbeard's killer, Lieutenant Robert Maynard, was thought to have fled the area because he feared reprisals at the hands of the community. It was said that Blackbeard kept a nice home in Bath. In light of the short duration of his residence in the area, what would we expect to find in such a home relative to the homes of his neighbors?

While working on the golf course of the US Marine Corps Recruit Depot on Parris Island at the site of Santa Elena, the capital of La Florida from 1566 to 1587, I accompanied Stanley South to Daufuskie Island. In those days Daufuskie was only accessible by private boat. It was a Gullah-speaking community without any amenities.

We were greeted by a resident, Shorty Brown, who walked us around the small community of clapboard structures. Stanley noticed a house peeking out of the dense foliage and asked why it was overgrown and to whom it belonged (Figure 16.1). Without naming names, Shorty said the owner had asked the

Figure 16.1. Overgrown exterior of a clapboard rum-runner's house, Daufuskie Island, South Carolina, 1984. (Photo by author)

community to watch his home while he was gone. With some trepidation, he allowed us to peer through the windows into the house. Inside one room was a partially collapsed iron bedstead with a straw-filled mattress, pillows, sheets, and blankets (Figure 16.2). Hanging from the top of a closet door was a suit jacket with a narrow black necktie across its shoulder. Also in the room was a treadle sewing machine and a chest of drawers with a mirror on top. The ceiling was beginning to collapse. Another room still sported sheer once-white curtains as well as an upright organ and hand-cranked Victrola (Figure 16.3). On the wall was a calendar from the 1920s. This was the "embalmed" home of a person of means, located in a hard-to-reach impoverished community. Why was it untouched?

It turned out the owner of the house was a bootlegger or rum-runner involved in moving alcohol south to Savannah and north to Beaufort. During

Figure 16.2. Interior of the bedroom of a rum-runner's house, Daufuskie Island, South Carolina, 1984. *Left*: bed and dresser with mirror. *Right*: treadle sewing machine. (Photo by author)

Prohibition in the 1920s, Daufuskie Island was the perfect place to be invisible to law enforcement. The locals were marginalized in many ways. Living on an island, they were cut off from the mainland. Being of African descent and speaking Gullah added social distance to this physical distance. They made their livelihood at sea gathering oysters and fishing and no doubt carrying alcohol from "mother ships" to the island and on to the mainland for redistribution. As in the case of Blackbeard two hundred years earlier, their allegiance was to their neighbor. It was a promise they kept for sixty years, through the collapse of the fishing and oyster industry in the years after World War II and into the 1980s.

Pirates and Popular Culture

At the turn of the twenty-first century, when this journey to discover pirates and piracy in the archaeological record began, popular views of piracy were broadly embraced. Many of the individuals (ranging in age from eighteen to eighty-seven) in interviews and surveys conducted in the United States and the Philippines drew on ideas taken from films and literature (Skowronek

Figure 16.3. Interior of the living room of a rum-runner's house, Daufuskie Island, South Carolina, 1984. *Top*: organ, with Stanley South outside window. *Bottom*: Victrola (*left*) and mirrored sideboard. (Photo by author)

2006; Skowronek and Ewen 2016). One of the informants cited centuries-old familial stories about the ravages of the pirate El Draque (Francis Drake). Another, living in Manila, mentioned the modern activities of Abu Sayyaf in the southern Philippines. What is significant is that only these two cited real people and not fictionalized characters, which underscores the power of popular culture (Skowronek 2006:292–293).

While many of these "traditional" popular images continue to influence the public, they are now joined by characters in video games. Over the past few decades, gaming has become an important venue to interactively expose people to the past. For some this may be their path into archaeology.

Idol and Thomas (Chapter 4) do a deep dive into the games and their inspiration for the depiction of pirates. Some, they note, are "counterfactuals": not accurate historical representations but a means of developing conceptual frameworks of historical knowledge. As we have seen elsewhere, "alternative facts" can undermine the tangible evidence of past behaviors that archaeology seeks to reveal. Nonetheless, some games like *Uncharted 4: A Thief's End* and *Assassin's Creed IV: Black Flag* do a good job exploring pirates and drawing on facts rather than on the mythology of Hollywood. These games may be the catalyst for the creation of new generations of archaeologists, just as books, films, and Disneyland were in earlier times.

Sunset or Sunrise?

As this retrospective shows, the archaeology of piracy has come far in the twenty-first century. Scholars from around the world study a topic that once was taboo. Their critical comparative perspectives provide a more nuanced picture of pirates, piracy, and more generally illicit behavior.

Moving forward, archaeologists might consider a Middle Range theory approach to gain deeper insights into pirate behavior. They might draw on the observed behavior and material culture of modern pirates such as those in Somalia, whose material record may prove to be analogous to the preserved behaviors that are testable in the archaeological record. This approach will move us from fiction to fact. Scholars should go beyond description and delve into social disorganization theory to explain the factors behind piracy.

This book and its companion volumes, *X Marks the Spot* and *Pieces of Eight*, were written by archaeologists not just for other archaeologists but for informed readers, with the goal of making academic esoterica relevant and interesting beyond the boundaries of academic archaeology.

In the past few years, the efforts of Jean Soulat and his colleagues have opened this door into the popular arena even further with the formation of Archéologie de la Piraterie in 2019 and the publication of "À la découverte des pirates" (Soulat 2019) and *Speaker 1702* (Soulat and von Arnim 2022). The "popular" genre captures the imagination of archaeologists and the general public alike. That said, publications such as the edition of *Wreckwatch Magazine* (Kingsley 2020) that focused on pirates and pirate archaeology have been seen as problematic by some because of connections to nonacademically sponsored excavation of sites. Does this mean that material recovered in this manner should be automatically discounted or ignored?

This leads back to questions that dogged the idea of pirate archaeology when *X Marks the Spot* was published in 2006, including evidence from the *Whydah* (C. Hamilton 2006). The controversy surrounding the government-sanctioned work on this wreck engulfed members of the Society for Historical Archaeology and led to revisions of the organization's code of ethics (Elia 1992). There is no question that archaeologists are loath to work with materials that lack good context or were obtained through nonacademically sponsored excavation or collecting. That said, museums and repositories are filled with poorly documented materials that have been the basis for a century of theses and dissertations. While some research questions could not be addressed with information derived from these materials, they did and will continue to serve as important sources of data for research. As Deagan (Ewen 2017:469) succinctly states in an interview,

> if those data exist, you can't ignore them. Refusing to acknowledge those sites and the artifacts recovered by treasure salvors and collectors would restrict the development of the discipline and does a disservice to the historical record and our interpretation of it.

Over the course of my career I have worked with poorly documented evidence collected by farmers (Reger et al. 2020), treasure salvors under contract with the State of Florida (Skowronek 1984), and treasure hunters contesting the primacy of the US National Park Service (Skowronek and Fischer 2009). Our evidence of the past is fleeting and the evidence for piracy is even more ephemeral, as we have seen. To paraphrase the late George Fischer, we get one chance to get it right in archaeology, "because they just don't make historic shipwrecks anymore" (Skowronek and Fischer 2009:184 and Skowronek 2017:460).

It is evident from the contributions to this publication, earlier volumes, and the broader public outreach efforts mentioned here that the future of pirate archaeology is in good hands, in the light of a rising sun.

It is time to weigh anchor and set sail. After decades of beating against the wind, there is now a following breeze. A secluded harbor and snug inn await. Should a fat prize be sighted, pipe me aboard for another round of adventure.

Yo ho ho, mates.

References

Allan, John

2001 The Medieval Pottery Found at Pig's Paradise, Lundy, in 2001. *Annual Report of the Lundy Field Society* 53(21):136–139.

Appleby, J. C.

1990 Settlers and Pirates in Early Seventeenth-Century Ireland: A Profile of Sir William Hill. *Studia Hibernica* (25):76–104.

2009 *Under the Bloody Flag: Pirates of the Tudor Age*. History Press, Cheltenham, United Kingdom.

Archives Départementales de la Charente-Maritime (La Rochelle, France)

1718 B 5713, f. 198.

Archives Départementales d'Ille-et-Vilaine (Rennes, France)

1718a Déclaration du capitaine navire *Le François*, 1718, 17 juin (SS. C4 330, no pagination).

1718b Rapport du capitaine navire *Princesse de Palma* le 30 juillet 1718 (SS. C4 330, C9 B 485, no pagination).

Archives Départementales du Calvados

1718 Amirauté de Honfleur 2 II 309.

Archives du Ministère de la Marine (Paris)

1718 Amirauté de Nantes B 4578.

Archives du Morbihan

1721 9 B 202 (copy of December 21).

Archives Nationales de France (Pierrefitte-sur-Seine, France)

1718a Manuscrits Marines, B3 251 and B3 241.

1718b Colonies/C8/A26 (February 14).

Archives Nationales d'Outre-Mer (Aix-en-Provence, France)

1635–1815 Secrétariat d'État à la Marine, Correspondance à l'arrivée en provenance de la Martinique: FR-ANOM COL C8A.

1660 FR-ANOM COL C8B 1, Doc. 3 (f. 1) and Doc. 6, pp. 21–22 (16600812).

1717a FR-ANOM COL C8A 22, f. 71.

1717b FR-ANOM COL C8B 4, Doc. 3.

Argote, Don Antonio, Spanish Consul, v. the Ship La Perla y Dolores *and Cargo*

1824 Account of Goods Received in the Custom House Store from on Board the Spanish Ship *La Perla*, February 4. Records of the District Courts of the United States,

1685–2009, Record Group 21, Law, Equity, Criminal, Habeas Corpus, and Admiralty Case Files. National Archives, Atlanta, Georgia.

Armstrong, Douglas V., Mark Hauser, and David W. Knight

2005 Historical Archaeology of Cinnamon Bay Shoreline Estate, Draft Report. On file at the Virgin Islands National Park, St. John.

Arquivo Histórico Ultramarino (Lisbon, Portugal)

1718 Piratas. Projeto Resgate: Biblioteca Luso Brasileira. http://resgate.bn.br/docreader/docmulti.aspx?bib=resgate (accessed October 2015).

1720 Conselho Ultramarino, Brasil–São Paulo. AHU_ACL_CU_023-01: Cx. 2/Doc.170 [1], Cx. 3/Doc. 242[2], Cx. 6/Doc. 691.

1731 Conselho Ultramarino, Brasil–São Paulo. AHU_ACL_CU_023-01: Cx. 9/Doc. 960[1].

Arquivo Nacional (Rio de Janeiro, Brazil)

1718a Secretaria de Estado do Brasil, Códice 84, vol. 1 (correspondência dos governadores do Rio de Janeiro com diversas autoridades).

1718b Secretaria de Estado do Brasil, Códice 85 (registro de cartas, provisões, ordens régias e alvarás ao governador do Rio de Janeiro).

Ascaron Entertainment and Gaming Minds Studios

2003–2012 *Port Royale* series. Tri-Synergy/Kalypso Media, Canton, Massachusetts/Worms, Germany.

Auer, Jens

2004 Fregatten *Mynden*: A 17th-Century Danish Frigate Found in Northern Germany. *International Journal of Nautical Archaeology* 33(2):264–280.

Ayres, Philip

1684 *The Voyages and Adventures of Capt. Barth. Sharp and Others in the South Sea*. B. W., R. H., and S. T., London.

Babits, Lawrence E., Joshua B. Howard, and Matthew Brencle

2006 Pirate Imagery. In *X Marks the Spot: The Archaeology of Piracy*, edited by Russell K. Skowronek and Charles R. Ewen, pp. 271–281. University Press of Florida, Gainesville.

Bailey, De Witt

2009 *Small Arms of the British Forces in America, 1664–1815*. Andrew Mowbray, Woonsocket, Rhode Island.

Barbour, Violet

1911 Privateers and Pirates of the West Indies. *American Historical Review* 16 (3):529–566. Published by Oxford University Press on behalf of the American Historical Association. https://www.jstor.org/stable/1834836 (accessed February 4, 2023).

Baring-Gould, S.

1926 *Devonshire Characters and Strange Events*. Mayflower Press, Plymouth, United Kingdom.

Barreiro-Meiro, Roberto

2002 The Bermuda Islands and Juan Bermúdez. *Bermuda Journal of Archaeology and Maritime History* 13:7–18.

Beal, Clifford

2007 *Quelch's Gold: Piracy, Greed, and Betrayal in Colonial New England*. Praeger, London.

The Beaufort Pirate Invasion

2021 The Beaufort Pirate Invasion. https://www.beaufortpirateinvasion.com (accessed February 4, 2023).

Beechler, W. H.

1890 The United States Navy and West India Piracy, 1821–25. *Frank Leslie's Popular Monthly* 29(1):2.

Bellamy, Martin

2006 David Balfour and Early Modern Danish Ship Design. *Mariner's Mirror* 92(1):5–22.

Bialuschewski, Arne

2009 Pirates, Markets and Imperial Authority: Economic Aspects of Maritime Depredations in the Atlantic World, 1716–1726. *Global Crime* 9(1–2):52–65. Taylor and Francis Online (November 27). https://www.tandfonline.com/doi/abs/10.1080/17440570701862769?journalCode=fglc20.

Biblioteca Digital Unesp (online)

1896 Documentos interessantes para a história e costumes de São Paulo. https://bibdig.biblioteca.unesp.br/items/03653020-0376-48d2-a283-2ded4709d9af (accessed February 4, 2023).

Biblioteca Nacional do Brasil Digital (online)

1928 Piratas. *Documentos históricos 1928*. http://memoria.bn.br/docreader/DocReader.aspx?bib=094536&pesq=piratas&pagfis=35 (accessed January 1, 2017).

1939 Piratas. *Documentos históricos 1939*. http://memoria.bn.br/docreader/DocReader.aspx?bib=094536&pesq=piratas&pagfis=1 (accessed January 1, 2017).

1942 Piratas. *Documentos históricos 1942*. http://memoria.bn.br/docreader/DocReader.aspx?bib=094536&pesq=piratas (accessed January 1, 2017).

Bibliothèque Nationale de France (Paris)

1733 Département des Cartes et Plans: FR-BnF DCP, GE SH 18 PF 217 DIV 8 P 2/1.

Black, Clinton V.

1983 *History of Jamaica*. Longman Caribbean, Kingston, Jamaica.

Black, J. G. (editor)

1901 *Patent Rolls of the Reign of Henry III (1232–1247)*. Vol. 3. Her Majesty's Stationary Office, London.

Blackmore, Howard L.

1961 *British Military Firearms, 1650–1850*. Herbert Jenkins, London.

1976 *The Armouries of the Tower of London*, Vol. 1. Her Majesty's Stationary Office, London.

Blair, Claude

1962 *European and American Arms*. Crown Publishers, New York.

Blanchard, Émile

1872 L'île de Madagascar: les tentatives de colonisation. *Revue des Deux Mondes* 100(3)(1872):596–637.

Blaufarb, Rafe

2016 Arms for Revolutions: Military Demobilization after the Napoleonic Wars and Latin American Independence. In *War, Demobilization and Memory: The Legacy of War in the Era of Atlantic Revolutions*, edited by Alan Forrest, Karen Hagemann, and Michael Rowe, pp. 100–118, Palgrave Macmillan, New York.

Borgens, Amy A.

2016 Small Arms and Munitions from a Texas Coastal Shipwreck. *Historical Archaeology* 50(2):127–151.

Borrelli, Jeremy R.

2020 An Initial Assessment of Lead Artifacts Used for Hull Repair and Maintenance on North Carolina Shipwreck 31CR314, *Queen Anne's Revenge* (1718). *International Journal of Nautical Archaeology* 49(2):357–370.

Borrelli, Jeremy, and Lynn Harris

2016 Bricks as Ballast: An Archaeological Investigation of a Shipwreck Site in Cahuita National Park, Costa Rica. *Society for Historical Archaeology Conference Proceedings, Washington DC*:8–16.

Bratten, John

2018 What They Left Behind: The Artifact Assemblage. In *Florida's Lost Galleon: The Emanuel Point Shipwreck*, edited by Roger C. Smith, pp. 122–206. University Press of Florida, Gainesville.

Briand, Jérôme

2014 Saint-Martin, Grand-Case, route de *l'Espérance*, parcelle BK 77. Rapport de diagnostic archéologique, Inrap Grand-Sud-Ouest, Guadeloupe.

Bridenbaugh, Carl, and Roberta Bridenbaugh

1972 *No Peace beyond the Line: The English in the Caribbean 1624–1690*. Oxford University Press, New York.

British History Online (BHO)

1717–1718 *Calendar of State Papers Colonial, America and West Indies: Volumes 29 and 30*. https://www.british-history.ac.uk/search/series/cal-state-papers—colonial—america-west-indies (accessed October 11, 2019).

British Library (London)

1625 Journal du voyage faict par les peres de familles envoyes par Mrs les Directeurs de la Compagnie des Indes occidentales pour visiter la coste de Gujane (ca. 1625). Manuscripts: GB-BL Ms 179b.

British Museum (London)

2020 Database: Portable Antiquities Scheme, British Museum, London. http://finds.org.uk/database (accessed June 19, 2020).

Bro-Jørgensen, J. O.

1966 Dansk Vestindien indtil 1755. In *Vore Gamle Tropekolonier*, vol. 1, edited by Johannes Brøndsted, pp. 3–148. Fremad, Copenhagen.

Brooks, Baylus C.

2018 *Sailing East: West-Indian Pirates in Madagascar*. Lulu.com, Morrisville, North Carolina.

Brown, Lane

2016 The Greatest Stories Ever Played. Vulture. https://www.vulture.com/2016/05/

uncharted-4-and-gamings-greatest-storytellers-c-v-r.html (accessed February 20, 2021).

Brown, Ruth

2007 Bronze Signalling or Saluting Gun: Second Report (No. 90). North Carolina Department of Natural and Cultural Resources, Queen Anne's Revenge Conservation Lab, Greenville, North Carolina.

Bru, Lorenzo, v. Schooner Filomeno

1819 Inventory of the Trunk Captured on Board the Privateer Bravo by Revenue Cutter *Louisiana*, November 12. Records of the District Courts of the United States, 1685–2009, Record Group 21. National Archives, Fort Worth, Texas.

Bruce, John (editor)

1858 *Calendar of State Papers, Domestic Series, of the Reign of Charles I (1625–1649)*, Vol. 1. Longman, London.

Burgess, Douglas R.

2008 *The Pirates' Pact: The Secret Alliances between History's Most Notorious Buccaneers and Colonial America*. Ragged Mountain Press, Camden, Maine.

Burnett, John S.

2002 *Dangerous Waters: Modern Piracy and Terror on the High Seas*. Dutton, New York.

Calado, Rafael Salinas

2003 *Faiança portuguesa da Casa Museu Guerra: Junqueiro, séculos XVII–XVIII*. Câmara Municipal do Porto, Porto, Portugal.

Cally, Jean William, and Jacques Gasser

2019 *La Buse, l'or maudit des pirates*. Éditions Dorotheos, Sainte-Marie, France.

Camp, Helen

1975 *Archaeological Excavations at Pemaquid, Maine, 1965–1975*. Maine State Museum, Augusta.

Cartland, J. Henry

1914 *Twenty Years at Pemaquid; Sketches of Its History and Remains, Ancient and Modern*. L. A. Moore, Boothbay Harbor, Maine.

Casimiro, Tânia Manuel

2013 Faiança portuguesa: datação e evolução crono-estilística. *Revista Portuguesa de Arqueologia* 16:351–367.

Cassin, Joseph

1822 Letter to Captain Stephen Cassin, October 7. Letters Received 1789–1906, Miscellaneous Letters, M179, Record Group 59. National Archives, Washington, DC.

Cassin, Stephen

1822a Letter to Secretary of the Navy, October 10. Letters Received 1789–1906, Miscellaneous Letters, M179, Record Group 59. National Archives, Washington, DC.

1822b Letter to United States District Attorney in New Orleans, October 3. Manuscript. Letters Received 1789–1906, Miscellaneous Letters, M179, Record Group 59. National Archives, Washington, DC.

Chapman, Adam

2016 *Digital Games as History: How Videogames Represent the Past and Offer Access to Historical Practice*. Routledge, New York.

Charleston Daily Courier

1825 Escape from a Pirate. July 18.

Charleston Mercury

1825 Copy of a Letter from John Holmes. March 8.

1826 From Our Correspondent. November 11.

Chet, Guy

2014 *The Ocean Is a Wilderness: Atlantic Piracy and the Limits of State Authority, 1688–1856*. University of Massachusetts Press, Amherst.

Christensen, Tilde Hoppe, and Tilde Strandbygaard Gabriel Jessen

2012 Fragments of the Colonial History of St. John: Beverhoudtsberg and Mary Point in a Historical Archaeological Perspective. University of Copenhagen for Virgin Islands National Park. On file at Virgin Islands National Park, St. Thomas.

Clifford, Barry M., and Kenneth J. Kinkor

2007 *Real Pirates: The Untold Story of the Whydah from Slave Ship to Pirate Ship, 1717*. National Geographic Exhibition, Washington, DC.

Clifford, Barry, and Paul Perry

2000 *Expedition Whydah: The Story of the World's First Excavation of a Pirate Treasure Ship and the Man Who Found Her*. HarperCollins, New York.

Coimbra, Álvaro

1959 Noções de numismática brasileira (I). *Revista de História* 18(37):201.

Collectif

2017 Sainte-Marie, Madagascar 2015 Report. Center for Historic Shipwreck Preservation, Brewster, Massachusetts.

Cooke, Edward

1712 *A Voyage to the South Sea and Round the World*. B. Lintot and R. Gosling, London.

Coolidge, A. J., and J. B. Mansfield

1859 A *History and Description of New England, General and Local*. Austin J. Coolidge, Boston.

Cordingly, David

2006 *Under the Black Flag: The Romance and the Reality of Life among the Pirates*. Random House, New York.

Coulaud, Alexandre, and Nathalie Sellier-Ségard

2019 Les preuves matérielles d'une occupation littorale inédite de la fin du XVIIe siècle à Saint-Martin (Petites Antilles): témoins de la presence flibustière? In *Archéologie de la piraterie des XVIIe et XVIIIe siècles: étude de la vie quotidienne des flibustiers dans les Caraïbes et l'Océan Indien*, edited by Jean Soulat, pp. 125–136. Éditions Monique Mergoil, Drémil-Lafage, France.

Coustet, René, and Jacques de Cauna

1987 Mission à l'île de la Tortue. *Conjonction: Revue Franco-Haïtienne* 174–175 (March 16–30):6–12.

Cragg, Jessie

2019 Squad Goals: The West Indies Squadron and Suppression of Piracy in the Early Republic. Master's thesis, Department of History, University of West Florida, Pensacola.

Crawford, Michael J., and Christine F. Hughes

1995 The Reestablishment of the Navy, 1787–1801: Historical Overview and Select Bibliography. Naval History Bibliographies 4. Naval History and Heritage Command. https://www.history.navy.mil/research/library/bibliographies/reestablishment-navy-1787-1801.html (accessed November 15, 2020).

Crawford, S. D., and A. Márquez-Pérez

2016 A Contact Zone: The Turtle Commons of the Western Caribbean. *International Journal of Maritime History* 28(1):64–80.

Creative Assembly

2000–2020 *Total War* series. Redwood City: Electronic Arts/Activision/Sega, Redwood City and Santa Monica, California/Tokyo.

2009 *Empire: Total War*. Sega, Tokyo.

2014 *Total War: Rome II, Pirates and Raiders*. Sega, Tokyo.

2018 *Total War: Warhammer II, Curse of the Vampire Coast*. Sega, Tokyo.

Crouse, Nellis Maynard

1940 *French Pioneers in the West Indies, 1624–1664*. Columbia University Press, New York.

Dampier, William

1697 *A New Voyage Round the World*. James Knapton, London.

1906 [1697] *A New Voyage Round the World: 1679–1691*. Vol. 1. John Masefield, New York.

1937 [1697] *A New Voyage Round the World*. Adam and Charles Black, London.

Daviau, Marie-Hélène

2008 La pipe en pierre dans la société canadienne des XVIIe, XVIIIe, et XIXe siècles: une approche archéologique. Master's thesis. University Laval, Québec.

Davis, William C.

2006 *The Pirate Lafitte: The Treacherous World of the Corsairs on the Gulf*. Houghton Mifflin Harcourt, Boston.

Davis-Marks, Isis

2021 17th-Century Coins Found in a Fruit Grove May Solve a 300-Year-Old Pirate Mystery. *Smithsonian Magazine* (April 12). https://www.smithsonianmag.com/smart-news/17th-century-coins-found-fruit-grove-solve-pirate-mystery-180977401.

Deagan, Kathleen

1987 The Material Assemblage of 16th Century Spanish Florida. *Historical Archaeology* 12:25–50.

2016 Pirates as Providers. In *Pieces of Eight: More Archaeology of Piracy*, edited by Charles R. Ewen and Russell K. Skowronek, pp. 239–259. University Press of Florida, Gainesville.

de Aranguren, Captain Bartholome de

1794 Account of Attack by Pirates from Captain of Schooner *San Juan Nepomuceno*, September 11. GM, Legajo 685-556. Transcribed and translated by Alicia Gardner and Michael Thomin. PARES, Archivos Españoles, Seville, Spain.

de Bry

2006 Christopher Condent's *Fiery Dragon*: Investigating an Early 18th-Century Pirate Shipwreck off the Coast of Madagascar, In *X Marks the Spot: The Archaeology of Pi-*

racy, edited by Russell K. Skowronek and Charles R. Ewen, pp. 100–130. University Press of Florida, Gainesville.

de Bry, John, and Marco Roling

2011 Archaeological Report Madagascar 2010: Research on 17th and 18th Century Pirate Shipwrecks at îlot Madame, Sainte-Marie. Melbourne Beach, Florida.

2016 Revisiting the *Fiery Dragon*. In *Pieces of Eight: More Archaeology Piracy*, edited by Charles R. Ewen and Russell K. Skowronek, pp. 57–92. University Press of Florida, Gainesville.

de Comte, Bois

1825 Letter to Francisco de Zea Bermúdez, April 13. Pares (Portal de Archivos Españoles). Embajador de Francia sobre los desórdenes en las Antillas. Archivo General de Indias, Estado 17, No. 116 http://pares.mcu.es/ParesBusquedas20/catalogo/show/62684?nm (accessed February 4, 2023).

Defoe, Daniel

2010a [1724] *Le grand rêve flibustier: histoire générale des plus fameux pyrates II*. Translated by Henri Thiès. Edited by Guillaume Villeneuve. Éditions Libretto, Paris.

2010b [1726] *Les chemins de Fortune: histoire générale des plus fameux pyrates I*. Translated by Henri Thiès. Edited by Guillaume Villeneuve. Éditions Libretto, Paris.

Dell, Harry J.

1967 The Origin and Nature of Illyrian Piracy. *Historia: Zeitschrift für Alte Geschichte* 16(3):344–358.

De Putter, Thierry

2014 Quelques réflexions à propos de l'étude des bouteilles d'usage en France au XVIIIe siècle. *Bulletin de l'Association Française pour l'Archéologie du Verre*20:136–139.

de Souza, Philip

2008 Rome's Contribution to the Development of Piracy. *Maritime World of Ancient Rome* 6:71–96.

Digital Archaeological Archive of Comparative Slavery (DAACS)

2004 The Digital Archaeological Archive of Chesapeake Slavery. http://www.daacs.org (accessed September 13, 2017).

Donachie, Madeleine J.

2001 Household Ceramics at Port Royal, Jamaica, 1655–1692: The Building 4/5 Assemblage. PhD dissertation, Department of Anthropology, Texas A&M University.

Dookhan, Isaac

1975 *A History of the British Virgin Islands, 1672 to 1970*. Caribbean Universities Press in association with Bowker, Epping, United Kingdom.

Dow, Douglas N.

2013 Historical Veneers: Anachronism, Simulation, and Art History in *Assassin's Creed II*. In *Playing with the Past: Digital Games and the Simulation of History*, edited by Matthew Wilhelm Kapell and Andrew B. R. Elliott, pp. 215–232. Bloomsbury Academic, New York.

Dow, George Francis

1969 *The Pirates of the New England Coast: 1630–1730*. Marine Research Society, Salem, Massachusetts.

Drake, Samuel Adams

1875 *Nooks and Corners of the New England Coast*. Harper and Brothers, New York.

Draper, Mary

2017 Timbering and Turtling: The Maritime Hinterlands of Early Modern British Caribbean Cities. *Early American Studies: An Interdisciplinary Journal* 15(4):769–800.

Duco, D. H.

1987 *De Nederlandse Kleipijp*. Stichting Pijpenkabinet, Leiden, the Netherlands.

Ducoin, Jacques

2001 Compte rendu de recherches dans les Archives Françaises sur le navire Nantais *La Concorde* capturé par des pirates en 1717. North Carolina Department of Natural and Cultural Resources, Queen Anne's Revenge Conservation Lab, Greenville, North Carolina.

Duplessis, Robert

2015 *Material Atlantic: Clothing, Commerce, and Colonization*. Cambridge University Press, Cambridge.

Dutertre, R.-P. Jean-Baptiste

1667 *Histoire générale des Antilles*. Thomas Jolly, Paris.

Earle, Peter

2006 *The Pirate Wars*. Macmillan, New York.

Elia, Ricardo

1992 The Ethics of Collaboration: Archaeologists and the *Whydah* Project. *Historical Archaeology* 26(4):105–117.

Emory University

2019 Trans-Atlantic Slave Trade Database, Slave Voyages. Emory University, Atlanta. https://www.slavevoyages.org/voyage/database (accessed December 8, 2020).

Ensemble Studios

1997–2020 *Age of Empires* series. Microsoft Game Studios, Redmond, Washington.

Ernaud, François

1718 Deposition of François Ernaud, April 17. ADLA B 4578 ff. 56–57. Archives Départementales Loire Atlantique, Nantes, France.

Esquemeling, John

1967 [1684] *The Buccaneers of America: A True Account of the Most Remarkable Assaults Committed of Late Years upon the Coasts of the West Indies by the Buccaneers of Jamaica and Tortuga Both English and French*. Reprint: Dover, New York.

Ewen, Charles R.

2017 An Interview with Kathleen Deagan. *Historical Archaeology* 51:463–470.

Ewen, Charles R., and Russell K. Skowronek

2006 "Identifying the Victims of Piracy in the Spanish Caribbean." In *X Marks the Spot: The Archaeology of Piracy*, edited by Russell K. Skowronek and Charles R. Ewen, pp. 248–267. University Press of Florida, Gainesville.

2007 A Pirate's Life for Me! But What Did That Really Mean? In *Box Office Archaeology: Refining Hollywood's Portrayals of the Past*, edited by Julie M. Schablitsky, pp. 51–69. Left Coast Press, Walnut Creek, California.

Ewen, Charles R., and Russell K. Skowronek (editors)

2016 *Pieces of Eight: More Archaeology of Piracy*. University Press of Florida, Gainesville.

Exnicios, Joan M.

2006 On the Trail of Jean Lafitte. In *X Marks the Spot: The Archaeology of Piracy*, edited by Russell K. Skowronek and Charles R. Ewen, pp. 31–43. University Press of Florida, Gainesville.

Exquemelin, Alexandre Olivier

1684 *Bucaniers of America*. Vol. 1. William Crooke, London.

1685 *Bucaniers of America: The Second Volume*. William Crooke, London.

1969 [1684] *History of the Buccaneers of America*. Dover, New York.

2005 *Histoire des aventuriers flibustiers*. Edited with a glossary and index by Réal Ouellet. Introduction and notes by Réal Ouellet and Patrick Villiers. Les Presses de l'Université Laval, Québec.

Farragut, Loyall

1879 *The Life of David Glasgow Farragut, First Admiral of the United States Navy*. D. Appleton and Company, New York.

Farrell, Erik, Kimberly Kenyon, Sarah Watkins-Kenney, Kay Smith, and Ruth Brown

2018 Message in a Breech Block: A Fragmentary Printed Text Recovered from *Queen Anne's Revenge*. *North Carolina Historical Review* 95(2):231–248.

Figueredo, Alfredo E.

1978 The Early European Colonization of St. Croix (1621–1642). *Journal of the Virgin Islands Archaeological Society* (Frederiksted, St. Croix) 6:59–63.

Finamore, Daniel

2006 A Mariner's Utopia: Pirates and Logwood in the Bay of Honduras. In *X Marks the Spot: The Archaeology of Piracy*, edited by Russell K. Skowronek and Charles R. Ewen, 64–78. University Press of Florida, Gainesville.

Fisheries and Oceans Canada

2006 Commercial Fisheries for Atlantic Cod. Ottawa, Ontario. https://www.dfo-mpo.gc.ca/fisheries-peches/commercial-commerciale/atl-arc/cod-morue-eng.html (accessed February 4, 2023).

Floore, Peter, and Ranjith Jayasena

2010 In Want of Everything? Archaeological Perceptions of a Dutch Outstation on Mauritius (1638–1710). *Post-Medieval Archaeology* 44: 320–340.

Floore, Peter, and Carmel Schrire

1997 Reports on the Archaeological Survey of the Ruins of Vieux Grand Port, 2–30 July 1997. Preliminary Report, Friends of the Environment, Mauritius.

Florida Museum of Natural History (FLMNH)

1995–2010 *Historical Archaeology: Digital Type Collection*. University of Florida, Gainesville, http://www.flmnh.ufl.edu/histarch/gallery_types/type_list.asp, (accessed September 2017).

Fox, Edward

2013 "Piratical Schemes and Contracts": Pirate Articles and Their Society, 1660–1730. PhD dissertation, Maritime History, University of Exeter, United Kingdom.

Fox, Russell, and Kenneth J. Barton

1986 Excavations at Oyster Street, Postmouth, Hampshire, 1968–71, *Post-Medieval Archaeology* 20:31–255.

Frézier, Amédée-François

1717 *A Voyage to the South Sea, and along the Coasts of Chili and Peru, in the Years 1712, 1713, and 1714.* Jonah Bower, London.

Froidevaux, H. M.

1896 *Un explorateur inconnu de Madagascar au XVIIe siècle.* Imprimerie Nationale, Paris.

Funnell, William

1707 *A Voyage Round the World.* James Knapton, London.

Fusaro, Maria, Bernard Allaire, Richard Blakemore, and Tijl Vanneste

2020 *Sailing into Modernity: Comparative Perspectives on the Sixteenth and Seventeenth Century European Economic Transition.* University of Exeter, Centre for Maritime Historical Studies, Exeter, United Kingdom. https://humanities.exeter.ac.uk/history/research/centres/maritime/research/modernity (accessed June 26, 2020).

Gallegher, John

1823 Letter to the Secretary of Navy, May 21. Letters Received 1789–1906, Miscellaneous Letters, M179, Record Group 59. National Archives, Washington, DC.

Gardiner, Julie

2005 Navigation and Ship's Communication. In *Before the Mast: Life and Death Aboard the Mary Rose,* edited by Julie Gardiner and Michael J. Allen, pp. 264–292. Mary Rose Trust, Portsmouth, United Kingdom.

Gardner, Andrew

2007 The Past as Playground: The Ancient World in Video Game Representation. In *Archaeology and the Media,* edited by Timothy Clack and Marcus Brittain, pp. 255–272. Left Coast Press, Walnut Creek, California.

Gardner, Keith

1972 *The Archaeology of Lundy: A Field Guide.* Landmark Trust, n.p., United Kingdom.

Garrard, Timothy F.

1973 Studies in Akan Goldweights (III): The Weight Names. *Transactions of the Historical Society of Ghana* 14(1):1–16.

Gawronski, Jerzy, and Peter Kranendonk

2020 Below the Surface: The Archaeological Finds of the North/Southline, Department of Archaeology, City of Amsterdam. https://belowthesurface.amsterdam/en (accessed December 16, 2020).

Germain, Jean-Christophe

2007 Claude de Beulayne, premier commandant de la partie française de l'île de Saint-Martin (1630–1633). *Bulletin de Généalogie et Histoire de la Caraïbe* 199:5067–5069.

Gibbs, Charles

1831 The Confession of Chas. Gibbs Alias James Jeffreys, Who Has Been Sentenced to Be Executed at N. York, on the 22d April 1831 for Piracy and Murder on Board the Brig *Vineyard.* Rhode Island Historical Society Vault F 2161.G44 L34: *The Confessions of Charles Gibbs, the Pirate, Who Acknowledges That He Has Assisted in the Murder of Four Hundred Human Beings!* (n.p.: Printed for the Purchasers, 1831). https://wp.me/p7ud3-6U. Library of Congress, Boston, Massachusetts.

Gibbs, Joseph
2012 *On the Account: Piracy and the Americas, 1766–1835*. Sussex Academic Press, Brighton, United Kingdom.
Gilbert, W. S., and Arthur Sullivan
1879 *The Pirates of Penzance*. Royal Bijou Theatre, Devon, United Kingdom.
Godden, Geoffrey
1966 *An Illustrated Encyclopaedia of British Pottery and Porcelain*. Herbert Jenkins, London.
Goguet, Christian
1987 Mémoire sur l'île de la Tortue et devis descriptif du fort. *Revue de la Société Haïtienne d'Histoire et de Géographie* 45:156–161.
Goodall, Jamie
2016 Navigating the Atlantic World: Piracy, Illicit Trade, and the Construction of Commercial Networks, 1650–1791. PhD dissertation, Ohio State University.
Gooding, James S.
2003 *Trade Guns of the Hudson's Bay Company, 1670–1970*. Museum Restoration Service, Ontario, Canada.
Goodrich, Caspar F.
1916 *Our Navy and the West Indian Pirates: A Documentary History*. Proceedings 42(4):1171–1192. US Naval Institute, Annapolis, Maryland.
Goodwin, Peter G.
1987 *The Construction and Fitting of the English Man of War, 1650–1850*. Naval Institute Press, Annapolis, Maryland.
Goslinga, Cornelius C.
1971 *The Dutch in the Caribbean and on the Wild Coast 1580–1680*. University of Florida Press, Gainesville.
Gough, Barry, and Charles Borras
2018 *The War against the Pirates: British and American Suppression of Caribbean Piracy in the Early Nineteenth Century*. Palgrave Macmillan, Basingstoke, United Kingdom.
Green, Mary Anne Everett
1857 *Calendar of State Papers, Domestic Series, of the Reign of James I (1603–1625)*. Vol. 1. Longman, London.
Gregory, Francis
1823 Letter to Daniel Patterson, May 3. Letters Received by the Secretary of Navy from Captains (Captains Letters) 1805–1885, Microfilm 125, Record Group 260, Department of the Navy. National Archives, Washington, DC.
Gulseth, Chad M.
2016 "Black Bart's Ranger." In *Pieces of Eight: More Archaeology of Piracy*, edited by Charles R. Ewen and Russell K. Skowronek, pp. 93–109. University Press of Florida, Gainesville.
Hackelton, Maria W.
1869 *History of Pemaquid Maine—Jamestown*. Hurd and Houghton, New York.
Haddad, Ken
2019 Prohibition Ended 86 Years Ago Today: Here's What It Looked Like in Detroit.

All About Michigan (December 5). https://www.clickondetroit.com/all-about-michigan/2018/12/05/prohibition-ended-85-years-ago-today-heres-what-it-looked-like-in-detroit.

Hallett, C.F.E. Hollis

2007 *Butler's History of the Bermudas: A Contemporary Account of Bermuda's Earliest Government.* Bermuda Maritime Museum Press, Old Royal Navy Dockyard, Bermuda.

Hamilton, Christopher E.

2006 The Pirate Ship *Whydah.* In *X Marks the Spot: The Archaeology of Piracy*, edited by Russell K. Skowronek and Charles R. Ewen, pp. 131–159. University Press of Florida, Gainesville.

Hamilton, Donny L.

2006 Pirates and Merchants: Port Royal, Jamaica. In *X Marks the Spot: The Archaeology of Piracy*, edited by Russell K. Skowronek and Charles R. Ewen, pp. 13–30. University Press of Florida, Gainesville.

Hamilton, Nathan

2010 Isles of Shoals Archaeology Artifacts Revealed: Seacoast New Hampshire. http://www.seacoastnh.com/Places-and-Events/Smuttynose-Murders/isles-of-shoals-archeology-artifacts-revealed (accessed May 21, 2010).

Hamilton, Nathan, Ingrid Brack, and Robin Hadlock Seeley

2009 *Environmental Archaeology on Smuttynose Island, Isles of Shoals.* New Hampshire Archaeological Society, Mount Kearsarge Indian Museum, Warner, New Hampshire.

Hamilton, William Douglas, and Sophia Crawford Lomas (editors)

1897 *Calendar of State Papers, Domestic Series, of the Reign of Charles I: Appenda: March 1625 to January 1649.* Vol. 19. Eyre and Spottiswoode, London.

Hampton, Fred

1823 Public Instrument of Declaration and Protest of Captain John Hampton of Ship *Josephina*, June 11. Letters Received 1789–1906, Miscellaneous Letters, M179, Record Group 59. National Archives, Washington, DC.

Handler, Jerome S.

2009 The Middle Passage and the Material Culture of Captive Africans. *Slavery and Abolition* 30(1):1–26.

Hanselmann, Frederick H.

2019. *Captain Kidd's Lost Ship: The Wreck of the Quedagh Merchant.* University Press of Florida, Gainesville.

Hanselmann, Frederick H., and Charles D. Beeker

2016 The Wreck of the Quedagh Merchant: The Lost Ship of Captain William Kidd. In *Pieces of Eight: More Archaeology of Piracy*, edited by Charles R. Ewen and Russell K. Skowronek, pp. 110–132. University Press of Florida, Gainesville.

Harfield, C. G.

1996 In the Shadow of the Black Ensign: Lundy's Part in Piracy. *Annual Report of the Lundy Field Society* 47(16):60–71.

Haring, C. H.

1910 *The Buccaneers in the West Indies in the XVII Century.* E. P. Dutton, New York.

Harrington, Faith

1992 Deepwater Fishing from the Isles of Shoals. In *The Art and Mystery of Historical Archaeology: Essays in Honor of James Deetz*, edited by Anne Elizabeth Yentsch and Mary C. Beaudry, pp. 249–263. CRC Press, Boca Raton, Florida.

Harris, J. R.

1966 Copper and Shipping in the Eighteenth Century. *Economic History Review* 19(3):550–568.

Harris, Lynn

2020 The Serendipitous Saga of Danish Slave Trade Frigates *Christianus Quintus V* and *Fredericus Quartus IV*, Wrecked in 1710. *Coriolis: Interdisciplinary Journal of Maritime Studies* 10(1):1–31.

2021 Maritime Cultural Encounters and Consumerism of Turtles and Manatees: An Environmental History of the Caribbean. *International Journal of Maritime History* 32(4):789–807.

Harris, Lynn, and Nathan Richards

2018 Preliminary Investigations of Two Shipwrecks in Cahuita Park, Costa Rica. *International Journal of Nautical Archaeology* 47(2):405–418.

Harris, Lynn, Nathan Richards, and Jeremy Borrelli

2015 Tantalizing Tales of Two Shipwrecks: Cahuita National Park Site Report. Report to Sistema Nacional de Areas de Conservación (SINAC), Costa Rica. Fieldwork Report, Program in Maritime Studies, East Carolina University, Greenville, North Carolina.

Harris, Lynn, Nathan Richards, Jason Raupp, et al.

2016 Community Maritime Archaeology in Costa Rica: Cahuita National Park Site Report 2016. Report to Sistema Nacional de Areas de Conservación (SINAC), Costa Rica, Program in Maritime Studies, East Carolina University, Greenville, North Carolina.

Hatch, Heather

2016 Signaling Pirate Identity. In *Pieces of Eight: More Archaeology of Piracy*, edited by Charles R. Ewen and Russell K. Skowronek, pp. 208–227. University Press of Florida, Gainesville.

Haviser, Jay

1988 An Archaeological Survey of St. Martin–St. Maarten. Reports of the Institute of Archaeology and Anthropology of the Netherlands Antilles 7.

Head, David

2015 *Privateers of the Americas: Spanish American Privateering from the United States in the Early Republic*. University of Georgia Press, Athens.

Heisen, Johan

2016 Dissonance in the Danish Atlantic: Speech, Violence and Mutiny, 1672–1683. *Atlantic Studies* 13(2):187–205.

Helms, Mary W.

1983 Miskito Slaving and Culture Contact: Ethnicity and Opportunity in an Expanding Population. *Journal of Anthropological Research* 39:179–197.

Henderson, Bruce

2018 He Maimed, Killed, Plundered: Why Will NC Fly Blackbeard's Creepy Black Flag

Again? *Charlotte Observer* (April 6). https://www.charlotteobserver.com/news/local/article208056714.html#storylink=cpy.

Hennessy-Fiske, Molly

2018 On the Texas-Mexico Border, No One Knows Who's Smuggling the Border Crossers: Everyone's a Suspect. *Los Angeles Times* (December 17). https://www.latimes.com/projects/la-na-roma-texas-immigration.

Highfield, Arnold R.

2013 *Sainte Croix 1650–1733: A Plantation Society in the French Antilles.* Antilles Press, Christiansted, St. Croix, United States Virgin Islands.

Historic Environment Record

2012 Devon and Dartmoor Historic Environment Record (online). Heritage Gateway, Devon, United Kingdom. https://historicengland.org.uk/research/current/discover-and-understand/landscapes/aerial-investigation-and-mapping-the-south-devon-coast-to-dartmoor-survey (accessed January 10, 2021).

Hobsbawm, Eric J.

1985 *Bandits* (1969). Penguin, New York.

Höglund, Patrik

2019 Symbols of Power: Attributes of Rank on Warships in the 17th Century. In *On War on Board: Archaeological and Historical Perspectives on Early Modern Maritime Violence and Warfare*, edited by Johan Rönnby, pp. 39–50. Södertörns Högskola, Huddinge, Sweden.

Holm, John A.

1978 The Creole English of Nicaragua's Miskito Coast: Its Sociolinguistic History and a Comparative Study of Its Lexicon and Syntax. PhD dissertation, University College of London. University Microfilms International, Ann Arbor, Michigan.

Holman, R. G.

1975 The *Dartmouth*, a British Frigate Wreck off Mull, 1690 2: Culinary and Related Items. *International Journal of Nautical Archaeology* 4(2):253–265.

Hopkins, Fred

2008 For Freedom and Profit: Baltimore Privateers in the Wars of South American Independence. *Northern Mariner* 18(3–4):93–104.

Horrell, Christopher E., and Amy A. Borgens

2014 Interpreting the Past by Exploring the Abyss: Archaeological Investigations of an Early Nineteenth-Century Shipwreck in the Gulf of Mexico. Paper presented at the Offshore Technology Conference, Houston, Texas.

2017 The Mardi Gras Shipwreck Project: A Final Overview with New Perspectives. *Historical Archaeology* 51(2):1–18.

Hostin, Geraldo

2019 *The Pirate of Cotinga Island (1718): A Historical and Archaeological Study of a Mysterious Shipwreck in the South of Brazil.* Published by the author, Lakelands, Australia.

2020 *The Identification of the Pirate and Shipwreck: A Second Preliminary Report* (February). https://www.researchgate.net/publication/340732038_The_Identification_of_the_Pirate_and_Shipwreck_A_Preliminary_Report.

Hoving, A. J.

2012 *Nicolaes Witsen and Shipbuilding in the Dutch Golden Age*. Texas A&M University Press, College Station.

Humphrey, C. J.

1915 Tests on the Durability of Greenheart (*Nectandra Rodiaei Schomb*). *Mycologia* 7(4):204–209.

Hutchins, John G. B.

1941 *The American Maritime Industries and Public Policy, 1789–1914: An Economic History*. Russell and Russell, New York.

India Office Library (London)

1700 Document E3/70 (letter signed by Bowen and Both on April 18, 1700, stipulating that they captured the *Speaker*, a ship they encountered on April 16, 1700).

Israel, Jonathan

1989 *Dutch Primacy in World Trade, 1585–1740*. Oxford University Press, Oxford.

Jambu, Jérôme

2019 Les "monnaies des pirates": entre imaginaire collectif et réalité archéo-numismatique. In *Archéologie de la piraterie des XVIIe–XVIIIe siècles: étude de la vie quotidienne des flibustiers dans les Caraïbes et l'océan Indien*, edited by Jean Soulat, pp. 365–381. Éditions Mergoil, Drémil-Lafage, France.

Jenness, John Scribner

1875 *The Isles of Shoals: An Historical Sketch*. Riverside Press, Cambridge, United Kingdom.

Johnson, Charles

1724a *A General History of the Pyrates: Their First Rise and Settlement in the Island of Providence, to the Present Time*. 2nd ed. T. Warner, London.

1724b *A General History of the Robberies and Murders of the Most Notorious Pyrates*. C. Rivington, J. Lacy, London (facsimile edition 1962: Folio Society, London).

Jones, Evan

2012 *Inside the Illicit Economy: Reconstructing the Smugglers' Trade of Sixteenth Century Bristol*. Ashgate Publishing, Farnham, Surrey, United Kingdom.

Jornal do Brasil (Rio de Janeiro)

1966 Como achar (mesmo) um tesouro. March 17.

Kampfl, Jeffrey

2019 The Historical and Archaeological Analysis of the Swords of *La Belle*. PhD dissertation, Department of Anthropology, Texas A&M University.

Kapell, Matthew Wilhelm, and Andrew B. R. Elliott

2013 Conclusion(s): Playing at True Myths, Engaging with Authentic Histories. In *Playing with the Past: Digital Games and the Simulation of History*, edited by Matthew Wilhelm Kapell and Andrew B. R. Elliot, pp. 357–369. Bloomsbury Academic, New York.

Kearney, Lawrence

1823 Letter to David Porter, August 10. Letters Received by the Secretary of Navy from Captains (Captains Letters) 1805–1885, Microfilm 125, Record Group 260, Department of the Navy. National Archives, Washington, DC.

Kelleher, Connie

2016 Ireland's Golden Age of Piracy: History, Cartography, and Emerging Archaeology. In *Pieces of Eight: More Archaeology of Piracy*, edited by Charles R. Ewen and Russell K. Skowronek, pp. 165–192. University Press of Florida, Gainesville.

2020 *The Alliance of Pirates: Ireland and Atlantic Piracy in the Early Seventeenth Century*. Cork University Press, Cork, Ireland.

Kenyon, Kimberly P.

2016 Prioritizing the Concretions from *Queen Anne's Revenge* for Conservation: A Case Study in Managing a Large Collection. In *ACUA Underwater Archaeology Proceedings 2016*, edited by Paul F. Johnston, pp. 84–89. Advisory Council on Underwater Archaeology, Washington, DC.

Kert, Faye

2015 *Privateering: Patriots & Profits in the War of 1812*. Johns Hopkins University Press, Baltimore, Maryland.

Kingsley, Sean

2020 Pirates. *Wreckwatch Magazine* 3–4 (December). www.wreckwatchmag.com.

Kinkor, Kenneth J.

2016 Artifacts That Talk Like Pirates: Jolly Roger Iconography and Archaeological Sites. In *Pieces of Eight: More Archaeology of Piracy*, edited by Charles R. Ewen and Russell K. Skowronek, pp. 228–238. University Press of Florida, Gainesville.

Klooster, Wim

1998 *Illicit Riches: Dutch Trade in the Caribbean, 1648–1795*. Kitlv Press, Leiden, the Netherlands.

Knight, David W,

1999 A Documentary History of the Cinnamon Bay Plantation 1718–1917. Compiled for the Virgin Island National Park's Cinnamon Bay Archaeology Project. On file at the Virgin Islands National Park, St. John.

Knox, John P.

1852 *A Historical Account of St. Thomas, W. I.* Charles Scribner, New York.

Konstam, Angus

2003 *The Pirate Ship 1660–1730*. Osprey Publishing, Oxford, United Kingdom.

2006 *Blackbeard: America's Most Notorious Pirate*. John Wiley and Sons, Hoboken, New Jersey.

2008 *Piracy: The Complete History*. Osprey Publishing, Oxford, Oxford, United Kingdom.

2019 *The Pirate World: A History of the Most Notorious Sea Robbers*. Bloomsbury, London.

Kouadio, Auguste Y.

2018 Akan Gold Weights: Values Perspectives of a Non-Western Cultural Artifact. Master's thesis, Department of Interdisciplinary Humanities, University of California–Merced.

Labat, Jean-Baptiste

1730 *Voyage du Chevalier des Marchais aux Isles et à Cayenne, fait en 1725–1727*. Pierre Prault, Paris.

Landstrom, Björn
1961 *The Ship: An Illustrated History*. Doubleday, Garden City, New York.
Langham, A. F.
1989 Thomas Benson's Convict Slaves on Lundy. *Annual Report of the Lundy Field Society* 40(14):50–52.
1994 *The Island of Lundy*. History Press, Stroud, United Kingdom.
Lassure, Jean-Michel
2005 Le décor des plats et assiettes de Giroussens (Tarn) au XVIIe siècle. *Mémoires de la Société Archéologique du Midi de la France* 65:197–214.
Launders, John L.
1823 Affidavit to Mayor John Holt, February 11. Letters Received 1789–1906, Miscellaneous Letters, M179, Record Group 59. National Archives, Washington, DC.
Lawson, Russell M.
2007 *The Isles of Shoals in the Age of Sail*. History Press, Charleston, South Carolina.
Lefroy, John Henry
1877 *Memorial of the Discovery and Early Settlement of the Bermudas or Somers 685*. Longmans, Green, London.
Levett, Christopher
1628 *A Voyage into New England*. William Jones, London.
Lincoln, Captain Barnabas
1822 *Narrative of the Capture, Sufferings and Escape of Capt. Barnabas Lincoln and His Crew, Who Were Taken By a Piratical Schooner, December 1821, off Key Largo; Together with Facts Illustrating the Character of Those Piratical Cruisers*. Ezra Lincoln, Boston.
Lizé, Patrick
1984 The Wreck of the Pirate Ship *Speaker* on Mauritius in 1702. *International Journal of Nautical Archaeology and Underwater Exploration* 13(2):121–132.
2006 Piracy in the Indian Ocean: Mauritius and the Pirate Ship *Speaker*. In *X Marks the Spot: The Archaeology of Piracy*, edited by Russell K. Skowronek and Charles R. Ewen, pp. 81–99. University Press of Florida, Gainesville.
Lohse, Russell
2002 Slave-Trade Nomenclature and African Ethnicities in the Americas: Evidence from Early Eighteenth-Century Costa Rica. *Slavery & Abolition: A Journal of Slave and Post-Slave Studies* 23(3):73–92.
2005a Africans and Their Descendants in Colonial Costa Rica, 1600–1750. PhD dissertation, University of Texas, Austin.
2005b Africans in a Colony of Creoles: The Yoruba in Colonial Costa Rica. In *The Yoruba Diaspora in the Atlantic World*, edited by Toyin Falola and Matt D. Childs, pp. 130–156. Indiana University Press, Bloomington.
2014 *Africans into Creoles: Slavery, Ethnicity, and Identity in Colonial Costa Rica*. University of New Mexico Press, Albuquerque, New Mexico.
Lords of Commons
1830 Affairs of the East India Company: Minutes of Evidence, July 6. In *Journal of the House of Lords: Volume 62, 1830*, pp. 1168–1172. His Majesty's Stationery Office,

London. *British History Online* (December 20, 2020). https://www.british-history.ac.uk/lords-jrnl/vol62/pp1217-1223.

Lordy, Roberto de Aquino

1982 Da importância da pesquisa subaquática na arqueologia brasileira. *Revista Paulista de Arqueologia* 1 (no pagination).

LucasArts Entertainment

1990 *The Secret of Monkey Island*. LucasArts Entertainment, San Francisco.

LucasArts Entertainment and Telltale Games

1990–2010 *Monkey Island* series. LucasArts Entertainment/Telltale Games, San Francisco/San Rafael, California.

Lusardi, Wayne R.

2002 Cannon, Munitions, and Small Arms from the Wreck of the Pirate Vessel *Queen Anne's Revenge* (1718). *Man at Arms* 24(2):32–39.

2006 The Beaufort Inlet Shipwreck Artifact Assemblage. In *X Marks the Spot: The Archaeology of Piracy*, edited by Russell K. Skowronek and Charles R. Ewen, pp. 196–218. University Press of Florida, Gainesville.

Macleod, Murdo

2010 *Spanish Central America: A Socioeconomic History, 1520–1720*. University of Texas Press, Austin.

MacNeill, Ben Dixon

1958 *The Hatterasman*. John F. Blair, Winston-Salem, North Carolina.

Mahaffy, Robert Pentland

1900 *Calendar of the State Papers Relating to Ireland, of the Reign of Charles I (1625–1632)*. Vol. 1. Her Majesty's Stationary Office, London.

Maillard, Bruno

2014 L'impossible bagne: les "envoyés" de l'île Bourbon à Sainte-Marie de Madagascar. *Annales Historiques de la Révolution Française* 375:115–138 (January–March, online). http://ahrf.revues.org/13070.

Maine Department of Agriculture, Conservation, and Forestry

2013 The Village at Pemaquid. https://www.maine.gov/dacf/parks/discover_history_explore_nature/history/colonialpemaquid/village.shtml (accessed February 5, 2023).

Malcolm, Corey

2017 Continued Investigations of Sites and Artifacts Believed to Relate to the Pirate-Slaver Guerrero and HMS *Nimble*, 2005–2014. Report to Florida Keys National Marine Sanctuary from Mel Fisher Maritime Heritage Society, Key West.

Marley, David F.

2011 *Modern Piracy: A Reference Handbook*. ABC-CLIO, Santa Barbara, California.

Martin, Colin J. M.

2017 *A Cromwellian Warship Wrecked off Duart Point Castle, Mull, Scotland, in 1653*. Society of Antiquaries of Scotland, Edinburgh.

Martindale, Karen

2018a On the Verge: The Pocket Watch from *Queen Anne's Revenge*. In *ACUA Underwater Archaeology Proceedings 2018*, edited by Matthew Keith and Amanda Evans, pp. 15–20. Advisory Council on Underwater Archaeology, New Orleans.

2018b Report on Mystery Object QAR1108.010. North Carolina Department of Natural and Cultural Resources, Queen Anne's Revenge Conservation Lab, Greenville, North Carolina.

Mattingly, Garret

1963 No Peace beyond What Line? *Transactions of the Royal Historical Society* 13:145–162. Online (February 12, 2009). https://doi.org/10.2307/3678733.

McBride, J. David

2006 Contraband Traders, Lawless Vagabonds, and the British Settlement and Occupation of Roatan, Bay Islands, Honduras. In *X Marks the Spot: The Archaeology of Piracy*, edited by Russell K. Skowronek and Charles R. Ewen, pp. 44–63. University Press of Florida, Gainesville.

McCarthy, Michael

2005 *Ships' Fastenings: From Sewn Boat to Steamship*. Texas A&M University Press, College Station.

McKeever, Isaac

1825 Letter to Captain Lewis Warrington, April 1. Letters Received by the Secretary of Navy from Captains (Captains Letters) 1805–1885, Microfilm 125, Record Group 260, Department of the Navy. National Archives, Washington, DC.

McKillop, Heather

1985 Prehistoric Exploitation of the Manatee in the Maya and Circum-Caribbean Area. *World Archaeology* 16(3):337–353.

Mendiola, Daniel

2018 The Rise of the Mosquito Kingdom in Central America's Caribbean Borderlands: Sources, Questions and Enduring Myths. *History Compass* 16:1–10.

Metropolitan Museum of Art

2020 The Met Collection. Metropolitan Museum of Art, New York. https://www.metmuseum.org/art/collection (accessed December 18, 2020).

Meulen, J. van der

2003 *Goudse Pijpenmakers en Hun Merken*. Pijpelogische Kring Nederland, Leiden, the Netherlands.

MicroProse

1987 *Sid Meier's Pirates!* MicroProse, Hunt Valley, Maryland.

MicroProse and Firaxis Games

1991–2021 *Civilization* series. Hunt Valley: MicroProse, Hunt Valley, Maryland/Infogrames Entertainment/Novato: 2K Games, Paris.

Mol, Angus A. A., Csilla E. Ariese-Vandemeulebroucke, Krijn H. J. Boom, and Aris Politopoulos (editors)

2017 *The Interactive Past: Archaeology, Heritage & Video Games*. Sidestone Press, Leiden, the Netherlands.

Mollat, Hartmut

2003 A New Look at the Akan Gold Weights of West Africa. *Anthropos* 98(1):31–40.

Moore, David, and Mike Daniel

2001 Blackbeard's Capture of the Nantaise Slave Ship *La Concorde*: A Brief Analysis of the Documentary Evidence. *Tributaries* 11:15–31.

Moore, Peter
2000 Tilbury Fort: A Post-Medieval Fort and Its Inhabitants, *Post-Medieval Archaeology* 34:3–104.
Morales, Edgardo
2018 *No Limits to Their Sway: Cartagena's Privateers and the Masterless Caribbean in the Age of Revolutions*. Vanderbilt University Press, Nashville, Tennessee.
Moreau, Jean-Pierre
2006 *Pirates*. Tallandier, Paris.
2016 *Un flibustier français dans la mer des Antilles, édition présentée par J.-P. Moreau*. Éditions Payot, Paris.
Moreau de Saint-Méry, M.L.E.
1797 *Description topographique, physique, civile, politique et historique de la partie française de l'isle Saint-Domingue*. Vol. 1. Dupont, Paris.
Morelle, Nicolas
2019 Des fortifications de pirates dans le port de l'île Sainte-Marie (Madagascar) à la fin du XVIIe siècle. In *Archéologie de la piraterie des XVIIe–XVIIIe siècles: étude de la vie quotidienne des flibustiers dans les Caraïbes et l'océan Indien*, edited by Jean Soulat, pp. 187–195. Éditions Mergoil, Drémil-Lafage.
Mueller, G.O.W., and Freda Adler
1985 *Outlaws of the Ocean: The Complete Book of Contemporary Crime on the High Seas*. Hearst Marine Books, New York.
M. W.
1699 *The Mosqueto Indian and His Golden River: Being a Familiar Description of the Mosqueto Kingdom in America, &c., &c.* Verzameling Buitenlandse Kaarten Leupe, 16e–19e Eeuw: NL-HaNA 4.VEL. Nationaal Archief, The Hague.
National Archives of the United Kingdom (Richmond)
1718 Francis Hume's Papers. Admiralty Records, ADM 1/1879, f. 5.
Naughty Dog
2007–2016 *Uncharted* series. Sony Computer Entertainment, San Mateo, California.
2016 *Uncharted 4: A Thief's End*. Sony Computer Entertainment, San Mateo, California.
Niles, Hezekiah (editor)
1823 Documents, Essays, and Facts. *Niles' Weekly Register* (Baltimore, Maryland) 24 (March to September).
Nintendo
2003 *The Legend of Zelda: The Wind Waker*. Nintendo, Kyoto, Japan.
Nørregård, George
1948 *Forliset ved Nicaragua 1710*. Årbog, Handels Søfartsmuseet på Kronborg, Helsingør, Denmark.
North Devon Magazine
1824 Island of Lundy. *North Devon Magazine: Containing the Cave and Lundy Review* 1:54–62.
Oexmelin, Alexandre-Olivier
2017 *Histoire des frères de la côte: flibustiers et boucaniers des Antilles*. Nouveau Monde, Paris.

Offen, Karl

2020 Subsidy from Nature: Green Sea Turtles in the Colonial Caribbean. *Journal of Latin American Geography* 19(1):182–192.

Olien, Michael D.

1998 General, Governor, and Admiral: Three Miskito Lines of Succession. *Ethnohistory* 45(2):198–199.

Oviedo, Gonzalo Fernández de

1851 *De la historia general y natural de las Indias*. Real Academia de la Historia, Madrid.

Owen, G. D. (editor)

1920 *Calendar of the Manuscripts of the Most Honourable the Marquis of Salisbury (1609–1612)*. Vol. 21. Historical Manuscripts Commission, Her Majesty's Stationary Office, London.

Page, Courtney, and Charles Ewen

2016 Recognizing a Pirate Shipwreck without the Skull and Crossbones. In *Pieces of Eight: More Archaeology of Piracy*, edited by Charles R. Ewen and Russell K. Skowronek, pp. 260–273. University Press of Florida, Gainesville.

Pajot, Bernard

2004 *Atelier de productions des verriers de la Grésigne, Colloque de Sorèze*. Imprimerie Messages, Toulouse, France.

Palmer, Paula

1993 *What Happen: A Folk History of Costa Rica's Talamanca Coast*. Distribuidores Zona Tropical, Miami, Florida.

Paradox Development Studio

2004–2020 *Crusader Kings* series. Paradox Interactive/Strategy First, Stockholm/Montréal.

Parisis, Denise, and Henry Parisis

1994 Le siècle du sucre à Saint-Martin français. *Bulletin de la Société d'Histoire de la Guadeloupe* 99–102:3–208.

Parker, Lucretia

1825 *Piratical Barbarity, or The Female Captive*. William Avery, Providence, Rhode Island.

Parthesius, Robert

2010 *Dutch Ships in Tropical Waters: The Development of the Dutch East India Company (VOC) Shipping Network in Asia 1595–1660*. Amsterdam University Press, Amsterdam, Netherlands.

Pennell, C. R.

2001 *Bandits at Sea: A Pirates Reader*. New York University Press, New York.

Perez, Josef

1823 A Correct Report of the Trial of Josef Perez for Piracy, Committed on Board the Schooner *Bee*, of Charleston, S.C.: before the Circuit Court of the United Sates [*sic*] for the Southern District of New-York: on Tuesday, Sept. 9th, 1823. Library of Congress, Washington, DC.

Peterson, Rolfe Daus, Andrew Justin Miller, and Sean Joseph Fedorko

2013 The Same River Twice: Exploring Historical Representation and the Value of Simulation. In the *Total War, Civilization, and Patrician Franchises in Playing with the*

Past: Digital Games and the Simulation of History, edited by Matthew Wilhelml Kapell and Andrew B. R. Elliott, pp. 215–232. Bloomsbury Academic, New York.

Pfister, Eugen

2018 "In a world without gold, we might have been heroes!": Cultural Imaginations of Piracy in Video Games. *Forum for Inter-American Research* 11(2):30–43.

Piat, Denis

2014 *Pirates & Privateers in Mauritius*. Éditions Didier Millet, Singapore.

Pickering, Vernon W.

1983 *Early History of the British Virgin Islands: From Columbus to Emancipation*. Falcon Publications International, British Virgin Islands, New York.

Pimentel, A.

1962 *Catálogo de moedas brasileiras de 1643 a 1962*. 9th ed. Santos Leitão, Rio de Janeiro.

Pitta, Rocha

1730 *História da America Portugueza*. Da Sylva, Lisbon.

Pope, Peter E.

2004 *Fish into Wine: The Newfoundland Plantation in the Seventeenth Century*. University of North Carolina Press, Chapel Hill.

Porcher, Kevin

2019 La piraterie en Guadeloupe dans les années 1720. *Bulletin de la Société d'Histoire de la Guadeloupe* 183:15–38.

2020 "Faire le métier de pirate" dans les Antilles, l'exemple de Thomas Dulain (1728–1729). *Annales de Bretagne et des Pays de l'Ouest* 127(1):151–179.

Porter, David

1823 Letter to Smith Thompson, April 24. Letters Received by the Secretary of Navy from Captains (Captains Letters) 1805–1885, Microfilm 125, Record Group 260, Department of Navy. National Archives, Washington, DC.

1825 Deposition of Daniel Collins, January 17. Letters Received by the Secretary of Navy from Captains (Captains Letters) 1805–1885, Microfilm 125, Record Group 260, Department of the Navy. National Archives, Washington, DC.

Quinn, David B.

1989 Bermuda in the Age of Exploration and Early Settlement. *Bermuda Journal of Archaeology and Maritime History* 1:1–23.

Rare

1995 *Donkey Kong Country 2: Diddy Kong's Quest*. Nintendo, Kyoto, Japan.

Rediker, Marcus

1981 "Under the Banner of King Death": The Social World of Anglo-American Pirates, 1716 to 1726. *William and Mary Quarterly*, 3rd series, 38(2) (April 1981): 203–227.

2004 *Villains of All Nations: Atlantic Pirates in the Golden Age*. Beacon Press, Boston.

2014 *Outlaws of the Atlantic: Sailors, Pirates, and Motley Crews in the Age of Sail*. Beacon Press, Boston.

Regele, Lindsay Schakenbach

2019 *Manufacturing Advantage: War, the State, and the Origins of American Industry, 1776–1848*. Johns Hopkins University Press, Baltimore, Maryland.

Reger, Brandi, Juan L. Gonzalez, and Russell K. Skowronek
2020 Lithic Raw Materials in the Lower Rio Grande Valley, South Texas and Northeast Mexico. *Lithic Technology* 45(3):184–196.
Reinhard, Andrew
2018 *Archaeogaming: An Introduction to Archaeology in and of Video Games*. Berghahn, New York.
Rigsarkivet Arkivalieonline (Copenhagen, Denmark)
1671–1754 Shipping (West Indies, The West India and Guinea Company, Board of Directors: Documents concerning Voyages to the West Indies and Guinea). *Kron Prins* Folder 618–619.
Ringrose, Basil
1685 *Bucaniers of America, The Second Volume, Containing the Dangerous Voyage and Bold Attempts of Captain Bartholomew Sharp, and Others; Performed upon the Coasts of the South Sea, for the Space of Two Years, &c. from the Original Journal of the Said Voyage*. Printed for William Crooke, London.
Rivers-Cofield, Sara
2011 A Guide to Spurs of Maryland and Delaware ca. 1635–1820. *Northeast Historical Archaeology* 40:43–71.
Robert, Sieur
1730 Description en général et en détail de l'Isle de Madagascar. Manuscript No. 3755, ff. 109-117. Bibliothèque du Dépôt de la Marine de France, Paris.
Roberts, O. W.
1827 *Narratives of Voyages and Excursions on the East Coast and in the Interior of Central America; Describing a Journey up the River San Juan, and Passage across the Lake of Nicaragua to the City of Leon: Pointing Out the Advantages of a Direct Commercial Intercourse with the Natives*. Constable, Edinburgh.
Rodgers, Bradley A., Jason T. Raupp, Ian Harrison, Jason Nunn, Deborah Atwood, Annie Wright, Sean Cox, Katie Clevenger, Samantha Bernard, Katrina Bunyard, Joel Cook, Anna D'Jernes, Andrianna Dowel, Paul Gates, George Huss, Stephen Lacy, Ryan Marr, Connor McBrian, Sara Parkin, Madeline Roth, Timothy Smith, Stephanie Soder, and Elise Twohy
2017 Preliminary Report on the Phase I Pre-disturbance Survey of the Morgan's Island Wreck Site, Somerset Bermuda, May 2017. Report to Department of Conservation Services, Government of Bermuda from East Carolina University Program in Maritime Studies, Greenville, North Carolina.
Rogers, Woodes
1712 *A Cruising Voyage Round the World*. B. Lintot, London.
Rogozinski, Jan
2000 *Honor among Thieves: Captain Kidd, Henry Every & the Pirate Democracy in the Indian Ocean*, Stackpole Books, Mechanicsburg, Pennsylvania.
Rojas, Eugenia Ibarra
2012 Exploring Warfare and Prisoner Capture in Central South America. *Revista de Arqueología Americana* 30 (Cambios Climáticos en la Antiguëdad):114–116.
Rollinger, Christian (editor)
2020 *Classical Antiquity in Video Games: Playing with the Ancient World*. Bloomsbury Academic, London.

Romon, Thomas

2012 Saint-Martin, Grand Case, Route de Petite Plage. Rapport de diagnostic, Inrap Grand-Sud-Ouest, Guadeloupe.

Roten, J.

2019 Assumption Iconography: Themes and Evolution. University of Dayton: All about Mary (online). https://udayton.edu/imri/mary/a/assumption-iconography-themes-and-evolution.php (accessed October 7, 2019).

Russell, Charles William, and John P Prendergast (editors)

1974 *Calendar of the State Papers Relating to Ireland, of the Reign of James I (1608–1610).* Vol. 3. Longman, London.

Rutledge, Lyman V.

1997 *Ten Miles Out: A Guidebook to the Isles of Shoals.* Peter E. Randall, Portsmouth, New Hampshire.

Saint-Yves, Georges, and Joseph Fournier

1898 *L'Expédition de M. de La Haye à Madagascar (1670–1671).* Impr. Nationale, Paris.

Sandler, Martin W.

2017 *The Whydah: A Pirate Ship Feared, Wrecked, and Found.* Candlewick Press, Somerville, Massachusetts.

Sands, Abraham

1822 Pirate's Inventory. Abraham Sands Papers, Box 1, French Archives Papers, Photocopies, and Files, Folder 9. UWF Archives and West Florida History Center, Pensacola.

Santos, Antônio Vieira dos

1951 [1850] *Memória histórica da cidade de Paranaguá e seu municipio.* Vol. 1. Museu Paranaense, Curitiba, Brazil.

Schmitt, Casey

2018 Pirates, Planting and the Rights of Mankind in the Seventeenth-Century Tortuga. *Latin Americanist* 10 (January 10). Southeastern Council on Latin American Studies and Wiley Periodicals, College of William and Mary. https://doi.org/10.1111/tla.12167.

Schwarz, Angela

2014 Narration and Narrative: (Hi-)Story Telling in Video Games. In *Early Modernity and Video Games*, edited by Tobias Winnerling and Florian Kerschbaumer, pp. 140–161. Cambridge Scholars Publishing, Newcastle upon Tyne, United Kingdom.

Seaborn, Laurel

2017 Gamming Chairs and Gimballed Beds: Seafaring Women on Board Nineteenth-Century Ships. *Journal of Maritime Archaeology* 12(1):71–90.

Sellier-Ségard, Nathalie, and Clara Samuelian

2016 Un village de bord de mer du Néoindien récent à Grand-Case (Saint-Martin, Petites Antilles): premiers résultats. In *Proceedings of the XXVIth International Congress for Caribbean Archaeology* (July 2015, Saint-Martin), 175–188. International Association for Caribbean Archaeology, St. Maarten, Dutch West Indies.

Senior, C. M.

1976 *A Nation of Pirates: English Piracy in Its Heyday.* David and Charles, Newton Abbot, United Kingdom.

Serrand, Nathalie

2013 Saint-Martin, Grand Case, Rue des Flamboyants, Parcelle BK 76. Rapport de diagnostic archéologique, Inrap Grand-Sud-Ouest, Guadeloupe.

Service Historique de la Défense (Vincennes, France)

n.d. Description en général et en détail de l'Isle de Madagascar. Manuscripts: FR-SHD Ms 196.

Shoemaker, Raymond L.

1976 Diplomacy from the Quarterdeck: The United States Navy in the Caribbean, 1815–1830. PhD dissertation, Department of History, Indiana University, Bloomington. University Microfilms International, Ann Arbor, Michigan.

Skowronek, Russell K.

1984 *Trade Patterns of Eighteenth-Century Frontier New Spain: The 1733 Flota and St. Augustine* (revised MA thesis). Volumes in Historical Archaeology 1, edited by Stanley South. South Carolina Institute of Archaeology and Anthropology, University of South Carolina, Columbia.

1992 Empire and Ceramics: The Changing Role of Illicit Trade in Spanish America. *Historical Archaeology* 26(1):109–118.

2006 X Marks the Spot—Or Does it? In *X Marks the Spot: The Archaeology of Piracy*, edited by Russell K. Skowronek and Charles R. Ewen, 282–298. University Press of Florida, Gainesville.

2016 Setting a Course toward an Archaeology of Piracy. In *Pieces of Eight: More Archaeology of Piracy*, edited by Charles R. Ewen and Russell K. Skowronek, 1–14. University Press of Florida, Gainesville.

2017 Memorial: George Robert Fischer (1937–2016). *Historical Archaeology* 51(3):451–461.

2021 Making the Exotic Mundane: The Manila Galleon, the Flota, and Globalization. In *The Archaeology of Manila Galleons in the Americas: The Wrecks of San Juanillo, San Agustín, and Santo Cristo de Burgos*, edited by Scott Williams and Roberto Junco Sanchez, 7–24. Springer Nature, Cham, Switzerland.

Skowronek, Russell K., and Charles R. Ewen

2006 Identifying the Victims of Piracy in the Spanish Caribbean. In *X Marks the Spot: The Archaeology of Piracy*, edited by Russell K. Skowronek and Charles R. Ewen, pp. 248–270. University Press of Florida, Gainesville.

2016 Shiver Me Timbers!: The Influence of Hollywood on the Archaeology of Piracy. In *Pieces of Eight: More Archaeology of Piracy*, edited by Charles R. Ewen and Russell K. Skowronek, pp. 193–207. University Press of Florida, Gainesville.

Skowronek, Russell K., and Charles R. Ewen (editors)

2006 *X Marks the Spot: The Archaeology of Piracy*. University Press of Florida, Gainesville.

Skowronek, Russell K., and George R. Fischer

2009 *HMS Fowey Lost . . . and Found!* University Press of Florida, Gainesville.

Smith, Aaron

1824 *The Atrocities of the Pirates: A Faithful Narrative of the Unparalleled Suffering of the Author during His Captivity among the Pirates*. G. and W. B. Whitaker, London.

Smith, Joshua M.

2006 *Borderland Smuggling: Patriots, Loyalists, and Illicit Trade in the Northeast, 1783–1820*. University Press of Florida, Gainesville.

Smith, Kiona N.

2021 17th-Century Pirates Might Have Stashed Middle Eastern Coins in New England. *Ars Technica* (April 13). https://arstechnica.com/science/2021/04/17th-century-pirates-might-have-stashed-middle-eastern-coins-in-new-england.

Smith, Robert, and Ruth Brown

2007 Bronze Signalling or Saluting Gun: Preliminary Report (No. 82). North Carolina Department of Natural and Cultural Resources, Queen Anne's Revenge Conservation Lab, Greenville, North Carolina.

Smithsonian National Museum of African Art

2020 Collection. Smithsonian Museum of African Art, Washington, DC. https://africa.si.edu/collection. (accessed November 30, 2020).

Soulat, Jean

2019 À la découverte des pirates. *Dossiers d'Archéologie* 394 (July–August).

Soulat, Jean, and John de Bry

2019 Archaeology of Piracy between Caribbean Sea and the North American Coast of 17th and 18th Centuries: Shipwrecks, Material Culture and Terrestrial Perspectives. *Journal of Caribbean Archaeology* 19:68–103.

Soulat, Jean, and Yann von Arnim

2019 *Speaker 1702: Mission archéologique sur le navire du pirate John Bowen, Grande Rivière Sud-Est, île Maurice*. Programme de Recherche Archéologie de la Piraterie, Rapport Scientifique de Préparation à la Mission de Novembre 2020, Samois-sur-Seine, France.

2022 *Speaker 1702: Histoire et archéologie d'un navire pirate coulé à l'Île Maurice*. Edition ADLP, Samois-sur-Seine, France.

Soulat, Jean, Yann von Arnim, and Patrick Lizé

2019 Le mobilier de l'épave pirate du *Speaker* 1702. In *Archéologie de la piraterie des XVIIe–XVIIIe siècles: étude de la vie quotidienne des flibustiers dans les Caraïbes et l'océan Indien*, edited by Jean Soulat, pp. 245–267. Éditions Mergoil, Drémil-Lafage, France.

South Carolina Court of Vice-Admiralty

1719 *The Tryals of Major Stede Bonnet and Other Pirates*. Benjamin Cowse, London.

Stack, Margaret

2011 An Archaeological and Archival Appraisal of "Spanish Indians" on the West Coast of Florida in the Eighteenth and Nineteenth Centuries. Master's thesis, Department of Applied Anthropology, University of South Florida, Tampa.

Steam

2022 Pirates. https://store.steampowered.com/search/?term=pirates.

Steffy, J. Richard

1994 *Wooden Shipbuilding and the Interpretation of Shipwrecks*. Texas A&M University Press, College Station.

Stelle, Lenville J.

2001 An Archaeological Guide to Historic Artifacts of the Upper Sangamon Basin. Center for Social Research, Parkland College (May 4, 2020). http://virtual.parkland.edu/lstelle1/len/archguide/documents/arcguide.htm.

Stevenson, Robert Louis

1883 *Treasure Island*. Cassell, London. https://en.wikisource.org/wiki/Treasure_Island_(1883) (accessed October 31, 2021).

1902 *Treasure Island*. Edited with notes and introduction by Hiram Albert Vance. Macmillan, New York.

Stevenson, W. H. (editor)

1916 *Calendar of the Liberate Rolls Preserved in the Public Record Office: Henry III (1240–1245)*. Vol. 2, Membrane 11. Her Majesty's Stationary Office, London.

St. Mary's University Archaeology Lab

2010 Ceramics Database. http://www.smu.ca/academic/arts/anthropology/ceramics/welcome.html (accessed September 13, 2017).

Stouvenot, Christian, and Christophe Hénocq

1999 Inventaire des sites archéologiques de la partie française de l'île de Saint-Martin, Guadeloupe. AAHE-DAC de Guadeloupe.

Takahashi, Dean

2016 The Comprehensive Interview with Uncharted 4 Creators Neil Druckmann and Bruce Straley. VentureBeat. https://venturebeat.com/2016/05/27/the-comprehensive-interview-with-uncharted-4-creators-neil-druckmann-and-bruce-straley/view-all (accessed February 20, 2021).

Ternstrom, M.

2008 Obituary: Keith Gardner. *Annual Report of the Lundy Field Society* 58(11):15.

Thackray, C.

1989 Lundy: National Trust Archaeological Survey Report. 2 vols. Unpublished. National Trust, Swindon, United Kingdom.

Thésée, Françoise

2008a Documents Colbert-Antilles: discours sur le stat présent des isles de l'Amérique appelées les Antilles. *Outre-Mers* 95(360–361) (l'Afrique des Indiens):242–296.

2008b L'ingénieur du roi François Blondel (1618–1686): sa mission aux isles d'Amérique (1666–1667). *Outre-Mers* 95(360–361) (l'Afrique des Indiens): 223–240.

Thomin, Michael

2018 Among Ships of Thieves on Waves of Change. *Coriolis: Interdisciplinary Journal of Maritime Studies* 8(1):12–32.

Tilley, Christopher

2013 Objectification. In *Handbook of Material Culture*, edited by Christopher Tilley, Webb Keane, Susanne Kuchler, Mike Rowlands, and Patricia Spyer, pp. 60–73. Sage Publications, London.

Tomadini, Noémie, Nathalie Sellier-Ségard, and Sandrine Grouard

2023 A Turkey on the Island of St. Martin (FWI) at the End of the 17th–Early 18th Century AD. In *Exploring the History of Turkey Domestication and Management*, edited by Aurelie Manin, Camila Speller, Eduardo Corona, and Erin Thornton (forthcoming). Collection Natures en Sociétés. Éditions Scientifique du Muséum National d'Histoire Naturelle, Paris.

Transatlantic Slave Trade Database

1710a Voyage 35157, *Christianus Quintus (a) Christian V* (1710). https://archive.slavevoyages.org/voyage/35157/variables.

1710b Voyage 35158, *Fredericus Quartus (a) Frederick IV* (1710). https://archive.slavevoyages.org/voyage/35158/variables.

Ubisoft

2007–2020 *Assassin's Creed* series. Ubisoft, Paris.

2007 *Assassin's Creed.* Ubisoft, Paris.

2012 *Assassin's Creed III.* Ubisoft, Paris.

2013 *Assassin's Creed IV: Black Flag.* Ubisoft, Paris.

2014 *Assassin's Creed: Rogue.* Ubisoft, Paris.

United States Circuit Court

1834 *A Report of the Trial of the Spanish Pirates before the United States Circuit Court.* Russell, Odiorne, and Metcalf, Boston.

United States v. Pegasus

1820 A List of Articles Found on Board the Schooner *Pegasus* Not Mentioned in Her Manifest. Records of the District Courts of the United States, 1685–2009, Record Group 21. Case Files, Fort Worth, Texas.

Urban, S.

1839 "Journal of the Time We Spent on the Island of Lundy in the Years 1752 and 1787" by a Gentleman. *Cave and Lundy Review and Critical Revolving Light* (Barnstaple, United Kingdom).

Vallejo Jorge, J. M.

2017 "Yo soy Cristóbal Linche": análisis bioarqueológico y contextualización de los restos del individuo no. 2 de la cripta de la Iglesia de Santo Domingo de Guzmán, La Laguna (Tenerife). In *Jornadas de jóvenes investigadores en arqueología, libro II,* edited by Asociación Jóvenes Investigadores de Arqueología, pp. 262–286. Asociación Jóvenes Investigadores en Arqueología, Madrid.

Van Broeck, Adrian

1709 *The Life and Adventures of Capt. John Avery, the Famous English Pirate (Rais'd from a Cabbin-Boy to a King) Now in Possession of Madagascar.* N.p., London.

van den Bel, Martijn

2015 Description des Caraïbes cannibales ou des îles sauvages @ 1627: un routier néerlandais des Petites Antilles collationné par Hessel Gerritsz. *Bulletin de la Société d'Histoire de la Guadeloupe* 171:1–53.

2020 How to make Cassava Bread: The Introduction of Metal Graters in the Guianas during the 17th Century. *Americae: Revue Européenne d'Archéologie Américaniste* 5. https://americae.fr/articles/make-cassava-bread-introduction-metal-graters-guianas (accessed February 4, 2013).

Van Duivenvoorde, Wendy

2015 The Use of Copper and Lead Sheathing in VOC Shipbuilding. *International Journal of Nautical Archaeology* 44(2):349–361.

Vaz, J. Ferraro, and Javier Salgado

1984 *Livro das moedas de Portugal.* 2 vols. Publicações Numismáticas, Braga, Portugal.

Victor, Megan Rhodes
2019 Under the Tavern Table: Excavations at the Tavern on Smuttynose Island, Maine, and Implications for Commensal Politics and Informal Economy. *International Journal of Historical Archaeology* 23(1):34–56.

Vitkus, Daniel J., and Nabil Matar
2001 *Piracy, Slavery, and Redemption: Barbary Captivity Narratives from Early Modern England.* Columbia University Press, New York.

von Arnim, Yann, Patrick Lizé, and Jean Soulat
2019 L'épave du *Speaker* 1702, navire pirate de John Bowen (Grande Rivière Sud-Est, île Maurice). In *Archéologie de la piraterie des XVIIe–XVIIIe siècles: étude de la vie quotidienne des flibustiers dans les Caraïbes et l'océan Indien*, edited by Jean Soulat, pp. 97–107. Éditions Mergoil, Drémil-Lafage, France.

Wafer, Lionel
1699 *A New Voyage and Description of the Isthmus of America.* James Knapton, London.

Wagner, Mark, and Mary McCorvie
2006 Going to See the Varmint: Piracy in Myth and Reality on the Ohio and Mississippi Rivers, 1785–1830. In *X Marks the Spot: The Archaeology of Piracy*, edited by Russell K. Skowronek and Charles R. Ewen, pp. 219–247. University Press of Florida, Gainesville.

Warrington, Lewis
1822 Deposition of David Eaton to Mayor Holt, July 24. Letters Received by the Secretary of Navy from Captains (Captains Letters) 1805–1885, Microfilm 125, Record Group 260, Department of the Navy. National Archives, Washington, DC.

Watts, Gordon Payne, Jr.
2014 *Shipwrecked: Bermuda's Maritime Heritage.* National Museum of Bermuda Press, Old Royal Naval Dockyard, Bermuda.

Webster, Jane
2005 Looking for the Material Culture of the Middle Passage. *Journal of Maritime Research* 7(1):245–258.

Westergaard, Waldemar
1917 *The Danish West Indies under Company Rule (1671–1754), with a Supplementary Chapter, 1755–1917.* Macmillan, New York.

White, Carolyn L.
2005 *American Artifacts of Personal Adornment, 1680–1820: A Guide to Identification and Interpretation.* American Association for State and Local History, Nashville, Tennessee.
2009 Knee, Garter, Girdle, Hat, Stock and Spur Buckles from Seven Sites in Portsmouth, New Hampshire. *International Journal of Historical Archaeology* 13:239–253.

White, Stephen W.
1975 On the Origins of Gunspalls. *Historical Archaeology* 9:65–73.

Whitehead, Ross
1996 *Buckles, 1250–1800.* Greenlight Publishing, Hatfield Peverel, United Kingdom.

Wild, Kenneth S.
2019 The Archaeology of Pirates, Privateers, or Planters: Locating and Identifying the

First European Settlers of St. John, U.S. Virgin Islands. Paper presented at the XXVII International Congress for Caribbean Archaeology, St. Croix, 2017.

Wilde-Ramsing, Mark U.

2006 The Pirate Ship *Queen Anne's Revenge*. In *X Marks the Spot: The Archaeology of Piracy*, edited by Russell K. Skowronek and Charles R. Ewen, pp. 160–195. University Press of Florida, Gainesville.

Wilde-Ramsing, Mark, and Linda Carnes-McNaughton

2018 *Blackbeard's Sunken Prize: The 300-Year Voyage of Queen Anne's Revenge*. University of North Carolina Press, Chapel Hill.

Wilde-Ramsing, Mark U., and Charles R. Ewen

2012 Beyond Reasonable Doubt: A Case for *Queen Anne's Revenge*. *Historical Archaeology* 46(2):110–133.

Williamson, James Alexander

1923 *English Colonies in Guiana and on the Amazon: 1604–1668*. Clarendon Press, Oxford.

Witsen, Nicolaes

1671 *Aeloude and Hedendaegshce Scheepsbouw en Bestier*. Amsterdam, the Netherlands.

Woodard, Colin

2007 *The Republic of Pirates*. Harcourt, New York.

Wright, Irene A.

1934–1935 *Nederlanse Zeevaarder op de Eilanden in de Caraibische Zee en aan de Kust van Columbia en Venezuela gedurende de Jaren 1621–1648(9)*. 2 vols. Werken van het Historische Genootschap Utrecht 63–64. Kemmink en Zoon, Utrecht, the Netherlands.

Contributors

Patrick J. Boyle received his MPhil at the University of Bristol in 2017 and his MA from East Carolina University in 2022. His research focused on the material culture of seventeenth-century English piracy. He is currently seeking a PhD in the Nautical Archaeology Program at Texas A&M University.

Alexandre Coulaud holds a Master 2 degree in archaeology from Burgundy University (Dijon, France). He is an archaeologist and has been project leader for Inrap since 2011, based in Gourbeyre (Guadeloupe) since 2016. He conducts archaeological investigations and studies metallic artifacts in the French West Indies. Coulaud is a specialist in the modern and contemporary period, especially in military contexts. He is also a member of the Unité Mixte de Recherche 8096, Archéologie des Amériques, Université Paris I—Panthéon/Sorbonne and a member of ADLP research program since its foundation. He recently contributed to *Archéologie de la piraterie* des XVIIe–XVIIIe siècles, edited by Jean Soulat.

Jessie Cragg is curator of exhibits at the University of West Florida Historic Trust, located in Pensacola, Florida. She has a MA in history/public history. Her thesis focused on piracy during the early republic. She also has a background in archaeology from her undergraduate studies at the University of Georgia, is dive certified, and is passionate about maritime archaeology. She recently worked for Gulf Islands National Seashore and the Pensacola Lighthouse & Maritime Museum before becoming a curator.

John de Bry is a historian, paleographer, and archaeologist, specializing in French and Spanish manuscripts from the sixteenth to the eighteenth centuries. He has done extensive research in European, Mexican, Central and South American, and Cuban archives. He is also an experienced underwater archaeologist and has participated in a large number of archaeological excavations in the United States, the Caribbean, Central and South America, Madagascar, and the Philippines. He holds a master's degree in history and a doctorate in modern history. He is the director of the Center for Historical Archaeology in Melbourne Beach, Florida, and is also a consultant to SEARCH, Inc. (Southeastern Archaeological Research). He founded the Archaeology of Piracy research program in 2019 and serves as its co-director with Jean Soulat. De Bry is a direct descendant of the Flemish engraver and publisher Theodore de Bry, who published *Grands voyages*, including the 1591 *Brevis* narration (based on the watercolors of Jacques Le Moyne de Morgues, the artist who accompanied the 1564 French expedition to Florida, and the account of René Goulaine de Laudonnière, who established Fort Caroline on the northeast coast of Florida).

Charles R. Ewen (PhD University of Florida, 1987) is professor of anthropology at East Carolina University, where he also serves as the director of the Phelps Archaeology Laboratory. He is the coeditor of *X Marks the Spot: The Archaeology of Piracy* (with Russell Skowronek) and its companion volume *Pieces of Eight: More Archaeology of Piracy* (with Russell Skowronek). Ewen is also the author or editor of a number of other books, including *From Spaniard to Creole: The Archaeology of Cultural Formation at Puerto Real, Haiti, Hernando de Soto among the Apalachee: The Archaeology of the First Winter Encampment* (with John Hann), *Artifacts*, and *Searching for the Roanoke Colonies* (with Tom Shields)

Lynn B. Harris is associate professor in the Program of Maritime Studies in the History Department at East Carolina University. She currently serves as codirector of the Coastal and Marine Interdisciplinary Program. She specialized in archaeology and African Studies at Stellenbosch University in South Africa, maritime history and archaeology at East Carolina University in North Carolina, and historic preservation and colonial history at the University of South Carolina. Harris is the author of *Patroons and Periaguas: Enslaved Watermen of the South Carolina Lowcountry* and editor of the compiled volume *Seaports and Sea Power: African Maritime Landscapes*. Among her journal articles are "African Canoe to Plantation Crew: Tracing African Memory and Legacy" in *Coriolis: Interdisciplinary Journal of Maritime Studies*, which won the annual award for best article. She has won several awards for fieldwork photography at the Society for Historical Archaeology and recently served as a consultant for *National Geographic* on slave ship history in the *Drain the Oceans* series. Harris teaches courses in underwater archaeology methods, maritime material culture, maritime landscapes, watercraft history, and coastal cultural resource management.

Geraldo J. S. Hostin is an Australian and Brazilian archaeologist, living in Halls Head, Western Australia. He has a master's degree in professional archaeology (University of Western Australia). Hostin is a marine surveyor and currently does research in maritime archaeology. His current projects are the clipper *Redemptora* shipwreck in Australia and a pirate ship sunk off Cotinga Island in Brazil.

Coy J. Idol is agricultural and life sciences lead educator at Old Salem Museum and Gardens. He uses this position to understand the role of interpreters and docents as NPCs (nonplayer characters) in the visitor's exploration of colonial North Carolina. As a video game player and archaeogamer, he has given presentations at archaeological conferences in Europe and the United States on how to use video games to teach the playing public about archaeology through video games.

Kimberly P. Kenyon, originally from Texas, moved to North Carolina to join the Queen Anne's Revenge (QAR) Project team in 2013. She is a graduate of the Nautical Archaeology Program at Texas A&M University, where she completed her MA in anthropology and earned a certificate in conservation. Her thesis is titled "Reconstructing the Assemblage of Iron Artifacts from the Late Hellenistic Shipwreck at Kizilburun, Turkey." She earned a BA in maritime studies from Texas A&M University at Galveston, minoring in both English and anthropology. Kenyon has worked as a field conservator on projects in Texas, North Carolina, Costa Rica, and Puerto Rico and served as a diver and conservator for both the Kizilburun Column Wreck Excavation near Izmir, Turkey, and the Cape Gelidonya Bronze Age Shipwreck near Finike, Turkey. She was interim head conservator for the Institute of Nautical Archaeology (INA) in Bodrum, Turkey, and continues to serve INA as a research associate. Kenyon also teaches a graduate-level introduction to conservation course at East Carolina University and currently holds a seat on the Monitor National Marine Sanctuary Advisory Council. She was appointed field director for the 2015 QAR excavation and is now a co–principal investigator for the QAR Project and a member of the Office of State Archaeology scientific diving program.

Patrick Lizé is a French historian, archivist, and archaeologist. With Jacques Dumas, he discovered in 1979 the wreck of the *Speaker* (1702), which ran aground on the east coast of Mauritius. He is the author of several articles on the *Speaker*, notably "The Wreck of the Pirate Ship *Speaker* on Mauritius in 1702" in the *International Journal of Nautical Archaeology and Underwater Exploration* and "Piracy in the Indian Ocean: Mauritius and the Pirate Ship Speaker" in *X Marks the Spot: Archaeology of Piracy*. He has written numerous works on the pirate John Bowen, captain of the *Speaker*, including a complete biography based on archival evidence: *La véritable histoire du pirate Bowen*. Lizé has discovered numerous wrecks since the *Speaker*, some of which are on the French Atlantic coast. He remains one of the top specialists in eighteenth-century maritime archives.

Laurent Pavlidis holds a doctorate in history from the University of Aix-Marseille and is the curator of the Maritime History Museum at the Citadel of Saint-Tropez. His research focuses on maritime history, particularly shipbuilding and the merchant marine in the eighteenth and nineteenth centuries. He also works on the history of coastal fortification and siege warfare in Europe and the West Indies from the seventeenth to the nineteenth century. These themes have led him to take an interest in freebooting in the Caribbean and the barbarian question in the Mediterranean. He is currently conducting a study on the French fortifications of the colonial period in the Republic of Haiti.

Jason T. Raupp is assistant professor in the Maritime Studies Program at East Carolina University and holds a PhD in archaeology from Flinders University. Over the past twenty years he has been involved with maritime and terrestrial archaeological research in the United States, West Africa, Australia, Asia, Europe, the Caribbean, and the Pacific region. Raupp's research interests include historical and maritime archaeology of the Pacific Ocean, Latin America, and the Caribbean, culture contact, historic fisheries, military technologies, battlefield studies, and contact-period rock art. He has authored or coauthored chapters in books, papers in conference proceedings, book reviews, and professional reports as well as numerous articles in the *Journal of Maritime Archaeology, International Journal of Nautical Archaeology, Bulletin of the Australasian Institute for Maritime Archaeology*, and *Florida Historical Quarterly*.

Bradley Rodgers recently retired from East Carolina University, where he was professor and former director of the Maritime Studies Program. His research has focused on the underwater archaeology of the Great Lakes, Bermuda, and numerous projects along the North Carolina coast and inland waterways. He is the author of numerous books and articles, including *The Archaeologist's Manual for Conservation* and *Guardian of the Great Lakes: The U.S. Paddle Frigate Michigan*.

Nathalie Sellier-Ségard holds a Master 2 degree in human and physical geography and prehistory from the University of Northern France (Lille). She has worked for Inrap for more than twenty-five years and is based in Gourbeyre (Guadeloupe). She studies lithic assemblages from the pre-Columbian and colonial periods in the French Caribbean. Sellier-Ségard is a member of the Unité Mixte de Recherche 8096, Archéologie des Amériques, Université Paris I—Panthéon/Sorbonne. She directed excavations at Grand Case Bay, St. Martin, in 2014 and 2016.

Russell K. Skowronek (PhD Michigan State University, 1989) is professor of anthropology and history at the University of Texas Rio Grande Valley, where he also serves as the associate dean for faculty research and diversity in the College of Liberal Arts and as the director of the Community Historical Archaeology Project with Schools (CHAPS) Program. He teaches an undergraduate and graduate class on maritime archaeology and history titled "Shipwrecks, Pirates, and the Sea." Skowronek is the coeditor of *X Marks the Spot: The Archaeology of Piracy* (with Charles Ewen) and its companion volume, *Pieces of Eight: More Archaeology of Piracy* (with Charles Ewen). He is also the author or editor of a number of other books, including *HMS Fowey Lost . . . and Found!* (with George Fischer), *Beneath the Ivory Tower: The Archaeology of Academia* (with Kenneth Lewis), *Recovering a Legacy: The Ceramics of Alta California* (with M. James Blackman and Ronald L. Bishop), *Situating Mission Santa Clara de Asís, 1776–1851: Documentary and Material Evidence of Life on the Alta California Frontier*, and *Blue and Gray on the Border: The Rio Grande Valley Civil War Trail* and *The Civil War on the Rio Grande, 1846–1876* (with Roseann Bacha-Garza and Christopher L. Miller).

Jean Soulat holds a PhD in medieval archaeology from the University of Paris 1 Panthéon-Sorbonne. He is an archaeologist and research engineer at the LandArc Laboratory in France and is attached to the Michel de Boüard Center at the University of Caen Normandy (Craham UMR 6273-CNRS). A specialist in postmedieval material culture, he conducts most of his research on the study of archaeological objects in France, the Americas, and the Indian Ocean. For several years, he has focused his work on the archaeology of seventeenth- to eighteenth-century piracy in connection with the analysis of terrestrial and underwater contexts, such as the *Speaker* wreck in Mauritius. He founded the Archaeology of Piracy research program in 2019, which he co-directs with John de Bry. Soulat edited Archéologie de la piraterie des XVIIe–XVIIIe siècles and coauthored "Archaeology of Piracy between Caribbean Sea and the North American Coast of 17th and 18th Centuries: Shipwrecks, Material Culture and Terrestrial Perspectives" (with John de Bry), in the *Journal of Caribbean Archaeology*.

Katherine D. Thomas is a CRM professional in California. She has presented at conferences in Europe and the United States on video games and archaeology, focusing on gender and feminist theory. She currently resides in the San Francisco Bay Area.

Michael Thomin is manager of the Florida Public Archaeology Network's Destination Archaeology Resource Center and faculty research associate at the University of West Florida. He has a MA in history/public history and has spent over a decade working as a museum professional in public archaeology. He is a certified guide with the National Association for Interpretation and has worked on a variety of heritage interpretive and heritage tourism projects across Florida with local, state, federal, and international agencies. Thomin has a passion for maritime history and is a certified computer nitrox/scientific diver. His published articles on topics including piracy and heritage management have appeared in *Legacy*, *Museum Review*, *ACUA Underwater Archaeology Proceedings*, *Interdisciplinary Journal of Maritime Studies*, and *Journal of the American Revolution*.

Martijn van den Bel is archaeologist and project leader for Inrap in the Lesser Antilles and French Guiana. He earned his PhD at Leiden University in 2015, focusing on the Ceramic Age of French Guiana. In addition to his work in project-led archaeology, he participates in various multidisciplinary projects as an archaeologist, addressing the impact of ancient human presence in the tropical forest of French Guiana. He also conducts archival research on the colonial encounter in the Lesser Antilles and the coastal Guianas during the seventeenth century.

Megan Rhodes Victor (PhD, William and Mary, 2018) is assistant professor of anthropology at Queens College, City University of New York. She received her BA in anthropology from the University of Michigan (2010) and her MA from William and Mary in 2013. She is an anthropological archaeologist with a focus on historical archaeology, encompassing sites from roughly 1500 to 1900. Victor examines three main topics: commensality; the archaeology of alcohol within public drinking spaces; and the archaeology of frontier spaces. She has worked extensively on archaeology of the English colonial world in North America, including excavations at the fishing village and trading post on Smuttynose Island, Maine (1623–1780s), Virginia's colonial capital of Williamsburg, including the eighteenth-century Raleigh Tavern, and sites throughout Chesapeake Bay. Much of her current research on negotiations and the informal economy takes place in the context of the Atlantic world and English colonial world. She previously worked as a project archaeologist for Colonial Williamsburg, leading the day-to-day excavations within the revolutionary city. Most recently, she was a postdoctoral scholar at the Stanford Archaeology Center at Stanford University (2017–2020), where she directed the archaeological excavations of the Arboretum Chinese Labor Quarters (ACLQ) Project.

Yann von Arnim holds a master's degree in oceanography and a master's degree in coastal resources exploitation. He is responsible for conservation of the underwater heritage within various Mauritian institutions and associations. He is currently a consultant in various fields of marine sciences, such as underwater archaeology, coastal environment, and aquaculture. His main interests are the development of maritime archaeology and the sustainable management of marine aquaculture in Mauritius. As president of the Mauritius Historical Society, vice president of the Mauritius Marine Conservation Society, and member of the Board of Directors of the Mauritius Museums Council, he has led several archaeological campaigns on the wrecks of the British frigate *Sirius* and the slave ship *Coureur*. In collaboration with the Stanford University Center for Archaeology, he is currently directing his research toward the inventory of the Mauritian underwater cultural heritage. He has published in the field of underwater archaeology and has written several books, such as *Les fonds sous-marin de Maurice et Rodrigues* and *Blue and White China from Shipwrecks in Mauritius: Symbolism in Decorations*.

Kenneth S. Wild holds an MS from Florida State University (1988) and was certified as a professional archaeologist by the Society of Professional Archaeologists (1995). He was a faculty scholar at Northern Illinois University in 2016. He is the 2002 recipient of the John L. Cotter Award for Excellence in National Park Service Archeology and served as the 2006 Virgin Islands rock art expert for a UNESCO transnational World Heritage proposal in 2006. Wild is the cultural resource manager/archaeologist for Virgin Islands National Park, where he develops and oversees archaeological research and directs a college-level intern program funded through private sources to support research and preservation efforts. The program's archaeological investigations report on a wide range of research topics, including shipwrecks, battlefields and fortifications, marine railways, epidemic hospitals, plantations, and prehistory, including rock art studies. Wild also oversees historic studies, museum development, artifact conservation, historic structures preservation, and ethnography studies. As a National Park archaeologist, Wild has written or coauthored over ninety reports on archaeological investigations conducted throughout the southeastern United States, such as *Underwater Archeological Survey and Site Assessment of Biscayne National Park* (with David Brewer), "Archeological Investigations at the Flanking Battery Wall of El Morro, San Juan, Puerto Rico" in *Historic Structural Report: San Felipe del Morro*, and *An Archeological Inventory and Assessment of Cultural Resources on Water Island, U.S. Virgin Islands* (with David Anderson). His articles published in the proceedings of the International Congress for Caribbean Archaeology include "Investigations of a 'Caney' at Cinnamon Bay, St. John, and Social Ideology in the Virgin Islands as Reflected in Pre-Columbian Ceramics," "Defining Petroglyphs from the Archeological Record," "A Timeline of Taíno Development in the Virgin Islands," and "The Archaeology of Pirates, Privateers, or Planters: Locating and Identifying the First European Settlers of St. John, U.S. Virgin Islands."

Index

www.ingramcontent.com/pod-product-compliance
Lightning Source LLC
Chambersburg PA
CBHW072000260326
41914CB00004B/875

* 9 7 8 0 8 1 3 0 6 9 7 4 6 *